Revelations of a
White Man in a Black Church

Revelations of a
White Man in a Black Church

*How society uses racism to divide
Christianity and what Christians can do about it*

Pierce Story

Revelations of a White Man in a Black Church

TABLE OF CONTENTS

PREFACE

Upon our early arrival at the St. Paul A.M.E. church, a few congregants already seated looked up but didn't budge as they saw us enter and seat ourselves. We sat quietly and undisturbed in one of the back pews as congregants arrived and strolled past us before the service began. Though I have trouble believing that we didn't stand out like sore thumbs, both as first-time visitors and the only white people in the building, no one said a word.

After a short while, as the church pews began to fill, a woman, whom we later determined to be the choir leader, finally walked up and squeezed herself boldly into the small space in the pew beside me. She sat for a moment, put her arm around me, leaned towards me slightly and looked me in the eye, as if studying me. For a tense moment, I didn't know what to expect next.

Then she leaned back, smiled broadly and said, "OK. I gotta ask. Two white folks at an A.M.E. church. What's up with that?!"

Asked in any other way, such an inquiry might have caused us to get up and leave. But she asked in such a friendly, precocious manner that there was never even a thought that she could have been anything but sincerely and warmly curious. She simply wanted to know. For her, and those congregants around us, we might have seemed as out of place as two rodeo clowns at a funeral.

But the question that came to my mind was, why was a white couple in a black church so strange that it elicited such a reaction? Why should it be so unusual that someone needed to ask "What's up with that?!" After all, though her demeanor was quite friendly, the question was important enough, and the situation strange enough, that it required her to approach two complete strangers and ask.

Had this been an isolated situation, based perhaps on the separation within a specific, highly segregated community, the question might have been justifiable. But, as I learned through years of visitation and interactions in churches throughout the southeast, this was not the case. It just isn't normal for a white man to be in a black church.

This was but one of many Sunday morning and weekday evening interactions that became part of a years-long calling to a path of discovery. The more I attended black churches, the more questions arose, and the broader my inquiry became. My dive into black church culture soon went well beyond weekly visitation. I began to delve deep / into the historical, social and political dynamics that have carved the moder Christian denominational landscape, both black and white. From this came many revelations about the past, current status, and significant risks for the future of Christianity in America.

By stitching together American Protestantism's racial history, current events, and modern society's evolutio and ongoing assault on our faith, it became clear to me that Christianity's racially tarnished history is allowing society to dictate its future. Christians are not only siloed within our individual, racially and socially isolated congregations, we are unwittingly aiding in the marginalization of our faith within American culture.

Today, Christian blacks and Christian whites fight as if on a smoke-engulfed battlefield, unknowingly waging war on one another even as we try to win the same spiritual and social battles around us. Our congregations, divided by race, denomination, politics, socioeconomics and doctrine, act more like individual soldiers battling the same enemies but without the unifying cause of a common flag. Thus, not only are we failing to have the impact we could and should, we are supporting society's efforts to simultaneously divide the races, split our nation, and, most disturbing, conquer any hope of Christianity's influence.

This book will take you on my journey of discovery, from the unbecoming history of race relations within the American Protestant church, to the clever but nearly silent, decades-long assault that society is waging on our faith, to the battles that Christians are unknowingly waging against one another on society's behalf, and finally to the need for a "Nehemiah Moment" and a new kind of Great Awakening in our faith.

Importantly, I will not only describe the tools of war that society is using against us, through us, and with our tacit approval, I offer the means by which Christian whites and Christian blacks can clear the smoke from the battlefield and together take aim at the common enemies surrounding us. I offer not only a clear and urgent justification for change but the mechanisms and means through which Christian whites and Christian blacks can simultaneously address important social issues and alter the course of our faith in our nation.

This is not an easy read. And the recommended path forward will be difficult, fraught with the perils of self-awareness, admissions of dramatic failure and the necessities of complete forgiveness. But only through dramatic change, and by doing radically different and not just better, can American Christianity unite as God has commanded, and become a true body of Christ to bring glory to Him and positive change to our society.

INTRODUCTION

Racism split us. Race still divides us.
And society is using this to defeat us.

Christian Americans need to hear this message: We are not as effective for God's Kingdom as we could and should be because we are a divided church. These divisions are not merely based on doctrine, denomination, or personal music and worship preferences. Those differences might seem understandable and inconsequential, as benign as hair styles, career choices, and favorite sports teams, even to non-Christians.

Rather, some of the most significant fissures in the American church landscape are based on race. And it is this racial separation that is the most disturbing and the most disabling for Christianity's impact on society. Because society is using our historical and current racial separation against both Christianity and Christ's message, our effectiveness in collectively impacting society and the world around us to the glory of God is and will be limited at best. Simply put:

"The Church must unite in action because a fragmented
church isn't much help to a fragmented world."[i]

The racism of many early American Christian whites created racially segregated churches and denominations that still exist today. Indeed, the American body of Christ is seen by many as being as historically tainted with racism as the worst parts of society. Though some great progress has been made in many parts of the country through interracial and interdenominational churches, Christians remain largely as racially isolated today as in 1958 when Dr. Martin Luther King, Jr. uttered the famous statement, "The most segregated hour in America is 11 a.m. on Sunday morning."

Ironically, this racial separation is now typically viewed as benign by most Christians, a relic of the past that is now based largely on personal preferences, geography, racial pride, socioeconomics, familial and social history, or even politics. We typically think little or nothing of it, often embracing it when we do. It just "is what it is."

Yet, these divisions impede our abilities to discuss, let alone address, key social and socio-economic issues. Christians often disagree on *both the causes of and solutions for* the social and economic disparities and outcome variations seen among racial and socio-economic groups. While the variations are clear to the naked eye, the discussion and identification of root causes is both necessary and legitimate, particularly among Christians.

Yet, we do not always deal with our opinions and differences as Christians and in Christian ways. Instead, our disagreements are most often couched in the same harsh and divisive terminology and messaging as the society around us. Thus, rather than leading society to solutions for its biggest racial and social problems, Christians follow society by using its antagonistic language and approaches. The toxicity that has infected our society has thereby infected our churches.

And as a result, far too many of Christianity's racial divisions are kept alive and enhanced by the same issues, mistrust, animosity, and resentment that drive American society's racial divisions. The same old traps continue to cause us to think, speak, and do the very things the Bible forbids, and make us act as much or more like the world from which we are commanded to be differentiated.[ii] The result is that, though perhaps unwittingly, racial divisions within the body of Christ are further solidified and exacerbated.

Moreover, any racial unity that occurs within society is typically not being driven by the unification of Christian blacks and Christian whites. Rather, Christians are often left trailing far behind the progress made by a society we claim Christ is able to save.

This, in turn, helps keep the message of Christ from taking its proper role in American culture, and prevents Christians from effectively and efficiently doing God's work in their communities. Moreover, these divisions support society's divisive narratives, thereby helping to keep the nation's youth away from Christ and our Christian youth from engaging with one another.

Meanwhile, as Christians have remained comfortably ensconced in racially siloed churches, America's racial divisions have flourished and, in many situations, worsened. Society has continued to divide the races by gradually altering the terminology used to define and discuss racism, keeping the Bull Conner imagery intact while spreading its application to nearly all white people, particularly Christian whites.

Importantly for our faith, society has been working for decades to equate many of Christianity's Biblically based values and social mores with racism and racist thinking, yielding an unbridled accusation of racism against Christianity in general and, more specifically, Christian whites.

This, in turn, has caused Christian blacks to inadvertently fight against their brothers and sisters as they fight for racial justice and racial equality, even becoming unwitting soldiers in society's battle with Christian whites and their own faith. Likewise, Christian whites unknowingly alienate and battle against their Christian black brothers and sisters through their words, actions, inactions, justifications, and self-imposed isolation.

Our racial divisions allow Christians to be seen as hypocrites by society, making the God we worship seem petty, foolish, incompetent, and completely unworthy of the respect we say He deserves. Even as society becomes more divided, secular, and harsh, churches remain far too divided and thus less able to serve as effective beacons for peace, joy, and the communion of loving saints. It is no small wonder, then, that non-Christians mock Christians as the fools and hypocrites they see us to be.

Add to this the fact that so many Christian charitable and sacrificial efforts go unnoticed by the broader society because they don't know or don't want to admit to God's power to change people for the better. Because Christians are so divided by so many boundaries, whether racial, doctrinal, or denominational, the messages of Christian service, actions and deeds are too often lost.

Society has thereby helped perpetuate Christianity's racial silos while they are simultaneously fortified by the ever-renewing cultural, political, and social divisions of these times. This is critical to understand, since this dual-pronged assault impacts Christians' ability to work together as Christian brothers and sisters by encouraging far too many of us to think, speak and act no better than our society does. The result is too many Christians isolated from one another in racially segregated groups, supporting rather than overcoming the racial divisions in society.

> *Christianity's racial silos are therefore the*
> *greatest restraints to coming together as*
> *a body of believers, as Christ commanded.*

And so, Christians are often our own worst enemies and the worst enemies of God's Kingdom.

But to be very clear, this is not a call for a United Church of America. Quite the opposite. Diversity in worship style, denominations, doctrine, music, and church culture means that more and more people are reached, and the body of believers is even larger than it might otherwise have been. Today, God's church in America consists of some 350,000 congregations, regularly attended by some 54 million Christians, with another 200 million Americans claiming Christianity as their faith. Christianity's ranks and the opportunities which these numbers reflect are huge.

Yet in many ways, those 350,000 churches are really individual silos from which Christians do great things within our own ranks and communities but too rarely, if ever, collaborate with the churches around the corner, down the street or on the other side of town. Working independently of one another within church silos, our efforts are inherently less efficient and effective, often overlapping and redundant, thus limiting our ability to have maximum impact, even within the same small community.

Thus, in practice and seemingly by design, Christians are isolated components of the larger body of Christ, like the gears and springs of a watch that are not joined together and synchronized. Christian diversity is thereby a tremendous strength that has only become a weakness as we've allowed it to keep us isolated from each other and thus less able to impact society for the glory of God and the expansion of our faith to others.

Fortunately, God has given Christians the means by which to bring Him glory and shine a new light on His truth. Christianity's numbers are strong and the latent capacity to serve is tremendous. Through the power of these numbers, Christians can break down the racial, doctrinal, cultural, and other barriers that keep us apart, impact the issues that plague American society, change the reputation of God's church, and awaken the next generations to a new impression of Christ, Christians, and Christianity. To achieve this relational transformation, several major steps must be taken.

First, Christians must all take on the "uprightness" that God defines and requires, and that Jesus exemplified. Uprightness, as a purely Christian term used over seventy times in our Bible, combines honesty, objectivity, and integrity into a singular description of a unique mentality, lifestyle, and way of communicating and interacting with others. Only Christians are called to possess such a unique trait, making us potentially uniquely qualified to take on society's biggest challenges.

Sadly, many Christians have taken on attitudes, positions, thoughts, language, and political stances that are much more like the world against which we are told to stand than that of the God we purport to obey. But if we are to change the world around us, we must first change ourselves and become "upright" by thinking, speaking, and acting with pure Godly honesty, integrity and objectivity.

This alone is daunting enough, as it flies in the face of the ways society encourages us to think and act. But uprightness will allow Christians to have difficult conversations and delve deeply into complex social and racial issues. We will be able to communicate, debate, and exchange ideas as the brothers and sisters of Christ rather than as the men and women of this world.

Uprightness will thereby make us far more unified, collaborative, and effective. Moreover, by becoming upright, Christians will inherently become different from, and a positive example for, the world around us. This, in turn, will enable Christians to do the work we are called to do.

Next, both sides of the Christian racial aisle need to do a few very important things. These are not small tasks, such as exchanging pastors, inviting another congregation to worship, or sharing a holiday meal. There are cultural barriers to be crossed, old wrongs to be righted, apologies to be made and accepted, and past sins shared and forgiven. There are difficult conversations to be had, wounds to be healed, and generations of divisions to be mended. Only Christians, bound by a duty to live as Christ directed, can overcome the racial, political, denominational, and sociological gaps that keep us and our nation divided. Only Christians, using Christlike uprightness as our measure, can move themselves into new Godly relationships and show the world a better way to live. And as Christians across America begin to come together across historic racial divisions, entire communities will share in "Nehemiah moments" as we bare our souls, forgive, love, and bond with one another.

Then and only then can Christians unite in specific yet non-constraining ways. Christians must break down the church siloes that keep us isolated while preserving the identity, personality, and uniqueness of each congregation and denomination. We must become what we are called by God to be: communal bodies of Christ, speaking with a voice from above and beyond the worldliness that drags others into sin, warring factions, hatred, arrogance, dishonesty, malicious self-righteousness, and despair.

Christians can then focus our collective efforts on a few important social issues. This "unity in action" will show society a better way to collaborate, interact, and live, while avoiding unnecessary battles over politics, parties, candidates, and non-essential social and doctrinal issues. Our unity will occur without the need to agree on every verb in the Bible, every ceremony of worship, or every theological nuance. Instead, unity in action will avoid the trappings of doctrinal and organizational disagreements and focus on the impacts Christians can have on our communities and our nation.

Next, Christians must act. We must, as bodies of Christ within our communities, address the issues and ills of society that we can and should impact while maintaining the many congregational efforts in missions, charity, and evangelism. Specifically, each community's united churches must focus on the root causes of issues within education, healthcare, justice, and racism. By uniting and using our collective capacity and passion to serve, Christians can draw on more resources without negatively impacting the other work our churches already do. Christians' vision for the future will come from God, our authority from our uprightness, and our power, strength, and perseverance from the power of God's people united under God's direction.

From this will come the means by which Christians can reach new generations of Americans. The next generations will not be brought to know Christ through threats of damnation, promises of eternal bliss, or even our acquiescence to the ways of the secular world. The revivals of the first Great Awakenings that brought so many to a knowledge of Christ will not draw America's younger generations. Indeed most have already heard of Jesus, yet don't like what they've seen and heard portrayed by society, the media and even some Christians.

But, as Christians unite and act, society will see us break down the barriers that it fortifies. Many will be opposed. But as non-Christians see this new image of Christianity, some will want to explore and learn more about a faith which has been discounted and damned by society for so much of their lives. They might become curious as to how Christians accomplish what we do, given the social stratifications that have kept so many racial, socioeconomic, and political divisions alive. They might approach God intellectually, questioning the very tenets of the Christian faith and core beliefs of the Bible. But through our uprightness, Christians will show a better way to be. Through our unity in action, Christians will open their eyes to a better way to live and impact society. And through their own intellectual inquires and spiritual curiosity, many will come to know that living with Christ is a perfectly reasonable and ultimately desirable way to live.

Mind you, this will not be easy work. There are powerful interests that are fully vested in the status quo. And those interests will readily unite against Christians, just as Christians unite in action. Furthermore, just at a time when society cries out for help as never before, God's church and its members are often portrayed as part (or most!) of the problem rather than the source of the solution. This will make Christians' work even more difficult, as the forces arrayed against us will be determined to see our failure.

It is up to Christian Americans of all races, doctrines, and denominations, to think, speak, and act uprightly, unite in action to release society of its ills, and restore God and God's church to a place of prominence and respect in modern American culture. America is broken. All you need to do is turn on the news or look at the internet to see it. America needs Christians, but not as we are and used to be. America needs a different kind of Christian and a different kind of Christianity.

Our churches need a "Nehemiah moment"
because America needs an Awakening.

In this book, I intend to expose the scars of the past and the ugliness that remains in the present. However, I will also attempt to show a better path for Christian Americans, both white and black and of all doctrines and denominations. A path based on truth, objectivity, uprightness, and a Godly perspective on the needs of society and our relationships with one another.

Specifically, I will spell out, in detail, what we as Christian blacks and whites can do to alter the course of history for our nation and the Kingdom of God as a united body of Christ through unity in action. With this, I believe that we can and will bring God glory and place God's church in its rightful place, respected, and valued, in society.

And with this, Christians can create what may become a Great Awakening to bring the next generations of Americans to a relationship with their loving, eternal Father.

I can only pray that this message is one that God himself is sending, and that it will achieve its intended purpose. For your consideration, the Psalmist put it this way:

¹ How good and pleasant it is when God's people live
together in unity! ² It is like precious oil poured on the
head, running down on the beard, running down on
Aaron's beard, down on the collar of his robe. ³ It is as if
the dew of Hermon were falling on Mount Zion. For there
the Lord bestows his blessing, even life forevermore.
(Psalms 133: 1-3)

CAVEATS

As you'll see in coming chapters, I do not claim to be a biblical or historical scholar, nor am I even a lifelong devout Christian. Yet this book deals with some thorny issues on the history and future of God's American church and the roles Christian blacks and whites need to play in uniting us in action. So before delving into the meat of this subject, there are several caveats that need to be stated.

OTHER CHRISTIAN GROUPS

Yes, I am fully aware that there are Christians among the many other races, nationalities, and creeds that make up our increasingly diverse American population. I am also fully aware that there are silo walls between and among the churches of Christian blacks and whites as well as those of our Hispanic, Asian, Native American, Middle Eastern, and other communities. And, most importantly, I am keenly aware that we will ALL need to come together, as believers, to impact American society and bring glory to God. Indeed, as Christians, we all suffer when any of us suffers from society's ongoing assault on our religion, our Biblically mandated standards and morals, and our way of life. Moreover, as important components of the larger body of Christ, all are needed because all are precious to God.

Yet, the reason for this book's focus on Christian whites and blacks is simply the history of strife, conflict, and racism and the current status of these still-estranged relationships. No other divisions seem as wide and difficult as the racial divide between blacks and whites and between Christian blacks and Christian whites. Therefore, the divisions I focus on herein are strictly those between these two groups, as if there were no other ethnically derived silos to worry with.

Thus, I hope that you will understand that examining the history of the relationships between Christians of each ethnicity throughout the history of this country would be a monumental task and would therefore detract from this more focused message. My scope is intentionally and consciously limited. And if this book influences the direction of the relationships between Christian blacks and Christian whites, my effort will have been a success.

If, however, this book moves Christians and churches of any ethnicity to join together with others to influence society for the glory of God, then it will have done a great service to God through the increased unity within our faith. In the end, God willing, we will bring together ALL Christians of ALL races for unity in action.

MULTI-CULTURAL CHURCHES

I am also fully aware that there are tens of thousands of multi-racial, multi-cultural churches scattered throughout our nation. If you, as a reader, happen to attend a multi-racial, Bible-preaching church, good for you! These can often serve as examples of what racial harmony and collaboration look like.

Yet, even these multi-racial churches are often just as siloed as the less diverse churches. They are often just as guilty as any of a failure to reach out to other churches down the street, around the corner or across town to collaborate on issues that impact their cities and towns. Indeed, it is ironic that churches are perhaps more likely to have a partnership with a church halfway around the globe than one just a few miles away.

Furthermore, for every one of these there is at least one if not several racially divided churches wherein there is little, if any, blending. This is particularly true of my experiences in the Southeast. Unless and until the big all-black A.M.E. church unites in action with the big all-white Southern Baptist church just a few miles away, God's impact on their communities will inherently be lessened.

While the concept and practice of multi-cultural churches is welcomed, having a multi-racial congregation is of less importance if that church still thinks and works in isolation. And having even tens of thousands of these is not enough until unity in action happens throughout ALL churches, uniting ALL Christians, not just a few.

THE JEWISH COMMUNITY

Likewise, I am aware that our Jewish community should not be ignored. Though there have long been differences, animosities, and clashes between the Jewish community and some Christians, we share a great heritage and should not exclude one another from our efforts to impact society. After all, the God-breathed ethical standards and social mores that we should all share are under constant and ongoing attack from a society hell-bent on our defeat.

Therefore, we should strive to create ample opportunities to look among and between our faiths in order to strengthen our efforts and grow the power of our numbers. Again, my concerns in this book are for the clear divisions between two specific groups of Christians. If, however, this book can serve as a means to promote new or ongoing collaboration between Jews and Christians on the key social issues of our day, then Heaven will rejoice.

TERMINOLOGY USED

My repeated use of the terms "black church," "Christian blacks" and the general use of the term "black" are likely to raise the ire of some readers. Some will likely read this and call me a racist and accuse me of being insensitive, irresponsible, and culturally unaware, among other things. (Ditto for the references to "negro" and "boy," two uses of the word "nigger," multiple uses of both "brother" and "sister," the several references to "African-Americans" and the instances in which I put "whites" before "blacks" in a sentence.)

However, the term "black church" and "black Christianity" is common in the academic and non-fiction literature. Furthermore, as the debate over proper and correct nomenclature continues, many blacks have come to dislike the term "African American" as well as the more modern, more generic "people of color," preferring instead "black" or "brown."

Certainly, the term it is not meant to do anything other than generally describe and differentiate, particularly from Christian whites. Thus, I use the word black in these contexts with no compunction, ill-will, or subliminal demeaning intent.

The term "black church" is also used generically, as is "white church". Yet, of course, there are no singular entities that represent either group. Indeed, there is great diversity and variation within the Christian faith and its many denominations and offshoots. Both terms are therefore used to describe generalized groupings within the landscape of American Christianity and not meant to imply some sort of unified coalition or over-arching organization.

PUTTING CHRISTIAN FIRST

I use the terms "Christian whites" and "Christian blacks" rather than using the secondary descriptor (e.g. "whites" and "blacks," respectively) first. Christians are Christians first and foremost, and certainly before they are anything else, whether American, Hispanic, white, black, Eskimo, disabled, etc. Therefore, I rarely use any adjective before Christian in this book. The exceptions are commonly when referencing the geographic location of a church or group of churches, such as "American Christian church."

FIRSTHAND ACCOUNTS

I can only reference what I have seen and heard first-hand. None of the personal experiences described are second or third hand. I do not let the experiences of others in similar circumstances taint what I have witnessed, nor do I pretend to have seen things that I haven't.

For instance, I have primarily been to churches in the southeastern United States. But, when attending churches elsewhere, I avoid letting any previous experiences taint what I see and hear to ensure that my writings reflect reality to the extent possible.

What I penned herein is as close to the actual events and words as memory and my notes will permit. I avoid embellishment, hyperbole, and "spin" at all cost. Thus, I can declare without pause that what is described herein is as objectively factual and tactfully stated as I could make it. Take it or leave it. It is what I saw, heard, and thought. However, there is one exception.

The circumstances of some of the conversations retold herein have been altered so as to avoid identification of certain parties. Out of respect to those who shared their innermost feelings and thoughts, I chose to keep their message and content without allowing them to be identified by those who know us either or both of us. This is why you will never see the name of a specific pastor mentioned herein. Instead, I captured the nature of the events and the meaning and words of the conversations, but not necessarily identifiable attributes of those who shared them.

That said, my intentions are to share my experiences and thoughts without offending. But if portions of this book hurt or offend, it was not my intention. If they sting a bit, perhaps it's a good thing. They are what they are. Of course, it is my sincere hope that this book drives people to act according to the will of God and the callings of the Holy Spirit to help unite Christians to important common causes. It is certainly not my intention to insult or injure along the way.

LIMITATIONS OF STUDY

Furthermore, there are only so many churches one can attend within a given timeframe, so my experience is inherently limited by virtue of the fact that a) Sunday only happens once per week, b) there are typically only two or three opportunities on any given Sunday to attend worship, and c) I haven't been doing this all my life.

While I haven't attended every white and black church throughout the nation, I am guessing that I've visited far more black churches than most Christian whites, and more white churches than most Christian blacks. And while the "n" (mathematically defined as the number of items in a set) may not be in the thousands, I have seen enough to detect patterns of behavior and the variation in that behavior to feel comfortable that what I write is directionally correct. That is, my experiences are consistent enough that I am confident that my conclusions are at least heading in the right direction. Importantly, my new experiences consistently fail to alter my existing conclusions.

CONCLUSION

I continue to learn with each visit to a new black or white church, and the education on the cultural differences and spiritual chasms has yet to cease. Therefore, as this book goes to publication, know that I am continuing to learn.

My prayer for this book is quite simple – that it influences, in some small or large way, the dynamics of the relationships between Christian blacks and Christian whites and thus impact the influence these groups can have on our society and its many growing problems. With the caveats set forth, let me share my personal experiences as a white man in a black church.

REFLECTIONS OF A WHITE MAN IN A BLACK CHURCH

INTRODUCTION

This chapter is written so that you, the reader, might understand my perspectives on the current potential for full unity and collaboration within the American body of Christ, and how those perspectives came to be. Laying this groundwork will hopefully help you understand more about the churches I attended and what I learned through years of attendance. This is a perspective that most Christian whites have never gotten on their own, and that some Christian blacks may need to hear for the sake of understanding their Christian white brothers and sisters.

Of course, racial divisions do not exist everywhere or in all denominations. There are tens of thousands of multi-cultural churches throughout our country, bringing together peoples of all races under single roofs each week to worship God. And where racial divisions do exist, they may be merely a reflection of personal preferences, old habits, historical communities, and doctrinal variations rather than historical or current racial animosity. Fortunately, in these latter scenarios, the church silos we have created can be more readily broken down for the sake of unity in action and the glorification of God in our society.

But where even two churches are racially separated for any reason, benign or not, and where collaboration and cooperation are thereby restricted by lack of Christian harmony, the power of the body of Christ is not optimized. Thus, there is a need to explore how racially divided our churches may be, as well as the cause, variation in degree and hardness of those divisions. This will reveal what may be required to open Christian hearts to one another and work together, unified in action for the glorification of God.

In this chapter, I share my reflections, thoughts, and perspectives as a precursor to the key message of this text, which is focused on the "to do's" of unified Christian action.

MY VERY CHRISTIAN WHITE BACKGROUND

I was raised in an all-white traditional Southern Baptist church, with a regular weekly attendance of two hundred or so. When we were boys, my brother and I were heavily engaged in church through choir, Boy Scouts, youth summer camps, and Vacation Bible School. Thanks to my mother's insistence, we regularly attended both Sunday School and "Big Church" (a.k.a. the 11 a.m. worship service).

Looking back, ours was a quiet church, filled with good Christian people and upstanding members of the community. These were by no means "upper class rich white folk." This was a working-class church, full of farmers, carpenters, teachers, secretaries, and hardworking furniture factory workers. I had wonderful Sunday School teachers who were true saints, some of whom I will never forget. We had a wonderful choir with some very talented musicians, and devoted pastors. Overall, it was a great church that positively influenced my life.

But our church was without a doubt and without exception all white. This was not due to hate or racism or even subtle rejection (though it may have been in decades past). Indeed, I cannot imagine the saints who worshipped there being anything but loving to every soul they ever met. But, because of the culture and history of racial divisions of my hometown, the churches in our town were nearly all racially divided and rigidly siloed.

And we thought nothing of it. It just "was what it was." We simply went about our Sunday and Wednesday night gatherings, and the missions and charity work that we were called to do, without a second thought as to the racial make-up of our congregations. I dare say that we were not at all unique.

THE CALLING

Fast forward to the 1990's. After many years away from Christ, my church visitation and attendance had ramped up. By this time, I was living in the northern suburbs of Atlanta, and had attended a number of churches before finding a biker church called God's Rolling Thunder ("GRT"). As a Harley rider, this was a perfect group for me. Not just because they nearly all rode Harleys, but because they did what some other churches didn't. They engaged directly with the addicted, the downtrodden, the working poor, the imprisoned, and those who had made the worst of life choices through drugs, alcohol, and crime. While perhaps not a stereotypical church crowd, they were collectively one of the warmest, kindest, most welcoming, Christ-filled groups of people I have ever known.

I then moved away from Atlanta for a number of years, and floated in and out of Catholic, Baptist and other denominations, mostly in all-white churches. I moved back to Atlanta for a third time, relocating nearer to the heart of the city where I met and later married my beloved wife. Though GRT was still a thriving church, the long commute from my new neighborhood made active engagement on any day other than Sunday difficult at best. So, my then fiancée and I began a search for a new church home close to our new location.

Of course, being good southern Baptists, we immediately gravitated to the "big white First Baptist" churches at the center of many of the local communities. However, though she was perfectly willing to attend any of them, I wasn't moved to join. For me, I didn't feel called to join in with a hundred or a thousand other average white congregants. Yes, they all had missionaries and active ministries and were no doubt doing great things in the community and the world. Yes, Christ was definitely worshipped there. But it didn't seem like the place for me. There was something missing.

We tried other denominations and met some wonderful, Christ-filled people along the way. The congregations were nearly all "lily-white" due to the seemingly strict racial segregation of Christians and churches in the local area. We also tried some smaller liberal churches nearby, which were both non-denominational and increasingly prevalent. But theologically we could not get behind some of the latter churches that seemed based only loosely on God's word. Indeed, we found churches where just about anything but the word of God was preached. Nice folks, but not much Jesus.

Frustration began to grow after months and months of searching. We even toyed with returning to our Biker church where we were at least spiritually fed and loved as part of the church family. Then one fateful day I drove past one of the largest churches around, just a few short blocks from my rental and in a relatively sketchy part of our urban, mixed-race neighborhood. It was a huge, block-filling A.M.E. church that had been around since the 1940's and expanded several times. It was at that traffic light, looking up at the white columns of the old sanctuary that I knew where we were to try next.

A road somewhat less traveled

Like most southern Christian whites, we'd never been to an all-black church before. In fact, it didn't occur to us that we might expand the focus of our search to include non-white churches. We had, as if by default, always focused our search on churches that were white. Not out of a specific goal to segregate ourselves, but rather out of habit, familiarity, specific denominational selection, geography/location, or "just because" nothing else. We simply hadn't even thought of the alternatives.

Looking back, I now believe that God didn't just bring me to a random black church. After all, there were a dozen o more black churches within a mile or so of my rental residence, and one Church of God in Christ church right next door. Instead, I believe that God brought me to this black church, with this pastor and this congregation at that time for His reasons (some of which I still do not fully grasp). I now feel that God brought me there not because it was a typical black church, but more that it wasn't completely atypical. I believe He wanted to show me something I'd never seen before, so that I would become that much more engaged and interested, and so that future interactions with black congregations would temper what I encountered here.

Indeed, had I attended another black church, more like the ones we attended in later years, I would not have received the in-depth education on the church, race, and politics that came from attending this kind of church. Nor would I have learned as much about the divisions between the Christian races that existed, since they were not quite as glaring in other congregations and from other pulpits. Thus, this our first church was a special introduction, with a very special pastor who not only opened my eyes but graciously helped me to understand things I might never have.

OUR FIRST A.M.E.

I vividly remember our first Atlanta black church. We were new, white, and unaccompanied, something not typical in all-black congregations. Upon our first visit on a sunny Sunday morning, we received a few friendly smiles and welcomes from the ushers at the front door and some of the congregants inside. As we found our way down long hallways to the doors of the Sanctuary, we also received a few looks that seemed to say, "You do know what the "A" in A.M.E. stands for, don't you?! That'd be African!"

Most congregants, however, seemed simply indifferent to our presence, which was not surprising given the size of the congregation (which numbered near 10,000 in total membership). Such an indifference is not uncommon in any large church of any denomination and race. There are just too many faces to keep up with in a large congregation, so it's just easier to just blend into a large crowd and not be noticed, even when you seem to stand out.

"Do we have any visitors?"

Before and since our first visit to this black church, I visited countless churches, including white, black, and multi-cultural. Being greeted as first-time visitors varies greatly between congregations, depending on variables such as denomination, church size, church culture and history, and even race.

In smaller white churches, it is obviously less easy to go unnoticed as a "first-timer," no matter your race. Someone commonly notices that you're new, especially if you aren't the guest of another congregant. This may result in a public acknowledgement, a welcome from an individual congregant, or a simple welcome from the pulpit.

In the larger, traditional white Southern Baptist churches that I frequently visit, white first-timers can usually come and go largely unnoticed. In large cities or vacation areas with weekenders coming and going for myriad reasons, visitation is commonplace. Some large white churches welcome visitors simply by asking for a non-compulsory raising of a hand to allow for the passing of church information to a visitor from an Usher.

Some don't even go that far. The pastor simply welcomes any and all visitors with a statement from the pulpit without forcing anyone to publicly acknowledge their status. Thus, I have come and gone from many a white church without much more than a few casual and courteous "Hellos" from congregants seated nearby.

In most Catholic and some white Protestant churches, there is a brief period during which the congregants are told to greet those seated close by, which commonly involves a simple handshake and a "Peace be with you", "God bless you", or "Good morning" to those seated within arm's reach. Commonly, first-timers are not formally recognized during this time but might be generally welcomed from the pulpit.

A few white congregations and denominations take this to the next level with what we came to call "meet, greet, and hug" time. During this period, commonly associated with the welcoming of visitors, congregants were told to mingle, greet one another, and welcome visitors. Depending on the church culture, this could take less than one minute.

But despite the inherent variation in cultures, in most white congregations I've visited there is just a simple verbal recognition of visitors and perhaps a request to fill out a visitor's card to be dropped into the offering plate as it passes. As a white Presbyterian friend jokingly quipped, "We don't hug at home, let alone at church!"

Yet in nearly every one of the black churches I attended, from the smallest to the largest, there is a specific "meet, greet, and hug" time. Depending on the church culture, this part of the service could go on for some time. Indeed, I've heard pastors put time limits on this period, as congregants would often mingle throughout the entire church, speaking to each and every soul in attendance.

During this time, the pastor will commonly welcome visitors by asking all first-time visitors to stand (never have I seen it suffice to sit without notice). Sometimes, after standing, visitors are asked to announce a home location, perhaps who brought them to church that morning, and even a reason for visiting. "Welcome! Glad you are here! Who are you and where y'all from?" was typical. This was nearly always the case in congregations of less than a few hundred. In the larger congregations, the dialogue was commonly dispensed with, but the rest of the process remained standard.

After visitors were recognized, thanked and still standing, the entire congregation would be asked to get up and circulate, shake hands and exchange hugs, hellos, and "God bless you's" with both the visitors and each other. As a southern Baptist, I wasn't used to this much interaction with fellow congregants during the service. I certainly wasn't accustomed to this level of attention and camaraderie.

But though strange at first, I learned to truly love this part of the worship experience. For me, it came to set the stage for corporate worship, the communion among saints and the joy of being with fellow Christians, and the experiencing of the Holy Spirit. Indeed, I miss it when visiting churches where it is not customary.

Yet this new experience also led to an interesting realization as I visited more and more churches. As white first-timers in black churches, we couldn't just "blend in." So, whether and to what degree we were welcomed was immediately and sometimes painfully clear by how we were received during this brief "hugfest" period, especially relative to black first-timers. I would suspect that a black person entering a white church might wonder, as I did, if race had anything or everything to do with the kind of greeting received.

Now that I have experienced so many first-time visits, I have sometimes seen the greeting gleefully welcoming. In other churches, I felt utterly shunned. I thereby came to understand that how any and all visitors are welcomed can be quickly taken as a sign of the culture of the church and, unfortunately, a possible sign, legitimate or not, of the openness to those of other races.

And having been a first timer in a variety of settings, I understand that both how visitors are greeted and how people interact during the "meet, greet and hug" time matters. Indeed, how a person of one race is received when visiting the church of another race may be indicative of the often-stark divisions between cultures and races within the larger body of Christ. Or, it may simply mean a less-than-positive culture within the congregation. Either way, it was certainly not as easy or automatic as I had hoped it might be.

The greeting we received on that morning wasn't the warmest, perhaps described as less than enthusiastic. Because of our lack of experience, we could not honestly say if we were actually being somewhat shunned, or if there was simply little interest in making the effort to greet us. Perhaps the black first-time visitors who were also in attendance that morning were there with friends and thus were known and greeted more warmly. It could be because we were white folks in the wrong place. Or simple indifference. Or, simply that the congregants wanted to quickly socialize with their friends during the short time allotted.

Regardless, whether from indifference or prioritization of time or genuine cold feelings, it made for an uncomfortable part of the service that, on that particular day, we were happy to see end.

Welcomed and ... not so much

Still, our lukewarm welcome at this service wasn't the coldest reception I've experienced at black churches I have visited. Perhaps the least welcoming was the ironically named Friendship Baptist. Here, not only was I not recognized, the black person sitting next to me and the black women seated directly behind me didn't say a word or even look at me during the "meet, greet, and hug" phase. It was not only unfriendly, I felt more like a leper in an elevator than a Christian in a Christian church. Again, this is probably what a black person might have encountered by visiting a white church fifty years ago. Simply not welcomed.

Of course, I have also experienced just the opposite. Years later, perhaps the warmest, friendliest welcome I've ever received came at an all-black Missionary Baptist church. During our first visit there, my wife and I were warmly welcomed by nearly each and every one of the eighty-some-odd attendees, including the members of the choir, the Pastor and his family, and even the youth (something rarely if ever duplicated!) Theirs were hugs and handshakes full of genuine Christian love. They didn't care why we were there and had no suspicions about our presence. No resentment, no indifference, no disdain. Simply joy! They made us feel incredibly welcomed, as much a part of their family as the Deacons. I can honestly say that if I were asked for the friendliest church I have ever entered, Mt. Zion would top the list without pause.

Naturally, depending on the culture and congregants of the visited church, there was everything in between warm and cold. I chatted with one black pastor after visiting his church for the first time. When he heard some of the stories of my visitations, he asked me how friendly his congregants were towards us, relative to other churches we'd visited. I thought about it and said, "I'd say about a six on a scale of one to ten." He nodded, smiled and said, "I'll take that."

At one of the several A.M.E. churches we visited in South Carolina the church members were initially quite cold. During the "welcoming of visitors" phase, I stood and responded to the usual questions about our visit by casually announcing the name of our home A.M.E. church in Atlanta. The Pastor gave me an odd look that said either skepticism or perhaps shock.

To this day, I don't know if his next question was meant to test me or if he genuinely didn't know. But it certainly felt like a test, since every A.M.E. Pastor in the Southeast likely knew of our church and the Pastor thereof. "Oh!! Well!" he said. "Let's see now … who is the Pastor of that church?" When I immediately responded with the correct name, he visibly perked up, smiled, and changed the demeanor with which he spoke to us. He repeated a now much warmer welcome and asked that we say hello to our apparently famous Pastor in Atlanta.

After the service, the reception we received changed from coolness and indifference to a few genuinely warm greetings from congregants. The Pastor even made his way from the pulpit to offer us another personal warm welcome. Perhaps there had been a negative experience or history with white visitors. Or, perhaps we just needed some "church cred."

Then there was the visit to an A.M.E. church in my hometown in rural North Carolina, as described in the Preface and repeated here. Upon our early arrival, a few congregants already seated looked up but didn't budge as they saw us enter and seat ourselves. We sat quietly and undisturbed as the congregants strolled in before the service began (though I have trouble believing that we didn't stand out like sore thumbs).

A woman whom we later determined to be the choir leader finally walked up and squeezed herself boldly into the small space in the pew beside me. She put her arm around me, smiled and said "OK. I gotta ask. Two white folks at an A.M.E. church. What's up with that?!" She asked in such a friendly, precocious manner than there was never even a thought that she could have been anything but sincerely and warmly curious. We all laughed as she broke the ice and made us feel completely at home. After a wonderful service, the Pastor greeted us warmly, and invited us back anytime we were in town.

Thus, I have received everything from cool to warm to officious greetings as a white man in a black church. These experiences, while mostly pleasant, continued to reiterate to me how segregated the Christian races are, and how strange blending the two still seems to be. And of course, this matters if we are to begin to try to unite as Christians to impact our society. If we cannot feel welcomed and loved in any house of God, where can we?

Settling into our new church home

Over the next several Sundays, we continued to attend our first black church. Though the services typically ran two and half hours, we never looked at our watches. For the most part, services were engaging and spiritually uplifting, with some of the best sermons I'd ever heard. This was no glossy, feel-good message from the pulpit. The subjects were quite meaty. The depth of our Pastor's spiritual knowledge was impressive, and he was an outstanding and passionate speaker. Soon, we began attending weekly Bible Study and continued to enjoy the Senior Pastor's deep knowledge of the Bible and his bold preaching style.

During the first several weeks, we also moved from the back of the large sanctuary all the way down to the front four rows. There were, of course, different congregants there, so our interactions began to spread to new people.

"What District are you from?"

This was perhaps the most striking question we received as newbies in a black church. During the "meet, greet, and hug" time on our second Sunday in attendance, a middle-aged black woman turned to my then-fiancée and, without even saying "Good morning" smiled and asked, "So, what district are you from?" Totally befuddled by the query, my fiancée replied cautiously, "Ummm, well, we're just here to worship." "Oh," she casually replied, "I assumed you were from one of the voting districts. We sometimes get white folks in here to check on us and make sure we're not talking too much politics and stuff." She then smiled, said "God bless you!" and turned away to greet others. We must've looked like two deer in headlights! We haven't received such an inquiry since, but her question spoke volumes to me about the divergence between the races and the mistrust between and amongst blacks and whites, even in church.

Commitment and acceptance

Despite that odd greeting, it was here in the front of the Sanctuary just fifty or so feet from the pulpit that we were befriended by some of the members. Several welcomed us with very open arms and graciously invited us to sit with them. One of these saints was particularly interested in adopting us. This kind, deeply Christian woman brought us into her realm as if we were her lost children and made sure that we understood more of what was going on in the services and behind the scenes. She graciously invited us to sit on "her" row, and eagerly got to know us. She shared much of the history of the church, the roles of the six to eight pastors on the staff, the role of the church mothers and other lay leaders, and a little of the "who's who" in the congregation. She introduced us to others in the church, held our hands when things got rough and periodically prodded us to join the membership. She was and is a true saint and a wonderful blessing as we tried to find our way in this new black church culture.

In the weeks following, we sensed that we were becoming part of this church. "Meet, greet, and hug" time quickly went from being an uncomfortable part of the service to a wonderful part of the corporate experience and fellowship with other Christians. The level of engagement with other members was helped, at least in part, in that we weren't just idle pew warmers or just there for a Sunday or two to check things out and "see the show." We kept showing up, and both wanted to be engaged in church activities and volunteer opportunities. We increasingly felt at home.

Indeed, after it was clear that we weren't going away, we began to be openly courted to be part of the many ministries and working groups of the church. My wife was asked repeatedly to be in the choir (it was obvious that she knew many of the traditional hymns by heart, singing as she did with great joy and no hymnal). Though business travel prohibited me from participating in any of the mid-week work, I was repeatedly asked to be a member of the dance ministry (talk about an inappropriate calling!), the Men's Choir (I can't carry a tune in a coal bucket!), and one of the Men's Usher Boards. We came to be viewed as one of the crowd by most congregants, and maybe even a little bit special due to our ongoing status as the only white, regular attendees out of a group of thousands. Opportunities continued to grow as we had clearly made the decision to stay in this church for the long haul.

Mind you, there were still those in the congregation who didn't seem to appreciate the white infiltration. There were just some folks who seemed to want the "A" in A.M.E. to mean "African" and nothing else. This is not unusual, and, as I later learned, was based on a distinct racial undertone. But these few became less and less significant as we started to become stitches in the larger fabric of the congregation.

And though we continued to visit other black churches in the area, we would typically take in one service at our home A.M.E. church, either the early- or late-morning service since the church was big enough to host two or even three full services each weekend. When we traveled, which I did frequently for work, I would always try to find a black church to attend, and/or view the live broadcast from our home church via the internet.

Within a few months of our first visit, and after much prayer, we made the decision to join. Joining this church, or any church, was significant for us. Even though we supported several ministries, this is where the bulk of out tithe would go, and where we would dedicate our time and energies. To our knowledge, we were the only regularly attending white couple out of thousands of others, some of whom drove long distances to attend this particular church. But we felt an irresistible pull, so the decision was anything but difficult.

One a selected Sunday morning, my fiancée and I walked the short walk to the front of the sanctuary during the Invitation period, accompanied by our dear sister and others who had encouraged us all along the way. We were accompanied by roughly six others who had either given their lives to Christ or had selected this church to be their new home. It was a moving experience, and one I'll never forget.

Our first black church became our church home for nearly two years.

POLITICS AND RELIGION

Let me first say that politics and religion should, in my humble opinion, be blended to some extent. Especially in today's America. In fact, Christian Americans cannot and should not ignore the ongoing slide of the American culture and the toxicity of modern American politics. That is the point of this text! Christians should hold public office, become deeply engaged in every aspect of their communities, attend local government-related meetings of all types, and unabashedly monitor and help manage the affairs of their communities. Believe me, non- and anti-Christians are there, actively involved in our communities. And they will be more than happy to dominate if we choose to sit idly by. Thus, part of the point of this text is the unification of Christians around key cultural maladies which we, as Christians, can and should influence.

Of course, that doesn't mean the church services should become political rallies for specific candidates or causes. Nor does that mean that sermons should ever become political speeches or worship a political function. Indeed, I grew up in a church in which politics were never discussed from the pulpit. Moreover, I cannot tell you of a single sermon from my years in Southern Baptist churches that was focused on politics.

Yes, there are certainly white pastors who have formed national organizations to influence politics and the direction of the country. And, I've heard of Christian white pastors who regularly preach politics from their pulpits, usually around topics related to abortion, immigration, local politics, and even civil rights. Some are on the left of the political aisle, some on the right. However, I was unfamiliar with these pastors and haven't attended their services, so was not accustomed to hearing politics in the church. And most certainly, I was not accustomed to politics directed against a single group of people of which I am a part. Therefore, my initial exposure to the politics of black churches was a bit of an awakening, to say the least.

POLITICS AND OUR FIRST BLACK CHURCH

Through the experience and my own research, I came to understand and appreciate how national politics became so tightly entwined with the black church and its pastors. Given the history of the church in black culture and the American political landscape, this should not be a surprise. Indeed, as described in the next chapter, the American black church is steeped in a history of political struggle that dates back to the beginnings of this country.

In some black churches, politics is a legitimate topic and subject matter for sermons and pastoral messages, whether delivered by staff or visiting pastors. And in the America of 2018-19, politics has become as prevalent in some black churches as it likely was in the 1950's and 1960's. Yet in many other black churches we visited, politics remains firmly separated from the word of God with pastors and congregations preferring to keep politics out of the pulpit. And so, just as in white churches, much depends on the pastor, the congregants, and the church and denomination culture.

But from the initial "What district are you from?" onward, it was clear that politics was an integral part of at least some black churches, most certainly our new church home. The Pastor of our church home described himself as both biblically conservative and a political leftist. Small wonder, he had marched with Rev. Dr. King in the 1960's and remained a steadfast activist for civil rights. Yet, he was theologically and socially conservative.

Thus, what we encountered was, for me, a fascinating blend of solid Christian doctrine occasionally peppered with strongly worded, politically charged statements. It was how those statements were worded and the language that was used by both our pastoral staff and visiting pastors that made these occasional, highly politicized diatribes rather uncomfortable for us.

White People Suck Day

I don't recall which service was our first such experience at our new home church, but over a short time we began to pick up on a periodic theme. Whether due to current events of the day, elections, specific racial issues, or specific politicians, the message on infrequent Sundays turned political and quite harsh if you happened to be a white person in a black church. So explicit were some of these messages and impressions that my wife and I came to use the phrase "White People Suck Day" to describe those services in which the sermons were particularly harsh towards whites.

To be clear, it is important to note that these politically focused sermons and pastoral messages were not a regular weekly occurrence. If it was made at all, most political commentary was offered in passing and without much ado, as a side note or quick jab about a policy or person tossed into a sermon or prayer. But there were those days when the message was largely driven by either what was going on in society and/or who might be preaching. For instance, after the death of Trayvon Martin and the subsequent trial and acquittal of George Zimmerman, there was an eruption of outrage throughout the black community, including within our church. Likewise, the political passions surrounding President Obama were deep and strident, for what might seem to be obvious reasons. President Trump brought forth additional negative passions. Therefore, the political seasons of presidential and mid-term elections came with more frequent political rhetoric from the pulpit.

Ironically, during the time we attended, the angriest and most extreme sermons seemed to come from visiting pastors, who might have felt freer to express political sentiments while away from their home churches. So hostile were some of the messages from some of the visiting pastors that we learned to avoid revivals and events where guests would typically speak, watching instead via the internet or attending another church. On more than one occasion, we were glad we did. The open display of what appeared to be raw anger from the pulpit could be as intense as it was infrequent.

Moreover, these sermons, sub-topics, sidebars and quick jabs were more likely to be directed against white political opponents, typically white political conservatives, than white political leftists or whites more generally. Thus, Tea Party supporters were called "asinine and ignorant" from our pulpit. Similar invectives targeted Presidential candidate Mitt Romney and his supporters. President Reagan was called "the most racist man ever to set foot in the White House," while multiple other Republican politicians were disparaged. And a visiting Elder in the A.M.E. church referred to conservatives as a group as wanting to "lynch our men and enslave our children" with their policies of "hate and Wall Street greed." White Christians were not spared, either. A visiting Pastor from a New York church said flatly "I am sick of white Evangelicals," due to their ongoing support of white conservative politicians.

Yet, we chose the name "White People Suck" instead of "White Conservatives Suck" or "White Republicans Suck" because there was often an overarching anti-white theme (intentional or not) that made political differences between right and left indistinguishable and unimportant. Politicizing preachers, whether guests or staff, didn't always specify the targets of their invective, leaving generalizations hanging that could readily be thought of as anti-white rather than anti-Conservative or anti-Republican. Thereby a message meant for a specific white politician could readily and easily be construed as meant for the entire white population.

As we'll discuss in a later chapter, the notion that all white people were inherently and uncontrollably racist has become pervasive in some political, media and academic circles via concepts such as modern racism, institutional and systemic racism, and white privilege. These concepts, whether valid or invalid, right or wrong in part or in whole, may have made their way into the thinking and pulpits of at least some black pastors. Thus, whites were generally called out as racists, bigots, oppressors, evil and a few other choice labels.

Today, as our nation's politics becomes more and more divided and visceral, the political element in some of our nation's pulpits has grown louder. However, now the target is more precisely and specifically President Trump and his supporters. As we continue to visit black churches, we have noticed that "Trump's People Suck" messages have even entered black pulpits where politics was heretofore rarely if ever mentioned. And in those churches where politics in the pulpit was already a norm, the "45th President" (some refuse to call him by his official title as a form of insult and defiance) has become a far more frequent target of invective.

For example, during a large, multi-church Thanksgiving Eve service in another southern city, a local Pastor used the evening's sermon time to hurl insults at the President, his wife, and his family, including accusations of racism, bigotry, misogyny, molestation, and falsely claiming to be Christians. Other pastors have used some rather unkind monikers, such as "Agent Orange" and "Liar in Chief." In another rather memorable holiday sermon in yet another city, a pastor rattled off a long list of rather viscous insults, accusations, and allegations directed towards President Trump that seemed far more appropriate for an Antifa internet blog than God's pulpit. And a bishop of the

A.M.E. church summed up the anti-white feelings succinctly by openly calling President Trump and all his supporters "hate-filled racists and bigots."

Like a drop of acid into pure water, otherwise loving, uplifting messages became peppered with unkind, even hateful political dialogue. I have now witnessed otherwise Godly pastors speak the worst of insults, accusations, innuendos, and even falsehoods about whites, white conservatives, previous white Presidents, and President Trump and his supporters. The rage, whatever its origin, has been renewed and fueled to levels I had not witnessed in any of my time in black churches. Indeed, if we were still in our old neighborhood, I wonder if we would still feel welcomed in our old home church due to the politics of the day.

Nothing displayed this animosity better than the list of people called out for specific prayers during the weekly Altar Call portion of our now-former home church service. Each week, one of the pastoral staff would invite any in the congregation to come to the front of the church to pray to God before the Altar. Prayers might include specific individuals in need of physical healing, families who had lost a loved one, prayers about personal issues and struggles, as well as words of thanksgiving that needed to be brought before God. A common theme in many black churches, the Altar Call was often a spiritually moving and emotional part of the service and a time for bonding with fellow congregants unified in prayer.

In our church (though not in all churches we attended), as congregants gathered down front, a list read from the pulpit would include specific members of the church known to be ill or in need of prayer, members and their families who had lost a loved one, those serving in the Armed Forces, local and district A.M.E. clergy, the Senior Pastor and his family, and elected leaders. During our time there, President Obama came to office, which began a specific call for prayer for President Obama and his family. Appropriate, perhaps, given the significance of President Obama's election. However, once President Obama left office, the calls for prayers for the President and his family abruptly ceased. Only prayers for the occasional local black politician and a general prayer for elected leaders are now still included in the weekly prayer list.

My fiancée and I struggled to make sense of these messages within the context of the day and history, and to see the perspectives of those both in the pulpit and the congregation. We tried very hard to avoid being offended, hurt, or angry. Nonetheless, White People Suck Day was both intriguing and particularly troubling, and spurred significant portions of this text and this call to action herein.

IRONIES AND IMPACTS

Importantly for the potentially united Christian church, none of these sermons or anti-white diatribes were ever accompanied by prayerful concern, prayers for forgiveness or for some divine "road to Damascus" realizations and enlightenment. There was none of that. Cynicism and bitterness, it seemed, overwhelmed love and prayer.

Yet, we all know that the Bible clearly demands that we pray for our enemies. As Dr. Martin Luther King, Jr. famously said, "Darkness cannot drive out darkness; only light can do that. Hate cannot drive out hate; only love can do that."

Indeed, Dr. King's message was one of forgiveness, with the sincere hope that the white racists would not so much be defeated as turned away from their sinful, abhorrent thinking and hateful actions to lives of Christian love, peace, brotherhood, and equality. "Never succumb to the temptation of bitterness," Dr. King said.

And, if whites and Christian whites are the racists that society would have us all believe, or if President Trump is the demon some pastors describe him to be, shouldn't there be prayers for the changing of hearts and minds?, Shouldn't the collective prayers of the congregants listening to the frustration and anger from the pulpit be focused on Godly interventions, or the means by which to bridge racial gaps? Shouldn't Christian love dominate the hearts, minds and messages on these pastors?

Instead, in those angry, targeted sermons or passing mentions within unrelated sermons, there were no prayers for those on the "other side." No prayer vigils. No fasts or other typical Christian approaches taken by prayer warriors in the face of adversity. If there was anything spoken, it was only invective, harsh allegations, and bitterness directed towards whites and white political conservatives. As will be discussed in later chapters, the irony is that many of those against whom the frustration and anger was directed are fellow Christians.

Thus, to me, there was a distinct missing element and thus a bit of worldliness about these messages on those occasional days. Indeed, one of the most ironic aspects of a few of the other black churches I've attended since is the blending of a definitive message of love, hope, and the God-given opportunities that come from following Jesus counterbalanced with messages of doom, gloom, oppression, mistrust, and bitterness bordering on hatred for white people. On occasion, those same messages might be blended together into a single sermon. This dichotomy remains difficult for me to navigate, but it may be one of the many reasons why God's American church remains as racially divided as the secular society around us.

Furthermore, and importantly, of major concern to us was the messaging for the children and youth of the church. We became deeply concerned about how this would taint their future opinions of whites generally and Christian whites and white conservatives specifically.

This was particularly concerning given the role of the black Pastor as a true leader in the Christian black community. As local pastors, particularly those of large or influential congregations, they carried great authority through their positions and as expositors of the Holy Word of God. Minor comments, opinion, half-truths and biases might be taken as "gospel" as they came from the lips of these respected and revered men of God Almighty, many of whom proudly wore the stripes and scars of the early Civil Rights movement. Any misconceptions about Christian whites, white conservatives, and whites in general carried great weight as they came forth from the pastors whom these young people had grown up to know, trust and respect.

Even if infrequently delivered, messages of distrust, oppression, hopelessness in the face of institutional racism and even hate no doubt rang in the impressionable ears of the church's youth. And since there was often no differentiation between Christian whites, white Republicans, President Trump, and whites as a racial group, a young person might justify their own feelings of hopelessness, mistrust, anger, and even hatred towards whites and Christian whites.

CONTRASTS AND CONFLICTS

As mentioned repeatedly, I don't want the reader to think that these sorts of politicized, angry sermons and messages or even passing jabs were a weekly event or the norm in every black church we attended. Certainly not! The vast majority of the sermons at nearly all black churches I have attended, including our first church, have been about Godly principles, valuable life lessons drawn from scripture, and uplifting messages of hope.

Indeed, except for the occasional White People Suck Days, we rarely walked away from church feeling unfulfilled, unenthusiastic, or un-revived. Routinely, we came away excited about our faith, rejuvenated by the service and the message, and ready to take on whatever evil came into our paths during the week. On most Sundays, it was just plain hard to walk out without feeling good all over! Likewise, Bible study was typically equally uplifting and spiritually deep.

Yet, given what I've seen and heard in our former home church and other black churches of various denominations, I am comfortable saying that this church is not an outlier. That is, it is not one of a kind or wholly unique. Rather, it is somewhat exemplary of churches with similar congregational cultures and similar congregational attitudes and feelings.

Eventually, we became so concerned that we began to question giving our tithes and support to a church that seemed to be doing more to divide the races than to bring them together though God's Holy word. Given my wife's deep passion for young people, we were worried that what we saw as an inaccurate impression of whites and/or white political conservatives would stick with these impressionable youth and do them harm as they went forth into the world and an already integrated workforce.

Yet, despite the negatives, our time at our first black church was a true blessing for me. It also opened my eyes to the often-gaping chasms between Christian blacks and Christian whites, helping me understand better than ever before the deeper issues, history, and current status of those gaps.

This led to the alarming realization that our faith was further in trouble than many of its followers ever imaged, unaware as they are of the deep but often unseen divisions. The experiences were therefore invaluable, setting me on the current course. As painful and troubling as it sometimes was, I am forever thankful.

MOVING ON OUT

Well over a year into our tenure at our first black church, I felt a call to be elsewhere. The concerns began to become more and more prominent, and I could not shake the frustration with how we and others like us were being referenced and targeted. While I'd made friends and had come to know many of the congregants, I pondered how we might seek to educate and offer a different perspective. Yet, initial conversations had done little good to sway opinion. At the time, even I didn't realize the holistic magnitude of the divisions within God's church. I was only coming to understand the breadth and depth of these divisions and had no idea how pervasive they were in certain parts of the country.

Yes, we could have stayed on and tried harder to have an impact. But in the moment, I felt the need to move on, take advantage of the lessons learned, and seek out a new church home. Our final decision to move away from our home church was a very difficult one. Difficult, in part, because of the people we'd met, the positive experiences we'd had, the time invested and the hopes for the future.

Of course, despite the mixed feelings and frustrations of our first black church, I didn't even consider turning away from where we both felt I was called to be. Indeed, I was more determined to explore the obvious divisions, whether political, racial, or cultural, and see for myself to degree to which Christianity was split. Therefore, we continued to feel strongly that God had placed a thought in my head, and I remained determined to continue down this path. Thus, we began a search for a new black church home.

Since we'd continued to visit black churches throughout our nearly two years at our first black church, we knew of several in the community around us. There were churches, large and small, of various denominations.

We were able to quickly find another black church, a Missionary Baptist Church, nearby our home, perhaps the friendliest church I'd visited, before or since. The congregants were, to a person, warm, friendly and welcoming. The pastor was a genuine man of God, passionate about his gifts and calling. During our subsequent visits over the next several months, politics didn't come up once during the service.

I began to get to know our new pastor, and he certainly wasn't oblivious to the issues of the day. He and I began a great relationship that included racial, social, and spiritual discussions at a local coffee shop. He, too, was a Biblical scholar who offered great insights and thoughts on the current days' events and the relationships to scripture. I never knew how he voted because he was more concerned with the message of God than the political messages of men. He simply chose to focus on God's word each week, delivering powerful, poignant messages on relevant topics to his multi-generational congregation. This was a refreshing change from the periodic politicized messages. And we never worried that White People Suck Day would happen there.

Sadly, shortly after beginning our stay there, we moved out of state once again to what we hope will be our permanent home. There, we found both black and white churches and a few multi-cultural ones. After some searching, we quickly settled into and now regularly attend two great churches, even as we continue to visit new ones.

CONCERNS AND SUMMARY

In private conversation, I have heard from more than a few pastors that healing the current divide between Christian blacks and Christian whites may now actually be impossible. Yet, surely, we must know that if the leaders and members of our churches cannot stand up for Godly honesty, pure integrity, love, and mutual respect even among the widest gaps in political opinions, something or someone else will stand up in their place. Satan has already taken his place in our society and his influence is spreading right before our eyes.

Meanwhile, our churches remain racially divided, often exacerbated by political differences, while Satan takes on an ever-larger role in guiding our society, our children, public opinion, and decisions about right and wrong. Through our divisions, indifference, and worldliness, God's church seems to be opening more doors for him than we are closing.

In the remainder of this text, I will try to present my opinions, feelings, and research to two very different groups. There is a section for Christian whites, Christian blacks, and both. If we are to ever come together as a united Church – the church God intended us to be – we will have to do a much better job of being honest with each other and ourselves, relating to one another, and serving one another as we show a very, very different image to the world. Unity should be our goal. It is my prayer that this text might help that cause.

WHAT CHRISTIAN WHITES NEED TO KNOW ABOUT BLACK CHURCHES

BLINDERS

My wife and I had recently met a couple at a charity event and, as often happens among strangers in social settings, struck up a conversation. We wanted to get to know them better after that event, so we decided to meet them for dinner at a convenient, casual Italian restaurant during the following weekend. He is a surgeon, well-known in the local medical community, and she is a former stay-at-home-mom who had successfully raised three children and now helped manage their rental properties around town. Both are well-educated. They lived in an upscale suburban neighborhood ten or so miles away from our home. Both are devout Christians who regularly attend, financially support, and volunteer at their church. They are fine people with loving, Christ-centered hearts.

As we chatted over pizza and linguini about college football, our churches and preachers, and a little local politics, the conversation shifted to our experiences in the black churches we'd visited. I began telling some of the stories of our previous interactions, the friends we'd made, the things I'd learned, and the differences I'd detected. They were intrigued, even fascinated, by what must have seemed like our out of the box Sunday experiences.

In telling these tales, I casually mentioned some of the acronyms of the denominations we'd visited. Since I knew what these acronyms meant, I carelessly rattled them off without thinking to explain or define, as if I were a Marine using commonly understood military acronyms.

But as I rambled on, I could tell that they were distracted by something I'd said. At one point, they looked at each other, as if to confirm that they both had the same question. I stopped and asked, "You seem puzzled. What is it?"

His next question helped me understand the relative lack of knowledge within the Christian white community and some of the unknowns that still exist between the Christian races. As innocently as a child, he asked "What do you mean by A.M.E.?"

INTRODUCTION

Race certainly isn't the only element that keeps churches and congregations in their siloes. There are also doctrinal and denominational differences, personal preferences, locations, historical traditions and habits, and even socio-economic barriers. But of all the differences, race should not prevent us from collaboration and cooperation in addressing our society's most important issues. Bringing glory to God simply cannot be done properly from within racially fortified silos, as they limit our capabilities far too much.

Importantly, history has provided American churches with a unique opportunity like we have never seen. Christianity's numbers, though siloed in 350,000 congregations across the nation, have tremendous potential to impact key issues in our society. If Christians can unify within communities and across racial boundaries, there is no limit to the good that might result.

Sometimes, breaking out of these siloes is easy. Other times, not. But in order that Christian blacks and whites unify around action and impact society, it is imperative that each group know and understand the other and the perspectives from which we all see ourselves, each other, society, the world, and our God.

My education on the roles of the black church in America came later in my life through interactions, church attendance, discussions with pastors and lay people, and questioning the things I heard, saw, and thought. Through this, I came to have an admiration and deep respect for the abiding, stalwart faith of Christian blacks throughout America's history.

Moreover, I came to understand and appreciate the very different perspectives and passions that my Christian black brothers and sisters brought to their faith, their worship and their politics. I have learned much from the way in which Christian blacks worship, the words and songs they use, the role of the black pastor in the black church, and the racial divide that helped create the historical and current separations of Christian Americans. Most was learned through an education by immersion, through seeing and interacting with people with profoundly different social and political viewpoints, and seeking the truth with as objective a lens as I could muster.

Indeed, I write this book assuming that there are other Christian whites who know as little or perhaps even less than I did when I started. I have dear, Christian white friends who are all too unfamiliar with this topic, so I am guessing that there are more.

The history offered below is meant to be extremely brief and succinct. If you would like to dig deeper, there are many volumes on a variety of these subjects written by great historians. This, however, is not meant to be a complete history of Christian black culture and people, the black church, or the sources of the racial divisions within God's American churches. It is a Reader's Digest version, if that and at best.

Yet I hope that this overview will offer enough information to be enlightening to Christian white readers who may want or need to know more. Moreover, it is my hope that this book will help pave the way, for a few or many, toward a broader education and a deepening bond between and among God's children who have for so long been divided by race, culture and animosity.

A VERY BRIEF HISTORY OF THE BLACK CHURCH IN THE UNITED STATES

Christianity in Africa

Christianity was introduced in North Africa as early as the first century AD,[iii] such as was seen with the eunuch mentioned in Acts 8. Clearly, Europeans were not the first Christians on that continent. But it was the colonialization of Africa from the 15th century onward that served to ramp up the introduction of Christianity from Europe to the African people. Exposure to the teachings of Christ began to grow in the late 1400's as European missionaries first began to come in growing numbers to sub-Saharan Africa. Further mission work came as exploring and/or conquering Europeans came to the continent from Portugal, Spain, Britain, and other European powers. For instance, Catholicism was spread via the Portuguese in conquered territories of what is now Angola and the Congo in the 1700's. During the same period, Christian missionaries throughout Europe and of all denominations began to see Africa as a destination for missionary work, resulting in missionaries from a wide spectrum of denominations, many of them in competition and conflict with each other.[iv]

All the while, of course, the global trade in African slaves had begun and continued to grow until its peak in the 1780's. So, despite the newly born enthusiasm for the conversion of the African people and the gradual increase in distaste for the slave trade, there was also an increasing demand for slave labor from the African colonies.

Unfortunately, some Europeans and even Christian Europeans misused and abused Biblical references, such as the "Curse of Ham"[v] and Paul's admonition for slaves to obey their masters, as religious justifications for slavery and/or the sub-humanization of Africans and blacks. Used improperly and without the context of the times in which they were written or the entirety of the

42

Scriptures, the Bible was made to appear to condone slavery in both the Old and New Testaments.

Thus, while some Christians were interested in saving the souls of Africans, others were justifying their enslavement to the Christians who were supposed to see all people as equal before the eyes of God. It was an ironic blend of two messages taken from the same Bible – soul-saving and second-class citizenship; equality in the eyes of God and an errant allowance for slavery via a divinely ordained racial hierarchy. So, while Christian compassion for the plight of slaves meant that money could be raised for missions work in the African continent, money was simultaneously being made through shackles and bondage.

Over time, of course, anti-slavery Christians and the Abolitionist movements (which Christians helped birth) gradually won the day, starting in Britain. Britain banned the Atlantic slave trade in 1807 and slavery in its colonies in 1834. Indeed, it was British Christians who helped shut down the global slave trade by pushing for legislative action in Parliament and, eventually, military assistance. Since British influence was so strong, as went Britain, so went the world. Other European capitals therefore followed Britain's direction and outlawed the trading and/or use of slaves within their colonies. Spain in 1811, Sweden in 1813, the Netherlands in 1814, France in 1817.

To implement these bans, the British government eventually used its powerful Navy, at great expense to its national coffers, to patrol the waters off the coast of Africa to search for vessels still engaged in the trade of slaves, usually Arab Muslims who remained actively engaged in slave trading throughout the 1800's. Indeed, the horrific stories of the deaths of Africans in the deserts and on the seas while in the hands of Arab Muslim slave traders brought more vigilance and determination to the task of breaking the slave trade.

The changing political and economic dynamics throughout this period also increased the power of the abolitionist movements in the U.S. and across the globe, while general enthusiasm for mission work among freed slaves and the African peoples increased. In the early- to mid-1800's, both Catholic and Protestant missionary expeditions were launched with new vigor. The results included a huge increase in the number of non-European Christians. In 1800, only roughly one percent of Protestant Christians lived in Asia, Africa, and Latin America. By 1900, this number had grown to ten percent. Today, at least sixty-seven percent of all active Protestant Christians live in countries once considered foreign mission fields.[vi]

Christianity and slavery in the United States

According to many history books, the first African slaves arrived on U.S. soil as indentured servants in 1619, in Jamestown, VA.[vii] However, such a definitive date and event may be overly simplistic, since African peoples are thought to have been brought to the United States nearly one hundred years earlier[viii]. Nonetheless, by the late 18th and early 19th centuries, slavery was alive and well, particularly in the American South. As in Europe, Christian slave owners often justified their economic and physical dominance over their slaves through the misuse and abuse of Biblical scripture. Indeed, the so-called Curse of Ham was still being used by the Ku Klux Klan in the twentieth century as justification for segregation, slavery, and the supremacy of whites.

American slaves could have, but did not, seek solace in the other religions and beliefs that were known to the African peoples, such as Islam,[ix] or in the works of white philosophers like Hume, More, or Leroux, or the later egalitarianism of Marx and Engels. Some clung to their historical roots and the beliefs of their ancestral homelands, including derivatives of African rituals such as Conjure.[x] But these latter practices became increasingly difficult as high death rates, separation of families and social units through the trading of slaves, and the growing number of Protestant evangelists served to dissuade the preservation of African traditions. For instance, as slaves were bought and sold, it was common for families to be separated, which caused their African religious customs to begin to be lost. Moreover, as the importation of slaves ended in the early 1800's, the ties with African culture and customs were further severed, increasing the tendency towards the Christian denominations. And as more and more slaves and freed blacks were American native born, ties to the cultures and practices of Africa even further severed.

There was also a concerted effort by some slave owners to eradicate "heathen" customs. Some slave masters were, to varying degrees, tolerant of Christianity among their slaves, even seeing a moral responsibility to convert their slaves to Christianity and away from their "heathen" beliefs while keeping them in bondage.

Moreover, if they allowed it at all, many slave owners preferred preaching that included a deep concentration in a [false, out of context] justification of slavery and God's ordinances for the segregation and enslavement of peoples. This perhaps gave the slave masters some sense of comfort that slaves were saved while justifying the continuation of the economic and physical power to repress and subjugate.

However, not all slave owners were so accommodating or gracious about the religious practices of their captives. American slaves were often severely punished for worshiping God among themselves and defying the teachings of their slave masters. Some slave owners were concerned that unadulterated worship and deeper knowledge of the teachings of the Bible and Jesus specifically might lead to insurrections or too much thought of freedom and equality, a concern that later proved to be valid.

In the 1820's and 1830's, two of the most significant slave rebellions were plotted by Nat Turner and Denmark Vesey, both Christians. In 1829, David Walker's inflammatory articles, written from Boston and entitled "An Appeal to the Coloured Peoples of the World,"[x] not only condemned Christians who supported slavery, but also used Christianity as validation of slave revolts.

Therefore in South Carolina, Virginia and throughout the South, these and other similar events resulted in government regulations for black religious services and preaching, including legal requirements for white supervision of all black religious services.

Hush Harbors

Yet even amid the miseries and oppression of slavery and the restrictive policies prohibiting free worship, blacks still found a way to worship God together more freely and without detection. One such practice was to meet in secluded places – woods, gullies, ravines, and thickets – aptly called hush harbors. Through signals, passwords, and messages not discernable to whites,[xii] slaves were called to hush harbors which allowed the free expression of the message of Christ and the singing, moaning, and dancing that slaves incorporated from their African culture.

Slave Kalvin Woods remembered preaching to other slaves and singing and praying while huddled behind tiny tents made of quilts and rags, which had been thoroughly wetted "to keep the sound of their voices from penetrating the air" and then hung up "in the form of a little room," or tabernacle.[xiii] (The name Tabernacle remains among the common names of independent black churches, e.g. Tabernacle Baptist). Of course, slaves could face severe punishment if caught attending these secret prayer meetings. Moses Grandy reported that his brother-in-law Isaac, a slave preacher, "was flogged, and his back pickled" for preaching at a clandestine service in the woods. His listeners were also flogged and "forced to tell who else was there."[xiv]

Yet, in spite of both harsh treatment and false doctrines, the message of Christ was still able to make its way into even the most repressive environments, as these new believers sought and found comfort in their pain

45

and suffering through Christ's teachings. Christianity thereby began to take on an even stronger role in African American life.

The Great Awakenings

Even as the slave trade and oppression of blacks went on and the decades-long fight for freedom began, Christianity managed to spread to both enslaved and freed blacks. Two of the important elements in the expansion of the Christian American black population were the First and Second Great Awakenings.

The First Great Awakening swept from Europe to the United States in the 1730's and 1740's and served to spread changes in denominations and worship styles as well a revised Christian message to a broader swath of the American public. Slow reductions in attendance and a staid, repetitive, and unenthusiastic preaching style had led to worries about the future of the faith and the fate of the remaining lost. Itinerant First Awakening preachers from Protestant Europe and New England therefore feared for the "deadness" of American churches.

These new-styled preachers used the aptly named "revivals" and powerful preaching styles to spread a message of redemption and personal spiritual conviction in place of ritual, ceremony, and church hierarchy. The First Awakening messages encouraged a strong commitment to personal morality and taught that salvation was based on pure grace rather than position in society, a concept that held great appeal to the masses. The First Awakening thereby reached thousands of converts, including freed and enslaved blacks, and helped spur the growth of newer denominations such as Baptists and Methodists.

The Second Great Awakening, a revival of church influence and attendance that began in the latter 1700's and continued into the early 1800's, was even more impactful to the new black American community. While emphasizing damnation for sin, as was common in the day, the preachers of the Second Awakening stressed the hope that man could act and live morally and have hope for a better life here on earth through choice and free will. The messages emphasized human beings' dependence upon God[xv] and His power to provide, yet opened the door to salvation for all humans, no matter of class, education or status.

Moreover, the Evangelical preaching styles of the revival movement were more attractive to blacks than the earlier, more stoic preaching styles. In the past, northern and much of southern white Christianity had taken on a look and feel that was more European, influenced as they were by their European ancestries in Catholicism and stricter versions of Protestantism.

By contrast, evangelical pastors preached in worship styles that included a more boisterous, plain-styled message of hope and redemption, some of which was brought from their ancestors in parts of England and Scotland. This catered to the mannerisms and worship styles that African men and women carried with them from Africa, including singing, shouting, and dancing, while offering a more hopeful message of deliverance.

Therefore, even though their African religious practices and beliefs had been or were being lost, the styles and preferences of worship that remained could be gelled with Christianity. This ready-made blending of religious practice, message, and worship style obviously appealed to the slave and free black populations far more than the restrictive, often pro-slavery message taught by slave owners and other Christian whites who wanted to maintain control of black independence.

Importantly, the Second Great Awakening led to large-scale and widespread evangelical efforts among slaves and freed slaves. Northern and some Southern Baptist and Methodist ministers, in particular, preached an important message of individual freedom while their denominational leadership supported the widespread establishment of new churches, particularly for slaves and freed blacks.

The Second Great Awakening also enabled northern blacks to reach out to assist their southern enslaved and freed brethren. Through their Protestant denominations such as the Baptists, northern free blacks helped southern blacks by establishing churches and associated schools. Black literacy was thereby greatly improved, moving it from just 5% in the early 1800's to 70% by the late 1800's.

Importantly, even as slavery continued, the ideas of freedom and "classless" salvation of the Second Great Awakening helped lay the groundwork for the Abolitionist movement, which many evangelical Christians joined and supported. Abolitionist ideas became increasingly prominent in Northern churches and politics beginning in the 1830s, which contributed to the regional animosity between North and South leading up to the Civil War.[xvi] Christian authors and leaders such as Theodore D. Weld, William Lloyd Garrison, Arthur and Lewis Tappan, and Elizur Wright, Jr. all spiritually nourished by revivalism, took up the cause of "immediate emancipation."

In early 1831, Garrison began publishing his famous newspaper, the Liberator, in Boston, supported largely by free African Americans. In

December 1833, the Tappan's, Garrison, and sixty other mostly Christian delegates of both races and genders met in Philadelphia to found the American Anti-Slavery Society, which denounced slavery as a sin that must be abolished immediately, endorsed nonviolence, and condemned racial prejudice. By 1835, the Society had received substantial moral and financial support from African American communities in the North and had established hundreds of branches throughout the Free states. They flooded the North with antislavery literature, agents, and petitions demanding that Congress end all federal support for slavery.

Through the expanded availability of the teachings of the Bible and the Gospel of Jesus Christ both slaves and freed blacks came to see meaning, hope, and power in Christ. The evangelism of both the First and Second Great Awakenings led to the rise of tens of thousands of Christian blacks throughout the south, and forever changed the role of Christ in black communities. And of course, the Christians of the Abolitionist movement forever changed the course of the history of God's church in America and the history of the nation, creating a foundational framework which exists today.

The black church: spread and division

However, despite the evangelism that began with Christian whites and continued with northern Christian blacks, and the initial racial unity and equality seen within many churches during this time, racial division in the church eventually took hold just as it had in the broader society.

Much of the split was, of course, due to racism and segregation. Since blacks had suffered under the same oppression, segregation, and subordination, there was a natural tendency to feel a deeper sense of solidarity within their own ranks. This solidarity was driven by myriad factors, such as the historical need for secret worship services and legal demands for white supervision of black services. This led to a growing desire to commune together in worship.

Thus, if blacks were to hold onto their Christianity, they were forced into or chose their own racially segregated denominations. Indeed, given their history in the U.S., it may seem striking that more blacks weren't turned away from Christ altogether and towards Islam and other religions, as Malcomb Little (a.k.a. Malcomb X) famously was. Having seen Christianity incorrectly and maliciously used by slave owners and southern white Christians as divine justification for slavery, oppression, and segregation, only the hope of Jesus Christ kept Christian American blacks from leaving what Malcomb X bitterly called "the white man's religion."

48

The denominations of the black church

The first black churches in America began to be established in the mid 1700's. Many recognize the first black church to be the Silver Bluff Baptist Church, founded in Beach Island, SC in 1750 by local slaves. Some recognize "Bluestone" Church in Mecklenburg Virginia as the first true African church. Still others point to the First African Baptist Church of Savannah (GA), established in 1777, which was originally known as First Colored Church.[xvii]

A.M.E.

Some of the largest black denominations came into being due primarily to racism and racial segregation of the Christian white community. For instance, one of today's largest black denominations in the country grew from restrictions on the mingling of Christian black with Christian whites within the Methodist church in Philadelphia.

As the story is told, Reverend Richard Allen was a black preacher and former Delaware slave who had purchased his freedom in 1780. He had requested to form an independent congregation as an offshoot of St. George's Methodist Church, the first Methodist Church in America, where he attended and had been asked to occasionally preach. Denied his request by church elders, Allen, Absalom Jones (later an ordained Episcopal Deacon and Priest), and a few other free blacks formed the Free African Society in 1787 as a secular group committed to service and charity to the black community to side-step those restrictions.

The final split with the Methodist Church finally came when white congregants voted to force black congregants to sit together in the balcony of the church and away from the whites. When the new restriction was enforced by church leaders, the Christian blacks walked out en masse, with Allen stating at the time "we all went out of the church in a body, and they were no more plagued by us in the church."[xviii]

The new church, under joint leadership of Allen and Jones, was formed in 1792 as the African Church. For myriad reasons, Allen and his followers split from this original body of believers and purchased a blacksmith shop in Philadelphia for $25 from which they worshipped and helped the poor and needy. In 1793 this became Bethel Church, meaning "house of God" (a.k.a. Bethel Methodist Episcopal Church, a.k.a. "Mother Bethel"). To establish Bethel's independence, Allen successfully sued in the Pennsylvania courts in 1807 and 1815 for the right of his congregation to exist as an institution independent of white Methodist congregations. Meanwhile, Jones and the remaining members of the African Church formed the African Episcopal Church of St. Thomas with Jones as its Lay Leader and Deacon.

Then in 1816, Rev. Allen of the aforementioned Bethel Church called together sixteen representatives from black churches in Philadelphia, Baltimore, Wilmington (DE) and nearby Attleboro (PA). A new Wesleyan church organization or "connection" was organized as the African Methodist Episcopal Church (A.M.E.). Richard Allen became the founder and first Bishop of what was thenceforth known as the African Methodist Episcopal Church, now one of the largest Christian black denominations in the world.

A.M.E.Z.

Allen, Jones, and this group of Methodist blacks were not alone in suffering under discrimination in white churches. Simultaneously, blacks in surrounding cities were dealing with their own segregation and discrimination issues and thus also desired religious autonomy from their Christian white congregations. Thus, during this same period, segregation also led to the formation of the Zion Chapel, which later became The Mother Church of Zion Methodism in Harlem and the founding home of what would later be called the African Methodist Episcopal Zion (AMEZ) denomination. (The "Zion" moniker was added in 1848 both to distinguish it from the black Methodist and Episcopal congregations of Philadelphia and to emphasize some of the core beliefs.) Due to its focus on racial justice, peace, and harmony, and its support of the abolitionist movement and the Underground Railroad, it is sometimes known by its congregants as the "Freedom Church." Sojourner Truth, Harriett Tubman, and Frederick Douglass were all members, the latter being an A.M.E.Z. pastor.

Presbyterians

Similarly, in 1807, the first black Presbyterian Church was formed in Philadelphia by former Tennessee slave John Gloucester. Gloucester was born enslaved in 1776. As a young man, Gloucester was taken under the wing of a local white Presbyterian preacher, Rev. Gideon Blackburn, who trained him in theology and purchased him with the intent of enabling his freedom.

Upon his release from slavery, Gloucester went to Philadelphia where he began preaching to groups that would later form the initial congregation of a new denomination. Chartered as the First Colored Presbyterian Church by the Pennsylvania Supreme Court in 1809, the first church was built on the empty lot where a tent once served as a church meeting space.[xix] The church name was later changed to the First African Presbyterian Church.

Methodists

Between 1860 and 1866, more than two-thirds of the black membership of the mixed-race Methodist Episcopal Church South (MECS, which later became the United Methodist Church) left that church to join other Methodist bodies that had begun competing for the membership of freed black men. Most joined one of two independent black denominations from the North, the aforementioned African Methodist Episcopal Church and the African Methodist Episcopal Zion Church where they enjoyed greater autonomy and freedom of expression.

In 1866, in order to prevent further losses of its membership and to recognize the growing desire for black congregations among freed blacks, the MECS began support for the creation of a separate black Methodist Episcopal denomination. In 1870, forty-six black delegates and a committee representing the MECS convened in Jackson, Tennessee, to establish the Colored Methodist Episcopal Church, the first African American denomination established in the South.[xx] This became the Christian Methodist Episcopal (CME) Church in the 1950's, with nearly one million members today.

Baptists

The Baptist denomination had spread quickly through intense missions work and denominational support for new and independent churches within the black community. In 1808, the Abyssinian Baptist Church was formed by blacks who refused to tolerate the segregation within the First Baptist Church of New York City.

By the turn of twentieth century, there were millions of black Baptists throughout the young nation. Thus, in 1895, a meeting attended by more than 2000 clergy was held in Atlanta, Georgia, gathering the three largest black Baptist conventions of the day: the Baptist Foreign Missionary Convention, the American National Baptist Convention, and the National Baptist Educational Convention. They merged to form the National Baptist Convention of the United States of America (NBC), which formally brought both northern and southern black Baptist churches together. Among the delegates to the 1895 meeting was Rev. A.D. Williams, pastor of Ebenezer Baptist Church and grandfather of the Rev. Martin Luther King, Jr.[xxi]

The NBC's founding was perhaps the most significant institutional development in post-Reconstruction black religious life, as it became the nation's largest African American denomination. After other denominational splits, total membership in the various black Baptist denominations is now around five million.

Importantly, black Baptists later played a significant role in the Civil Rights movement. Black Baptist Pastors were the main force in the organization of the Atlanta-based Southern Christian Leadership Conference, which Dr. Martin Luther King Jr. led for eleven years. Black Baptist churches throughout the southeastern United States hosted mass meetings, staged sit-ins, marched in protests, and promoted black voter registration. They, along with other black denominations, gave the movement a distinct religious cast, as spirituals, sermons, and the practice of nonviolence blended into radical activism and protest.

Church of God

The evolution of the black church in the late 1800's and early 1900's also saw the rise of other black denominations. In 1897, the Church of God, later known as the Church of God In Christ (COGIC), was founded at the St. Paul Church in Mississippi by two black preachers, Rev. Charles Mason and Rev. Charles Jones. Mason's later experience with Pentecostalism led to a split within the congregation. Jones' group of Holiness-focused congregants moved to form the Church of God (Holiness) USA, a denomination that remains today.

Mason's more Pentecostal teachings remained under the Church of God in Christ and moved its new headquarters to Memphis, Tennessee, where the now famous Mason Temple was completed in the early 1940's. At the time, the roughly 4000-seat Mason Temple was the largest church auditorium of any black denomination in America, and attracted many famous black Americans including Dr. Martin Luther King, who delivered his Mountaintop speech there on the night prior to his assassination. COGIC would eventually become the largest Pentecostal denomination and the fourth largest Christian denomination in the United States.

Other black denominations sprang up in response to the growth of these newly formed congregations. Indeed, it is said that the movement of Christian blacks away from Christian whites throughout the 18th and 19th centuries was an initial form of rebellion against the restriction of civil rights and was perhaps the first Civil Rights protest.

Black Theology

Though there is no single denomination for it, Black Theology (a.k.a. Black Liberation Theology) grew out of the Civil Rights Movement in the late 1960's as both an intellectual and a spiritual movement. While there is great variation in the messaging and specifics, Black Theology generally holds that the dominant white culture has corrupted Christianity, its purpose for mankind, and the primary central themes and teachings of Jesus Christ.

Though its roots have been traced to the antebellum slavery period,[xxii] Rev. James Cone is widely known as the father of the movement. He penned many books on the subject of the purpose and intent of Jesus Christ relative to the plight of the oppressed, specifically black peoples in America. Cone's writings and teachings became the basis for a broader movement within the black church community that gave power and intent to bold ideas even if they lacked a specific denominational platform. Cone's many books, including the seminal "Black Theology and Black Power," "A Black Theology of Liberation," and "God of the Oppressed," describe the importance of understanding Jesus from the perspective of disenfranchised and oppressed black people. Though published several decades ago, they remain the essential texts of the movement.

Inspired by the works of Rev. Martin Luther King Jr, Malcomb X, and others, Cone's approach to theology saw God as concerned with the weak, the poor, and the oppressed. He saw Christ's most important messages told in Luke 4:16 – 20, and Matthew 25: 31 – 40, wherein Christ speaks of proclaiming good news to the poor, freedom to the prisoners, setting free the oppressed,[xxiii] and serving "the least of these brothers and sisters of mine."[xxiv] With this backdrop, Cone attempts to make the Bible relevant to the situation of American blacks, and differentiate Christ's messages to the weak, poor, and oppressed from what he saw as the Christian white messages of racial superiority and support of oppression.

Some scholars point to the beginnings of the spread of the Black Theology movement in a piece in the New York Times published on July 31, 1966, co-signed by forty-eight black church leaders from a variety of denominations, including A.M.E., Baptist, and U.C.C. Entitled "Black Power: Statement by the National Committee of Negro Churchmen," the article summed up many of the essentials of Black Theology, including the notion that the United States had failed to use its ample resources for the betterment of its own citizens, and that the black church should commit its resources to the advancement of human justice, equality, and freedom.

Black [Liberation] Theology commonly portrays Jesus as a brown-skinned revolutionary rather than a white man with brown hair and a distinctly European visage. Black Theology thereby remakes not just the message but the persona of Jesus Christ to be directly related to the historical suffering of American blacks, thus affirming the identity and humanity of black people while disavowing traditional white theology and its alleged deep roots in historical racism, segregation, and the oppression of blacks.

Black Theology's critique of white theology is broad and cutting. Many advocates believe that white theology is based on the self-serving support of oppression and is thereby focused on elements and actions other than aid to those in need. By lacking a direct and structured focus on justice and equality, white theology missed the essential messages and even the purposes of God's revelation in Jesus Christ. Thus, white theology was misguided, at best, intentionally and callously oppressive at worst.

Perhaps the most notable encounter many Americans have had with Black Theology came from the examination and critique of President Obama's long-time pastor, Dr. Rev. Jeremiah Wright of the Trinity United Church of Christ in Chicago. His often-misrepresented quote, "... God damn America ..." was used as a political weapon against the former President's campaign, highlighting what some perceived to be a radical, divisive, and even hateful and racist theology to which President Obama was said to subscribe. Rev. Wright unintentionally became a divisive figure in both politics and Christianity and a misunderstood example of Black Theology.

In the modern era, Black Theology remains a force in the Christian black community, and is often presented in a bold, forceful, point-blank fashion that can appear to Christian whites as harsh, angry, damning, and divisive. In a sense, it may be. Yet, understanding its history and its context is critical for Christian whites as they encounter its proponents and their messages, whether they agree with those messages or not.

The role of the black church

Racism and segregation thereby played a huge role in the development and growth of the black churches in America. Rather than constrain and control black worship, racism served to extend the spread of Christianity into a black community in need of God's grace, mercy and omnipresence. Just as racism and segregation shaped the modern political and social landscapes, so too did they shape the landscape of the Christian black community by creating the need for unique religious and social structures in which the black church would play a large role. There is little doubt that black churches played, and to a certain extent continue to play, a significant role in the black communities they serve.

Indeed, due to the racism and segregation blacks faced from their arrival onwards, there was and is a distinct role for the black church in black society unlike that of the white church in white society. Dating back to the days of slavery, the church represented much of the social structure and nurturing which blacks needed while in bondage. The church and faith in Jesus created a place of safety, comfort, communal love and bonding, and a respite from the realities of daily slave life. When they were allowed, and otherwise in secret, slaves could gather in relative peace, meet and bond in ways that might have been prohibited under other pretexts. Community and interpersonal relationships were built around the nexus of the worship of God and the hope He offered to both slave and free men and women. Thus, from the earliest days, the American black church took on a central role in black culture and became vital to the American black community.

During the days from Emancipation to segregation, the black church continued its role as a central part of Christian black life. Through the many ministries and intra-congregational assistance programs that sprung up in the black churches, blacks supplied their communities with services unavailable to them through traditional social venues used by whites. Services ranging from transportation to healthcare were aided or provided by fellow black congregants through various ministries. Even interstate travel might be aided by churches along the way, since many hotels and restaurants were often off limits to blacks during the era of segregation. And while ministries by similar names (e.g. health, shelter, food) might have existed in white churches, theirs were born more from a sense of duty or charity rather than group necessity and the open, flagrant denial of access to otherwise public services.

These ministries became and continue to be an important part of the soul of the black church, even as they have evolved into charity and community support.

Politics, the black church and the Civil Rights Movement

Volumes have been written on the role of the black church in the Civil Rights Movement,[xxv] so this book will only offer brevity. However, for perspective's sake and an understanding and appreciation of the Christian black church and its history, Christian whites need to grasp and deeply respect the role that religion played in bringing about dramatic social change. They also need to understand the roles that both supportive and unsupportive Christian whites played. Specifically, Christian whites need to appreciate the damage that was done to God's American church and how that history impacts efforts to unite as God's people today.

Throughout its history, the black church had taken on a bit of a political role, since it was here that blacks could freely and openly express frustration and anger without as much fear of reproach. The church was, in most instances and in most places, a safe place to voice opinions, frustrations, angers, and fears that might otherwise be withheld. Thus, the church was the perfect centralized place for the growth and support of the Civil Rights movement as it grew out of the 1950's.

Baptists, A.M.E., and other black denominations were instrumental in the Civil Rights Movement. Indeed, the great names of the Civil Rights movement were predominantly Christians. Think of the Reverends of the movement. Reverends Martin Luther King Jr., Andrew Young, Ralph Abernathy, Fred Shuttlesworth, Wyatt T. Walker, Joseph Lowery, Hosea Williams, John Lewis, and Jesse Jackson were just a few of the great black men of God who played national leadership roles in the movement.[xxvi] Moreover, Christian black laypeople played an enormous role throughout the period. For instance, Rosa Parks was a lifelong A.M.E. member, and become a Stewardess and Deaconess in the St. Matthew A.M.E. church in Detroit, Michigan where she moved after the Montgomery bus boycott.

Indeed, that game-changing boycott was no random event. It was well-planned by local Christians as part of a strategy for forcing peaceful change, learned from training in non-violent protests received at the renowned Highlander Folk School[xxvii] in eastern Tennessee.

But while great Christian black leaders created a central role for the black church in the movement, it also made the black church a natural target for those opposed to the movement. Attacks on black churches in the South were numerous, as segregationists tried to shut down the venues from which the movement was being supported. This culminated with the infamous deaths of four black girls in the bombing of the Sixteenth Street Baptist Church in Birmingham, Alabama on September 15, 1963. The event proved seminal, sparking a leap in the national awareness of the movement and the conditions against which it fought.

To grasp the power and presence of Christ in the inspired leaders of the black church during the Civil Rights movement, it is important to understand what was not present as much as what was. A good example is found in the words of a hymn, written by James Weldon Johnson in 1900 on the anniversary of President Abraham Lincoln's birthday. Long after Johnson's death in 1938, this song became known as the National Anthem of the Civil Rights Movement, the Negro National Anthem, the Negro National Hymn, and was even adopted by the NAACP as an anthem. Though it was penned some fifty years prior, its message was powerful enough to become a central, unifying theme in the movement. Indeed, it is still sung today in black churches across the nation, and is regularly part of Rev. Martin Luther King Day services.

Its words express a deep faith through troubled times and harsh treatment, as well as the determination to press onward to victory behind a stalwart God. Read these words, carefully and thoughtfully:

Lift every voice and sing,
Till earth and heaven ring,
Ring with the harmonies of Liberty;
Let our rejoicing rise High as the list'ing skies,
Let it resound loud as the rolling sea

Sing a song full of the faith that the dark past has taught us,
Sing a song full of the hope that the present has brought us;
Facing the rising sun of our new day begun,
Let us march on till victory is won.

Stony the road we trod,
Bitter the chast'ning rod,
Felt in the days when hope unborn had died;
Yet with a steady beat,
Have not our weary feet
Come to the place for which our fathers sighed?

We have come over a way that with tears has been watered.
We have come, treading our path through the blood of the slaughtered,
Out from the gloomy past,
Till now we stand at last
Where the white gleam of our bright star is cast.
God of our weary years,
God of our silent tears,
Thou who hast brought us thus far on the way;
Thou who hast by Thy might,
Led us into the light,
Keep us forever in the path, we pray

Lest our feet stray from the places, our God, where we met Thee,
Lest our hearts, drunk with the wine of the world, we forget Thee;
Shadowed beneath Thy hand,
May we forever stand,

True to our God
True to our native land.

Read aloud, even without its powerful accompanying tune (which you should hear if you haven't), it reminds us of an inspirational sermon that might have been given sixty years later by Rev. King himself.

Note that in these words there is no bitterness, only hope. No hate, only the promise of redemption. No negativity, only faith in a loving God whose ever-present love guides the path of the faithful through life's many troubles. And it is this faithfulness that enabled the Civil Rights Movement to become what it was.

Thus, were it not for Christians blacks and the role of deep-seated Christianity within the black community, America would likely have seen a much different, likely much more violent, end to segregation. The forces pulling the Civil Rights movement towards racial separation and violence during the prominence of Dr. King were numerous and strong. Had Malcomb X and Elijah Muhammed's version of Islam or other even more radical groups won the day, our nation might have faced a very different, less peaceful, Civil Rights Movement.

Christian whites and the Civil Rights Movement

Of course, there was tremendous moral and spiritual support for the movement from some Christian whites. Christian whites, as well as many Jews, became strong political supporters of the movement as voters and activists, helping push an agenda of freedom and fairness that rang true in their Christian hearts and minds. Indeed, the only person to die during the period of the three Selma marches in March 1965 was a white minister, Rev. James Reeb, while two other Christian whites (one pastor and one layperson) were murdered in the aftermath of the Selma marches. (The only black person to be murdered during the period was actually a Baptist Deacon, Jimmy Lee Jackson, whose murder by an Alabama State Trooper served to initiate the Selma protests). There are numerous photographs of Christian white pastors and priests marching alongside, arm in arm, with the great black Christian Civil Rights leaders of the day. Across the nation, Christian whites joined their Christian black brothers and sisters in support of the cause, while northern Christians and members of Congress pushed and finally attained the peaceful legislative end of segregation.

Despite this support, history shows us that Christian whites were not always helpful in the fight for black civil rights. Even though Christian whites spread the gospel to blacks in the Great Awakenings and through missionary efforts dating back to the 1400's, God's church in America was not united against either racism or segregation. Some churches tacitly or openly supported both. Both in the North and in the South, Christian whites were seen as unsupportive and even hostile to the cause.

Ironically, many white evangelicals were vehemently opposed to racism in their writings yet were opposed to the tactics advocated by popular Civil Rights leaders. They were resistant for several reasons, some of which they considered spiritual. For instance, some felt that Christians should focus on "personal regeneration ... instead of the social and systemic change advocated by"[xxviii] King and others. They believed that the preaching of "social gospel" undermined Christians' duty to proselytize and save souls. Issues such as justice were secondary, while saving souls should be the priority. To digress into society's fights would divert attention from more important objectives.

Indeed, some fundamentalists and evangelicals were adamant that the Civil Rights Movement was not of the church's concern, and furthermore believed that it was not the role of government to decide on such social matters.[xxix] Man's faults would be corrected only when hearts are changed, and no amount of legislation could do that. This penchant towards "limited government" led them to oppose legislation that might attempt to change the hearts of man through government diktat. Government legislation on civil issues like desegregation were thereby seen as both unnecessary and even dangerous. Thus, the middle ground of "voluntary segregation" was often the choice.

Still others opposed both the tactics and the purpose of the movement. In 1955, L. Nelson Bell, editor of *Southern Presbyterian* magazine, laid out evangelicals' and God's position on civil rights in an unflinching denunciation of integration. He wrote that though there were Christians who supported the Civil Rights Movement, there were others who were "as Christian ... as any in this world" who believed that it was "un–Christian, unrealistic and utterly foolish to force those barriers of race which have been established by God and which when destroyed by man are to his own loss."[xxx]

Following the 1954 *Brown vs. Board of Education* ruling, *Christian Life*, another leading evangelical journal, vowed to become "a (stronger) forum for resistance to desegregation." It urged principled believers to fight for "reversal."[xxxi]

The pastor of one of the largest Baptist churches in Alabama, stated plainly, "I am a believer in a separation of the races, and I am none the less a Christian. If you want to get in a fight with the one that started the separation of the races, then you come face to face with your God. The difference in color, the difference in our body, our minds, our life, our mission upon the face of this earth, is God given."

It would therefore not be out of the ordinary to see a Ku Klux Klan supporter also be a regular churchgoer or even church lay leader. All one need do is reference Rev. King's Letter from a Birmingham Jail[xxxii] (later published in *The Atlantic* as "The Negro is Your Brother") to understand the rift that existed between Christian blacks and some Christian whites and their churches and pastors.

Obviously, then, some Christian whites were complicit in and supportive of the divisions of God's church into racially segregated camps, a division that lives on today. Though this has changed, the reputation and stereotypes of Christian whites due to their lack of universal support for the Civil Rights movement haunts current efforts to be seen in a different light.

The black church in the post-Civil Rights era

In the decades after the Civil Rights movement, the role of the black church has evolved. Many churches remain the social and political hub of their communities. For those who remain members of black churches, the same support structures and mechanisms and political representation often remain intact, continuing the role of the church as an important component within the black community. Meanwhile, church ministries have expanded from fulfilling the necessities of a segregated and isolated black population to charity for the poor and needy of all colors and creeds while working to surmount the ongoing impacts of decades of segregation and racism. Many churches have become vital parts of their local education and healthcare systems in an effort to ensure equal opportunities for even the poorest among us, while continuing to spread God's word and pushing for social justice.

Sadly, more generally and throughout the American population, there has been a movement away from churches and religion in recent years. It is estimated that demographic shifts alone will cause many of our churches to close in the next twenty years. This is impacting both black and white communities and our nation's churches.

Therefore, like all churches, black churches continue to work to grow their congregations, minister to their local communities, reach the unsaved and lost, and generally expand God's Kingdom and the love of Christ here on earth. This, of course, is made more difficult by the current political and social environment described elsewhere in this book. And this is a primary reason why racial unity within God's church is so important.

THE ROLE OF THE BLACK PASTOR

To understand the history of the black church you must understand the role of the preacher in the black church. Accounts from the days of American slavery vary, but it is clear that the black pastor was vitally important in many slave communities. He might have been the only one literate enough to read the Bible, or simply the one God called to serve his fellow slaves through preaching, teaching, and the expression of Christian love. Clearly, the pastor stood as a prominent member of the community.

As discussed earlier in this chapter, the pastor's leadership within the slave community brought it together and offered a sense of hope, restoration and the love of Christ. And though he often had to walk a thin line between the wishes of the slave master and his desire to nurture the flock, he was a central and respected figure, certainly among the black enslaved Christians. Indeed, these early American Christian leaders were commonly the ones who organized the aforementioned hush harbors were they could preach without the inhibitions of white supervision. They were also the ones beaten and abused when hush harbors were discovered, or if slave owners disliked the message being delivered.

As the role of the church in Christian black society evolved, the church became a central gathering place for blacks where they could not only find the freely available love, hope, and peace of Jesus Christ, they could also find solace, refuge, needed services, and a political voice uninhibited by whites, racism, and segregation.

This, in part, explains the role that black pastors played in the Civil Rights movement. They were already well-spoken[xxxiii], articulate, and well-versed in the word of God, and certainly able to rally their congregants. And they were already anointed, respected leaders in their communities. Small wonder, then, that these men stood to lead their people out of the bondage of segregation. It is therefore not at all surprising to see the role of the black pastors become one of part-time social agitators, just as they had been in the days of the hush harbors.

As black clergy took front and center roles in the Civil Rights movement, black churches served as hubs for activism, mobilization, resistance training, and organization. They believed and preached that God Himself had ordained and codified the central demands of the Civil Rights movement, including freedom and equality. These messages combined with the role of the black pastor as a respected community figure made the black church a perfect place from which to foster this important movement.

Today, some black churches have maintained this political and social justice voice, with some pastors openly speaking from the pulpit on political and social issues relevant for today (as described elsewhere in this book). For other black pastors, politics are now best left outside the church walls, or at least out of the pulpit, since the public expression of political opinion is now more freely accepted. Either way, black preachers remain respected and loved figures and important to the lives of their flocks.

My thoughts on the future of the black pastor

Unifier. Disciple of God. Respected. Loved. An admired yet humble servant. Seeking the glory and plan of God rather than personal wealth, fame, or prestige. That is the description of the great religious and Civil Rights leaders of our past, of all races. This is what is needed in the American church today.

Now that many of the great historical leaders of the Civil Rights movement have faded away, there is a gap in the black church's national public-facing leadership. When whites are asked about modern Christian black leaders, the names Al Sharpton and perhaps Jesse Jackson will commonly come to mind. If the questioned person is Christian, perhaps T.D. Jakes, Dr. Rev. Tony Evans, or well-known black televangelists, such as Rev. Creflo Dollar, might come up.

But for the broader society, there are no central figures who appropriately represent the black church in the manner and impact of the great Civil Rights leaders of the 1960's. Perhaps that's with good reason. Indeed, it may be appropriate that men and women serve their local communities and collaborate, unite, and work with other Christians at a local level to impact society and bring glory to God.

Or perhaps there is now, as much as ever, a need for the rise of a group of national Christian black leaders, whose respectability comes from God-inspired humility, integrity, honesty, objectivity, and true Christian love for their fellow man. Perhaps these men and women could lead the charge towards racial unity arm-in-arm with their fellow Christian whites, showing America what God can do when Christians unite together to solve society's most pressing problems with the kind of honesty, objectivity, uprightness (defined in detail in Chapter 6), and love that only God Himself can muster within His children. Perhaps we need Christian black leaders to take leadership roles that society says we should never again have, and, in the name of Jesus, address that which society and government will never be able to address.

LESSONS FROM THE FORMATION OF THE BLACK CHURCH IN AMERICA

There are a few take-aways that might be gleaned from the formation of black churches in America and their roles in the black community.

The first is obvious: American Christianity would not have the racial divisions it historically had and currently has were it not for the broader society's racism and segregation. Simply put, American Christianity suffered from some of the same worldliness that surrounded it. White churches were anything but united against segregation and racism. Thus, it was required that blacks form their own denominations if they were to continue to worship a Christian God. While Christian whites can now look back and shake our collective heads over our foolish behavior, the damage was done to both society and the bride of Christ.

Yes, one could make the argument that Christian blacks and whites would have still separated based solely or partly on the varieties of worship and preaching style preferences and other non-economic and non-race factors. Freed blacks might have joined independent black denominations founded during the antebellum period simply for the sake of preferences and interacting with "people who look like me." Perhaps they might have preferred the preaching styles of certain denominations that might have more closely resembled the worship styles of their ancestors. Or they may have simply preferred the solidarity and unifying spirit of all-black congregations where communing with those of similar circumstances and life perspectives was easier and more comfortable.

Yet, even as these preferences continue to exist, there would not be the distinctive racial element that caused the initial separation and the growth of the black church as a separate manifestation of God's presence. Indeed, if racism was not part of our collective past, church unification would be as easy as the unification of any group of churches around any given important cause. While today we see great examples of multi-racial worship in churches across the country, without the racial divisions that plagued much of the nation in the early days of the Christian racial splits it is likely that many more congregations might resemble these multi-racial examples.

Furthermore, racism and segregation in America kept generations of blacks from attaining their full economic and productive potential, the results of which are still felt today. This manifests itself, in part, in where people live, how they interact, and the socio-economic stratifications that run throughout the nation. Thus, the socio-racial divisions of our country's past created and, to a certain extent, maintain the current environment and circumstances in which churches now abide, thus dictating some of the racial separations between churches we see today.

Again, all this division and separation may ultimately be either good or bad for God's church. Only God knows what plans He has for His church. But we know instinctively, as a Christian community of Believers that any separation based in worldliness is not in keeping with the messages of the Bible.

Second, the growth of the black church in America is impressive. During the days of slavery, despite the ironic harshness of often Christian slave owners, Christian blacks maintained their faith in Christ and expanded their ranks. When Christian whites discriminated against their Christian black brothers and pushed them out of their white churches, or misused and abused scripture to justify discrimination, slavery and segregation, Christian blacks did not give up their faith. Indeed, their faith strengthened, their ranks grew, and they formed tight church-based communities.

And even when some of the many Christian whites failed to come to the fight for Civil Rights, or joined in the discrimination and racism against blacks, Christian blacks did not leave their faith or give up on the love of Christ. Rather, the great leaders of the Civil Rights movement prayed for their errant brothers and sisters, that they might come to a better understanding of the word of God and His call for equality, justice, and love and thus join with their movement.

The growth and depth of the faith of Christian blacks speaks volumes about a relationship with God and Christ that is a model for those still under oppression around the world. It is far easier to praise God when you're on top than when you are at the bottom looking up at the heel of a boot.

Tens of millions of Christians suffer under oppression around the world. In the Middle East and Africa, thousands are murdered, chased from their homes and homelands, and abused for their faith by Muslim and autocratic oppressors each year. In many Middle Eastern Muslim countries, including allies of the United States, Christianity is outlawed.

Likewise, in Asia, Christianity and other religions are often outlawed or oppressed or both, making the worship of our loving God a crime, punishable by imprisonment, theft, extortion, rape, and even death. We see the turmoil, strife, and oppression which Christians suffer in China. The fact that so many Christian blacks, of all national origins, remained true to their faith, and flourished in their church communities where they found the love of Jesus ever-present in the face of oppression, murder, rape, and enslavement, is inspiring and humbling.

Third, the spread of denominations was a good thing … we just might not know it yet. Just as with the Christian white church, Christian black denominations grew, spread, and split. While some view this as a bad thing, the divisions helped diversify the membership and grow Christianity's ranks. Just as there are music, clothing, and architectural preferences among groups of individuals, so too are there preferences in the style, manner, and means of worshiping Christ. The sacraments and style of the Catholic Church appeal to some while the engaging spirit of the Pentecostal church appeals to others. Some prefer the preaching style of "hoopers," others prefer a more sedate style. The proliferation of denominations enabled more people to select their preferred approach to worship, preaching, and service, thus expanding opportunities for churches to extend their reach into local communities.

Perhaps, in other words, "God meant it for good" [Genesis 50:20]. How many more black souls were saved through the black church? How many more came to know Christ in a "like me" environment? How did black churches meet the needs of Christian blacks and black communities during the years of segregation, thus shining God's light of love and provision into a lightless world of hatred, racism, and oppression? How have Christian blacks come to rely on God's provision for their needs, showing even the richest of white men what it means to truly be thankful, prayerful, and Godly? How did God shine the light of forgiveness and Christian virtues through the many great Christian Civil Rights leaders of the period, overcoming the violent tendencies of other black leaders?

Most importantly, how might God have teed up His church to take the lead, at just the perfect time in America history, when America needs His leadership, His hope, His light, and His guidance the most? How has God brought us, 200 million plus strong, to a tipping point of our own history and role in American society? How has He, through machinations we may never be able to see much less comprehend, used the ugliness of our racist past to make His Kingdom glorified through the unification of His church?

CONCLUSION

Like most churches in America, Christian black churches work hard to grow and maintain active membership, engage within their communities, help those in need of assistance, and cast God's influence within society. Yet most Christian churches continue to act predominantly as individual silos, working and doing much good in our own "turf" but rarely collaborating with other Christians for more than occasional emergency relief efforts or holiday charity. Certainly, collaboration for long-term social changes doesn't happen nearly enough. And our racial divisions certainly don't help this. And while it is clear that denominational, doctrinal, historical, and personal preference divisions exist throughout the American body of Christ, racial divisions can even keep Christians of even the same Protestant denominations in separate siloes. Thus, no matter how we are siloed or what prevents our collaboration, we have not yet become a true body of Christ.

So, ask yourself if you can accept these premises:

- Racial divisions in the church may have served to bring more blacks to Christ than would have otherwise known Him. Thus, the American church is likely larger than it would have been had denominational splits not divided Christians by race.
- Regardless of the historical and current reasons, churches remain largely segregated along racial lines.
- There are some 350,000 congregations in the United States, attended by some 54 million Christians with another 200 million claiming Christianity as their faith. Yet, these are largely siloed from one another, even within denominations and racial groups.
- If those 54 million (or more!) Christians were to put aside the racial history and become the unified church that the Bible calls us to be, we would become an unstoppable force for good. We would show our nation and the world what God's Kingdom can do when united around Godly principles and action.
- America needs God's church NOW, perhaps more than ever before!

If you can accept these, then perhaps you'll agree with me that NOW is the time for God's church to put aside all our worldliness, our ungodly dishonesty and lack of pure integrity, our divisions and lack of communication, and our history of segregation and unite for the glory of God and betterment of our society.

RACE AND RACISM FROM A CHRISTIAN WHITE MALE PERSPECTIVE

BACKGROUND

When the racial divisions Christians display are the same or even more dramatic than society's divisions, we are seen as no better or sometimes worse than the society we seek to impact. No better because we are just as divided as our society is. Worse because we are seen as hypocrites for claiming a Savior who is supposed to inspire us to act and think better. It's one thing to claim no greater power or god as a guide and be socially, politically, or racially divided. It is another to claim to have the power and love of Christ in us and be divided in those same ways.

In light of our own sinful humanity, the history of Christian racial division is not hard to explain. Since Christians live in society and are commonly far more engaged in society than in the churches we attend or claim to attend, it's no small wonder that we can sometimes take society's overall norms as our own and make society's larger social and political splits our splits. Clearly, history shows that Christians can take on the same thoughts, emotions, stereotypes, and even hatred as the society in which we live.

So, rather than setting an example of how things could be, we instead often set the example of how things should not be and support the way things are. Indeed, we often mimic the words and deeds of our fallen society by reacting, thinking, and speaking in the very same ways or worse. Thus, our Christianity is at best seen as a secondary or tertiary characteristic rather than that which drives us.

It is therefore not outrageous to see how Christian whites might have been coopted by, or even participated in, historical segregation and overt racism, since it was such a deeply intrinsic part of American social history. Likewise, given several hundred years of blatant, violent, and ongoing injustices, it is not hard to imagine that Christian blacks might have become enamored of the enraged, hateful, and even violent rhetoric of some social justice and political movements. As Christians, we sometimes forget whose light we are supposed to shine and are instead consumed by the darkness around us.

Just as in the society around us, few issues have divided the church the way race has. Yes, there are divisions among churches on everything from doctrine to music style to baptism to gay marriage and even the support of abortion. Various congregations might differ on the approach to poverty, though I think we could all agree that it is an issue that needs to be addressed. Likewise, few would argue with the call in Micah 6:8 to "do justice," but we might disagree on the approach to attaining it or its relative importance in our evangelical efforts. Yet these differences should merely spawn creativity and encourage a variety of potential solutions to our problems but should not divide us.

In contrast, race continues to divide the church in ways these issues have not, perhaps now more than ever, even if in mostly benign ways. Not since the Protestant Reformation has the church split in such a fashion!

It is therefore no small irony that as our nation becomes more and more racially divided, our churches are not stepping forward and uniting across racial boundaries to take advantage of the opportunities these rifts offer to show a better path. Even if only by history, preferences, social differences, and other non-racial reasons, we are instead nearly as divided as ever. This leaves society, government, and non- and anti-Christian organizations to fill the void that Christ should fill in our broken world. Thus we, as Christian blacks and whites, are missing the great opportunity to bring glory to God by showing ourselves as a united people, having conquered the racial divide and united in action. Instead, we are too often a house divided.

And, as Jesus clearly tells us (three times in three chapters of the New Testament[xxxiv]), a house divided will not stand.

PERSPECTIVES

Before moving on to the meat of this chapter, I need to be clear that my goal here is to help Christians, particularly Christian whites, understand the social landscape in which they are being asked to work. To that end, I want to help ensure that all Christians have a full understanding of the current racial terminology so that they might be better equipped to undertake the necessary efforts to bring about unity in the body of Christ and social change in our nation. Without common terminology, one side will be speaking Greek, the other Latin … they won't even share the same alphabet. And thus, communication would be at risk, and certainly more difficult.

68

I therefore ask the reader not to infer that I am denying the existence of racism in our nation, nor that I am downplaying or amplifying its current or past implications. To the contrary. Part of the reason for this book is to help Christians to bring about the eradication of racism in all its forms, as you'll see in later chapters.

Furthermore, I ask the reader to avoid reading into my analysis of these definitions either support for or denial of their legitimacy or credence, or any opinion as to the dignity or intelligence of those who purport them. Whether one believes that, for instance, systemic racism exists as it is defined herein or elsewhere, or that racism is only a component of the current plight of blacks in our nation, is up to each individual. One may find it impossible to even suggest that racism no longer has an impact on blacks, or that its lingering effects have been fully removed. Likewise, one might believe that making racism the single culprit for each and every social malady in the black community is overly simplistic. Thus, a Christ-centered dialogue that deeply addresses these issues will be critical as Christians move forward toward unity.

But herein, I am not advocating for a particular side of any of these definitions. Therefore, I ask the reader to make your own judgments, understanding that how these definitions are used will likely have a significant impact on your intra-racial Christian dialogues and relationships.

THE MEANING OF RACISM

"The words of the wicked lie in wait for blood, but the speech of the upright rescues them." (Proverbs 12:6)

"The words of the reckless pierce like swords, but the tongue of the wise brings healing." (Proverbs 12:18)

Words have power, which can be used for good or evil. Therefore, an understanding of the transformation of the term racism over the past several decades is important for several reasons. One is simply a deeper understanding of the history of the changes to the definitions of the term, whether you agree with and support the newer definitions or not.

For instance, some of my Christian black friends[xxxv] did not fully understand how these definitions had changed over time and had not detected or even considered their slow transmutation within the modern lexicon. Likewise, some of my Christian white friends didn't understand the full implications of the changes in the terminology, and thus were clueless as to how they, as Christian whites, were perceived by modern society.

Thus, there is a need to understand the changing definitions within the context of modern social perceptions and interactions. And because of the very different perspectives on the issue, it is likely that some readers will accept the changes as positive, while others may find them devious, disturbing, and deceptive. Either way, it is important for our discussions that we all have a basic knowledge of the situation we face and the words we'll need to use.

Second, and most important for this book, is the application of the new and broader definitions of racism to Christian whites and Christianity in general. As you will see, modern definitions have turned important Biblical principles and guidelines into racist characteristics and attitudes, particularly among Christian whites. This is important for an understanding of the evolving sources of disunity and the possibilities for church unity across racial boundaries, the impacts these new definitions have on modern day racial dialogue, and on personal and social relationships.

And while many Christian black readers will already fully understand and even support these alterations, it is important to understand these changes within the context of the future impact of the church on modern American society and the relationships between white and black brothers and sisters within the body of Christ. As you will see, the justifiable zeal to fight racial injustices may have unintended consequences which our enemies are using against the faith and the faithful. The brush is broad that paints an ugly stripe, and how society views some of us taints how it views all Christians.

I offer the following as a very brief overview of the history and evolution of the term "racism" as a means to enlighten future discussions. This is not meant to be a granular analysis of each version of the terminology, nor is it meant to justify or condemn the use of any of the terms. Furthermore, it is not a complete anthology, as some lesser used terms and concepts are not listed. It is simply meant to offer a perspective on the evolution of the use of the word racism so as to analyze the implications for the future of the unity of American Christianity.

CHANGING DEFINITIONS

You might think that the definition of racism is something like the following: "A belief that race is the primary determinant of human traits and capacities and that racial differences produce an inherent superiority of a particular race."[xxxvi] Or, "Prejudice, discrimination, or antagonism directed against someone of a different race based on the belief that one's own race is superior."[xxxvii] You might also believe that racism refers to "hatred or intolerance of another race or other races."[xxxviii] If so, you'd be correct. And quite wrong. Correct in the sense that these were and remain textbook definitions of racism. Wrong in the sense that the cultural definitions and use of the term racism has changed dramatically since the 1960s.

The alteration of the meaning of the term racism began shortly after the initial successes of the Civil Rights Movement and continued in earnest throughout the 1980's and into the present age. During this decades-long period, racism's mid-twentieth century manifestations began to fade away as culturally and politically unacceptable. As if our society slowly began to sprout a collective conscience, the overt racism of early modern American history began to die as more white Americans realized its foolishness and the inherent, God-decreed equality of all people.

Yet, even as the textbook manifestations of racism slowly began to die away, racial discord and animus remained. There was no switch that our society could quickly and completely flip. Opportunity disparities, discrimination, what were seen as racist policies and laws, and overt and covert racial animus and discrimination continued to exist, seemingly unabated, throughout the country.

Thus, the term racism began to evolve in the 1970's as some in society and academia sought a way to continue to explain certain aspects of society, economics, and social practices in racial terms.

The Why: Socio-economic outcomes

This was brought on by what was seen as the long-term impacts of segregation and racism as well as the lack of immediacy of racism's dissipation. Socio-economic outcomes were and are not yet equalized. Of course, the results of any form of oppression can linger long after the actual oppression ends, with tentacles that reach well beyond the obvious and outward manifestations. And because the societal switch could not be flipped, racism, segregation, and other similar forms of maltreatment lived on, whether in minor or major ways. So, whether in education, job skills, or wealth accumulation, both the past and the present were thought to impact current outcomes. Commonly cited manifestations of racism's ongoing impacts include black incarceration rates, health disparities, job and career opportunities, and home ownership.

The existence and persistence of these and other disparities thus begged the larger causality questions: If racism in all its forms was truly dead, how could such disparities continue to be? If blacks were truly equal, why did their social and economic outcomes not reflect their newly found equality? And, most importantly, what role, if any, does racism currently play in the lives and opportunities of black people, and to what extent is its influence still felt?

Thus began the effort to explain the current social, economic, and even spiritual disparities and outcomes within the context of historical and ongoing racism.

Symbolic racism

Introduced initially through terms such as symbolic racism, racism was altered from the common textbook definitions by which some races thought themselves to be biologically superior to others thus justifying hatred and discrimination in both social practice and government policy.

The revised definitions instead attempted to broaden the traditional definition by including thoughts, policies, words, and actions that did not openly declare racial superiority, but yet continued to yield racism's outcomes. Symbolic racism, for example, was said to come from a blend of whites' underlying negative feelings towards blacks (acquired early in life through parenting, school, and media) with "the finest and proudest of the traditional American values,"[xxxix] notably individualism and the notion that a person could achieve success through effort. The adjective in the term, symbolic, thus referred to the more esoteric moral values from which the white racist sentiments are said to have emerged, rather than from its traditional manifestations.

Symbolic racism was defined as being characterized by four key beliefs said to be held by whites: That a) racism was/is no longer an ongoing issue (due to the changes in the social acceptance of racism), and therefore, b) blacks should put forth their own effort to achieve success. Furthermore, c) blacks had become overly demanding of society and government as their means of survival, and therefore, d) blacks had already received more than they deserved.[xl], [xli]

Thus, the focus and context of racism began to shift from overt policies (e.g. segregated bathrooms), sentiments (e.g. race-based restrictions to education) and the textbook sense of racial superiority and hatred toward the broader system through which negative outcomes for blacks were derived. Feelings of racial superiority and racial hatred were no longer required attributes for the racist. The only requirement was the existence of certain outcomes and a set of social and moral norms by which to judge the actions and attitudes of blacks.

Furthermore, and importantly, we see the initial linkage between racism and traditional (Christian) moral values, societal norms, and expectations derived from American Protestant behavioral standards.

Modern racism

Symbolic racism was later melded into the term modern racism, a phrase coined in 1976 and further defined in 1981 by John McConahay.[xlii] McConahay's further alterations continued to redefine racism as including ever more subtle, even subliminal, feelings, attitudes, beliefs, and thoughts. Racism lost its strict textbook application, evolving and broadening into an underlying, though potentially even more dangerous, manifestation. Indeed, the "new and improved" version of racism was thought to be even more insidious than the former, more blatant version, as it did not appear to be racism at all.

A major source of whites' alleged negative feelings towards blacks captured in the modern racism definition was said to lie in black Americans' newly found freedom and the resulting expectations for social and economic performance. For the modern racist, lack of black success was no longer necessarily due to genetic inferiority based on ethnicity, but rather the lack of key attributes and characteristics that commonly led to success and a fruitful life within "normal" white society.

Specifically, according to McConahay, modern racists believed that blacks had come to violate key social norms and values that "are associated with what we [McConahay and the other authors] call American civil Protestantism." Namely, blacks and black culture were thought to have rejected "hard work, individualism, sexual repression, and the delay of personal gratification, [along with] … patriotism and reverence for the past …"[xliii] This rejection of these important personal and social characteristics, not racism and its impacts, resulted in subsequent economic and social failures.

The linkage of traditional values with racist attitudes and sentiments thereby created the means by which racism and its discriminatory behaviors could be expressed in seemingly benign and socially acceptable ways. Racism became masked behind existing and long-standing social norms. So, for instance, racism towards blacks could be manifested in the opposition to food stamps, which could be easily couched in opposition to "hand-outs to the lazy and unproductive" in society. "Lazy and unproductive" was, according to the theory, a hidden but direct reference to blacks. Ditto for subsidized housing, single-parent households, and low literacy and graduation rates.

So, we see that the modern racist puts the onus and, to a certain extent the blame, for the black condition not on racism or discrimination or bias, but on blacks, black culture, and black attitudes and behaviors. *This turning of the blame was surmised to be part of the new incarnation of racism.*

Modern racism could thereby take on a subliminal yet impactful role as long as there was "a context in which there is a plausible, non-prejudiced behavior or intended behavior"[xliv] to be highlighted, as exhibited in white attitudes and expectations for good citizens, proper social norms, religious morality, and ethical and behavioral standards.

In other words, what most Christian whites would teach their children as "good, normal, socially-acceptable behavior becoming to a good Christian" became associated with racist thinking. And because racism was no longer a burning cross, a lynched body hanging from a tree, or a whites-only water fountain, and was instead an internalized, even subconscious thought, it was said to be harder to detect and call out yet undeniably present.

Politically, modern racism was said to cause whites to vote in ways they might not otherwise have voted. The new racism and the underlying animosity towards blacks was said to yield race-neutral political rhetoric but distinctly anti-black voting. So strong was the pull of racism that it caused whites to vote against politicians, parties, and ballot measures that might benefit blacks even if they might also benefit some whites. Examples include subsidized housing, extensions of unemployment insurance benefits, free healthcare, and other similar political causes.

For the purpose of this discussion, however, the direct and indirect references in these definitions to Protestantism and religious and moral standards meant that the relationship between racism, Christianity, and more specifically Christian whites, began to become codified and instilled as a truism within the American culture.

This linkage between Judeo-Christian ethics and beliefs and racism continued as the meaning of the term racism continued its evolution. Common social terms and norms associated with Judeo-Christian values, such as personal responsibility, came to be seen as racist and were thereby cast as hateful and oppressive rather than socially preferable or admirable personal qualities.

Thus, in today's society, Christian whites are now often defined generally and broadly as racist to their core, as their insistence on traditional values is seen as an indirect but intense assault on blacks and black culture. This helps explain some of the marginalization of Christianity and Christian whites in the modern lexicon as well as some of the subtle strategies for keeping Christian blacks and Christian whites separated, out of society and politics, and certainly out of key issues facing society.

These first iterations of modern racism have further morphed over time. In the more recent modern age, sociologists, political pundits, and academics have broadened the term modern racism to include *prejudice with power, white privilege, micro-aggressions, racial habits,*[xlv] *aversive racism,*[xlvi] and other similar terms and concepts. This kind of terminology was, in many ways, a natural outgrowth of the original modern racism theories. Importantly, however, this also served to expand the scope and reach of racism to include even those whites who feel that they harbor no conscious racism or racial animosity.

Micro's

For instance, micro-aggression is a term coined in the 1970's by Psychiatrist Dr. Chester Pierce and given greater voice in the last decade by psychologists, academics, and social pundits. Micro-aggressions are subconscious expressions of subliminal racist thoughts that are intentionally or unintentionally concealed behind words and actions. Psychologist Derald Wing Sue is credited for a common, modern definition of micro aggressions, who describes them as "everyday insults, indignities and demeaning messages, whether intentional or unintentional, that communicate hostile, derogatory, or negative messages to target persons based solely upon their marginalized group membership"[xlvii] (e.g. racial minorities). In daily language, these can be either positive or negative attributes or terms that subtly reference negative stereotypes or behaviors.

For instance, in the modern lexicon, "well-spoken" is considered a racist micro-aggression toward blacks as it references a negative, racist stereotype that claims blacks cannot speak well. It is considered insulting since its mention calls out the alleged general lack of the attribute, as if being a well-spoken black person were somehow a strange anomaly. Thus, *articulate* is also considered a racist term. Ironically, so are personal and cultural characteristics such as personal responsibility and traditional family values (which are simultaneously core tenets of Christianity and racial insults based on negative stereotypes of blacks).

So, while a stereotypical Christian white male may think that being a well-spoken, articulate, hard-working, and responsible individual would be a compliment and the basis for spiritual, financial, and social success, these terms are now said to be staples of subliminal racist insults.

The thinking driven in these new definitions thereby broadens the reach of racist thought to include common and previously appropriate behaviors, actions, and attitudes. In doing so, it allows nearly any white person to be accused of conscious or unconscious racist thoughts or at least tendencies while simultaneously neutering judgment on what might be considered socially unacceptable attitudes and behaviors.[xlviii] Simultaneously, it continues to make racist some of the core tenets of Christian lifestyles, theology, and ethical standards.

There are similar manifestations of this concept that include micro-assaults (e.g. deliberately serving a white person before a black person in a restaurant), micro-insults (verbal and nonverbal communications that subtly convey rudeness and insensitivity and demean a person's racial heritage or identity), and micro-invalidations (communications that subtly exclude, negate, or nullify the thoughts, feelings or experiential reality of a person of color).[xlix] All these terms have a similar theme in that all whites, consciously or unconsciously, harbor racist thoughts and express them in subtly hidden words, cues, and actions. And again, in many cases, the alleged racist thoughts are expected to be based on Judeo-Christian social norms and behavioral expectations.

Critical Race Theory

Another similar concept, Critical Race Theory (CRT), helped give birth to some of the concepts that are now part of the modern-day lexicon. CRT was developed out of legal scholarship and began to be espoused in legal and social advocacy circles in the 1980's. CRT is important today due to its ongoing influence on and adoption by social justice advocacy groups. By definition:

> "CRT recognizes that racism is engrained in the fabric and system of the American society. The individual racist need not exist [in order] that institutional racism [be] pervasive in the dominant culture. This is the analytical lens that CRT uses in examining existing power structures. CRT identifies that these power structures are based on white privilege and white supremacy, which perpetuates the marginalization of people of color.
>
> CRT also rejects the traditions of liberalism and meritocracy. Legal discourse says that the law is neutral and colorblind, however, CRT challenges this legal "truth" by examining liberalism and meritocracy as a vehicle for self-interest, power, and privilege.
>
> CRT also recognizes that liberalism and meritocracy are often stories heard from those with wealth, power, and privilege. These stories paint a false picture of meritocracy. That is, everyone who

works hard can attain wealth, power, and privilege while ignoring the systemic inequalities that institutional racism provides."[l]

CRT advocates such as Derrick Bell further maintained that the progress of the civil rights movement for blacks was in fact merely designed to augment white supremacy and support white dominion over blacks.[li]

Institutional and systemic racism

The notion of engrained, endemic racism began to be incorporated in other terminology. For instance, many of those trying to define and categorize cultural patterns based strictly or predominantly on racism suggest that institutional racism and systemic racism are now the root causes of the myriad issues faced by black Americans.

"Institutional racism" is generally defined as a pattern of social institutions, constructs, and systems, e.g. government, schools, banks, courts, etc., that negatively treat a specific group(s) of people based solely on their race. The Oxford dictionary defines it more broadly as "Racial discrimination that has become established as normal behavior within a society or organization."[lii] By contrast, the online Urban Dictionary defines it more specifically as "the process of purposely discriminating against certain groups of people through the use of biased laws or practices."[liii]

The impacts of this form of racism are depicted as the denial of access to healthcare, legal protections, housing, political representation, etc., for a certain group of people, usually minorities, by a more dominant, usually majority, group (i.e. whites). Simply put, institutional racism purports that blacks are treated differently (i.e. worse) within society's various institutions, the results of which are very different socio-economic outcomes for blacks and whites.

Furthermore, institutional racism is typically defined as being woven into the very fabric of society and the DNA of all white people, and thus neither blatantly manifested nor easily extracted.

Similarly, the term systemic racism holds that America was established as a racist nation, and thus racism is embedded in all social institutions, structures, and social relations within our society.

As described by sociologist Joe Feagan, "Systemic racism includes the complex array of anti-black practices, the unjustly gained political-economic power of whites, the continuing economic and other resource inequalities along racial lines, and the white racist ideologies and attitudes created to maintain and rationalize white privilege and power. Systemic here means that the core racist realities are manifested in each of American society's major parts - the economy, politics, education, religion, [and] the family - reflecting the fundamental reality of systemic racism."[liv] Our society is thereby said to be so indelibly stained by our history that whites, particularly Christian whites, may not be able to help but to think and act in racially oppressive ways.

According to its proponents, this fully and completely explains the lesser outcomes and life circumstances blacks endure, which are routinely worse than that of their white counterparts. Even within the same relative circumstances, blacks fare worse than whites. Thus, racism is the only reasonable source of disparities and must necessarily be a, if not the, root cause.

And since the historical Judeo-Christian values of our society have driven the creation of so many of the current systems, institutions, social norms, and acceptable behaviors, Christianity and white Christians are seen as part of, or at least linked to, the root causes of the racism within those systems. Here, again, there are specific references to religion and traditional Christian institutions (e.g. the family) as being inherently racist.

Example of the use of "Institutional racism"

As a personal example of the use of this terminology, I attended a school board presentation at a predominantly black school in a low-income area wherein most of the teachers, though certainly not all, were white. Given our involvement at this school through Christian after-school programs and our church, we knew many of the kids there were challenged with more than just learning. Some, though genuinely good kids, came from troubled home environments, challenging after-school scenarios, little or limited parental support, and the general and typical difficulties with middle-school social pressures.

But, we also knew the teachers to be highly committed, passionate about teaching and their students, and of at least good, if not relatively excellent, quality. These were not uncaring, unengaged teachers waiting for their pensions to kick in. They generally loved teaching. Likewise, the principal (a white woman) and school staff (mostly white) were engaged and committed.

As part of their ongoing analysis, the school board had studied this school's performance, and presented the results of the study to any parents, teachers, students, and locals of all ages, races, and genders who chose to attend. As the presenters gave their evaluations, one of the lead examiners, a middle-aged black female, stood and declared boldly that there was institutional racism within the school, based on some of the performance metrics.

Mind you, no evidence was presented, except poor performance. Indeed, though there was some discussion of possible related factors such as funding and access to technology, no direct correlation between the poor performance and any other factor was made or even attempted. Only institutional racism was declared as a definitive, singular factor. Certainly, there was no mention of the many social challenges these kids and their community faced.

Recall that the goal of these new definitions is to explain specific and general socio-economic and other outcomes that are known to vary between blacks and whites, even those living within the same or similar life circumstances. So, the implications of the use of this term in this context should be considered, regardless of its validity and even if racism was only partly to blame for the situation.

By the definition of the term, its use meant that the institution and all its components were racist, having been intentionally constructed by whites over many years to produce disparate outcomes. Therefore, all the teachers and administrators, regardless of their race, had decided, consciously or unconsciously, to offer the black children at this school a lesser education because they were black. Presumably, then, these teachers had spent years in undergraduate study, a few more years in preparation for becoming a teacher, and then as much as decades teaching, all so that they could do a great injustice to the kids they had committed to serve by refusing to teach them properly. Whether consciously or unconsciously, they routinely and habitually underserved a specific group of kids based solely on their race.

Mind you, no one challenged this viewpoint or demanded further exploration at the meeting. For if the accusation is true, more than just a report should have been generated. If they intentionally or unintentionally failed the children under their care, teachers, administrators, and staff should have lost their jobs and careers! Instead, the comment was accepted on its face, and the presentation moved on. This should demonstrate how concepts such as institutional racism have become part of our modern social lexicon, neither challenged nor debated even when entire schools are indicted.

Regardless of the outcome of the report, and damning though this accusation was, one might ask, what message did this send to the kids, to the teachers, and to the principal of the school? Was racism indeed the only major discernable factor in the students' poor performance? After all, this message came from someone who had deeply examined the school's function and outcomes. What did it say to and about those who had committed their lives and careers to teaching? What did it say to the community from which so many of those students came? What did it say to parents struggling to give their kids a better life, full of opportunities they might not have had?

Importantly, this scenario also demonstrates how far Christian whites have to go to change the relationships with our Christian black brothers and sisters. With these definitions now an integral part of the modern American discourse, and with the tainting of Christianity and Christian whites as racist due to the promotion of traditional values, ours is a steeper and harder climb.

Thus, the implications and impacts of the spread of these broader definitions have significant impacts on our ability to unite as Christians as well as our abilities to have an impact on society.

White Privilege

Out of the progression of this line of reasoning came the concept of white privilege or racial privilege. While there are many variations of the definition, white privilege generally refers to a set of advantages, immunities, and rights afforded to white people that are not afforded to black people. Taking both older and modern definitions and concepts one step further, white privilege is said to exist without the expressed knowledge of the white people it benefits, and generally helps maintain a racial, cultural hierarchy.

Advocates of the privilege concept will commonly purport additional special privileges that belong to myriad other groups, including male privilege, heterosexual privilege, and even beauty privilege. Generally, however, the term privilege is reserved for whites and their general socio-economic positions relative to blacks and other minorities.

White privilege is said to manifest in both subtle and blatant ways. Easier relationships with law enforcement; being given the benefit of the doubt when accused of wrongdoing (that is, *truly* presumed innocence); employer assumptions about work ethic, intelligence, and integrity; lesser penalties for bad behavior in school; and generally having access to greater power and resources when needed.

Like similar constructs such as institutional and systemic racism, white privilege assumes that racism is fully engrained in white people, developed like an age-old evolutionary mutation that whites no longer even consider. Privilege is said to be so much a part of whites that they no longer recognize its existence and can no more remove it than they could remove the flesh from their bones.

Furthermore, since Christianity is stereotypically and directly associated with wealthy white men who are said to be the root cause of racism and the holders of great privilege, the connection between Christianity and white privilege is easy for the proponents of the theory to manufacture.

Moreover, while the poverty, pain, struggle, and lack of opportunities exist for the poor in all communities (black, white, Hispanic, etc.), blacks have the distinction of suffering from the most obvious forms of racism. For those supporting the white privilege argument, the hardships of some whites and other minorities can therefore be excused without countering the belief in the holistic impacts of racism because that racism continues to be endemic throughout and deep within our social, political, and economic systems. In other words, just because there are poor and disadvantaged whites does not negate the existence of privilege. Rather, these outcomes simply mean that some whites fail to, or choose not to, take advantage of their inherent racial advantages. Regardless of their lot in life, they are not inhibited specifically by their race, as are blacks.

And even though other ethnic and religious groups have suffered discrimination throughout American history, white privilege supporters would argue that their suffering was neither as widespread, nor as concentrated, nor as long-lasting as that suffered by blacks.

To solve for white privilege, proponents insist that something must be done to remove the privilege of whites and spread that privilege to others in society, particularly blacks. Some insist upon reparations and due payment or recompense for the wrongs done and being done. This would likely come in the form of monetary redistribution, but could also include the denial of whites' access to jobs, universities, income, and other opportunities

However difficult such a redistribution of resources, relationships, and opportunities might be, and whatever the concept says about whites as supporters of a racist society, white privilege is now taught in schools and universities across the country as a social ill in need of correction, though often without specific recommended corrective actions. This may be why the white privilege argument, if not its accompanying redistribution of wealth, seems to be the most commonly used of these concepts, having become more engrained among both blacks and whites than the others.

Indeed, many Christian whites will quickly attest to their privilege, with or without supporting personal experiences or specific examples. Due to the decades and decades of racism, segregation, and abuse, it is not difficult to understand how whites might see themselves as privileged relative to the lives and experiences of their black brethren. Even though they may not have experienced clear and obvious privilege, such as being selected for a job over an equally qualified black person, the logic of privilege is not hard for many whites to grasp.

The implications of this and other definitions on race relations, public policy, and the future of Christianity will be discussed later. Importantly for this discussion, the correlation has once again been made between the historical entrenchments of racism, the historical dominance of Christianity in American society, and the Christian ethics and moral values that are said to be directly linked to white racial attitudes and feelings.

Other terms and phrases

Other terms for, and personal attributes of, racists that society has more recently begun using include the following.

Cultural Racism

Similar to institutional and systemic racism, cultural racism is often defined as the ability of a superior ethnic group (e.g. Christian straight white men) to define the standards for cultural norms in the society.

Cultural racism is also defined as using generalized cultural attributes, whether real or alleged, to explain social, economic, or political outcomes. For example, unemployed, recently arriving African refugees are said by cultural racists to be out of work due to an inherent lack of a cultural work ethic rather than the inherent racism that keeps them from job opportunities. This, like other forms of subliminal racism, is said to keep the white person from needing to openly express his/her racism while allowing for the full impact of racism to be felt and experienced by others.

Internal/Internalized racism

This is often defined as the racist thoughts and feelings that are instilled into blacks due to the constant barrage of racist messaging, both open and subliminal. Much like a brainwashed prisoner whose ongoing torture eventually leads them to side with their captors, blacks take racism's negative thoughts and feelings as real attributes of their race and culture.

Internalized racism thereby becomes the enablement of self-fulfilling negative outcomes. For instance, black children are said internalize and be at greater risk of acting upon the negative, anti-societal, and counter-productive behaviors which their white oppressors have long suggested they possess. This is said to explain some negative social outcomes, from crime to higher rates of out-of-wedlock births.

Likewise, racist stereotypes of blacks' abilities in sports leads to a focus on athletic achievements rather than scholarly successes. Black kids who might otherwise be good in school instead channel their energies into non-scholastic efforts on the playing field or basketball court. The result is a manipulation of self-worth and energy that leads to the reduction of opportunities, success, and achievements in specific areas of life.

Cultural appropriation

Though not explicitly racist, cultural appropriation describes the incorporation of particular aspects, attributes, genres, habits, or characteristics of another culture, race, people, or nation into one's own culture. Usually, it refers to whites appropriating the culture of minorities, particularly blacks.

Appropriation is sometimes associated with racism because it infers a sense of superiority and thereby an ability to select and adopt very specific, perhaps attractive, aspects of another culture while still assuming one's own overall superiority. Thus, whites might pluck hair styles, music, and dance styles, or even the use of certain colors in dress from African cultures while generally still assuming the superiority of European/Western/American culture. Appropriation has also been called out when white men find black women physically and sexually attractive, yet presumably thinking of themselves as racially superior.

Anti-racism

Another new term that has come to the present-day lexicon refers to white's attitudes and actions towards the eradication of racism. Like several others, the term starts with the assumption that American society is racist at its foundation and core (i.e. racism is systemic), and that white people are inherently racist by virtue of their whiteness, their historical positions of power, and the racist systems they have developed and sustained.

But, according to this term, it is no longer enough for a white person to be simply "non-racist" or even cleansed of all racist thoughts (were that ever possible). Being a non-racist still makes one a racist through the tacit support of existing racism within the system, even if only by being white. Being neutral in the presence of racism allows the system to move forward unimpeded and thereby contributes to its sustenance. In other words, neutrality (being non-racist) means complicity with and support of the systemic injustices that you see by merely mouthing objections and failing to take action. Therefore, being a non-racist is a bit like being a non-Nazi. The system goes on because of the failure to stop it.

Instead, one must be actively and fully engaged in battling racism ... being anti-racist. Anti-racism is therefore defined as the practice of identifying, challenging, and changing the values, structures and behaviors that perpetuate systemic racism. Whenever and wherever systemic racism exists, the anti-racist must be there to promote its cessation. And because racism occurs at all levels and spheres of society, anti-racism must also occur throughout society. This term broadens the systemic racism argument by demanding that all whites, regardless of their personality and willingness, participate in activities and actions to eradicate racism, else be dubbed a racist. Therefore, this requires the acceptance of the aforementioned premises, including but not limited to systemic racism. Whites must either accept the premises and the willingness to act or be called a racist.

Yet, while some might be offended or frustrated by the "do this or else" approach, calling out racism wherever and whenever it is detected should be part of Christian whites' approach to uniting with our Christian black brothers and sisters. Whether or not one feels that society's systems are inherently and completely racist, the concept of flushing it out should not be offensive if we are to unite as Believers.

Thus, "anti-racism" may be the least troubling of the terms described herein.

Variations on the themes

Of course, just as with nearly any subject, there is variation in how these and similar terms are used and what they are meant to convey. (And if you think this is complex, there are now said to be more than seventy definitions of specific gender types!). Indeed, many words in the English language have multiple definitions. Therefore, some users of terms like white privilege may not feel that all whites are inherently racists. Likewise, some will take the definition and application to its outermost extremes.

What I have presented here is both the textbook definitions of these terms, derived from those who developed or popularized them, and the manner in which they are commonly interpreted within society. This is not to say that everyone who uses these terms agrees completely on their use and the extent of their application. Nor is this to say that those who use them in daily life and general discussions fully understand their implications and textbook definitions. Indeed, it is common for some to misuse words without a full understanding of their meaning. And, particularly in today's society, it is far too common for harsh words and rhetoric to be tossed around too loosely, thus creating unnecessary damage and division.

Nonetheless, it is critically important for Christians of both races to have a full understanding of the words society uses and how those words and their definitions impact both our culture and our opportunity to impact that culture to the glory of God. As you will see, these definitions are having profound

Impacts on everything from our ability to unite to the perceptions of Christians and Christianity among America's younger generations.

IMPLICATIONS OF THE NEW DEFINITIONS

There are a great many issues and implications of these new definitions for our nation, our faith, and our potential to unite as a body of believers. Here are just a few of the more important ones that you will need to consider as you think about unity in action in your communities. As you consider these, think about the goals of their initial development and the variations in outcomes that each definition is trying to explain. This may help you understand the "why" of their development as you consider the "what" of the outcomes of their use.

The omnipresence of racism

Most of these modern constructs purport the notion that the genetic encoding of racism has, over many years, allowed a racist infrastructure to be developed that whites needn't consciously and openly realize, much less defend. All white people need to do is simply exist as white people within the constructs that their [Christian] forefathers established in order to maintain dominance and control over blacks and perpetuate the impacts of traditional racism. And in order to perpetuate an inherently racial social construct, white people do all that is necessary by supporting traditional values, morality, and ethics, "law and order," Judeo-Christian social norms, etc.

Thus, the new definitions hold that white people needn't think of themselves as genetically and inherently superior to blacks due to their own race. Rather, previous generations of whites developed a complete racist infrastructure that would survive without intentional thought or effort. The result is a foundational system built on racism that continues inequality through self-sustaining social, economic, and political mechanisms even without the conscious knowledge of those participating in the ongoing oppression. Racism is inherent and comes as a "built-in" which whites don't even need to know about to support.

Some examples include:
- Law and order politicians
- War on drugs, sounds good on paper but in fact inadvertently or intentionally targets young black men
- School funding by local tax base
- School detention and expulsion policies
- College entrance exams
- Business licensing

Importantly, these new definitions have the effect of spreading the accusation of racism to include any and all white people, even and especially those who profess no racist feelings or thoughts. As the modern terminology changed the definitions and the meaning of the word, they simultaneously created a universality to its application. Racism is both intrinsic and universal, inhabiting all white people, regardless of their personal opinions and feelings, by virtue of the social, political, and economic constructs in which whites live. Racism is in all white people, regardless of their personal opinions and feelings. And because of the manner in which it is said to exist within white people, it cannot be expunged.

This concept is important as Christians engage across racial boundaries. Christian whites need to understand that this concept is quite pervasive and can therefore be a barrier that must be crossed.

Christian black support of white racism

Once again, for our discussion herein, this inherent racism is born of, furthered, and continued by the core beliefs and tenets which Christian whites believe and teach their children. Since Christianity remains the dominant religion in America, Christian whites continue to instill racism, discrimination, and hatred in our society, even if unknowingly and unwittingly, through the teaching and preaching of God's word, morality, and values.

Likewise, these new definitions and variations could lead to the conclusion that Christian blacks are supportive of the ongoing oppression of their own people through the teaching and support of the Christian standards, values, and behavioral norms that sustain racism throughout the culture. For if racism is inherent in Christianity's social tenets and behavioral norms, Christian blacks who support and teach them are supporting the very social structures that have denied black people justice and fairness for generations. This may mean that Christian blacks are complicit in the subjugation of their black Americans and tacit supporters of the racism woven so deeply into the nation's social fabric.

Furthermore, these definitions hold that Christian blacks who support what are known as traditional Christian moral and ethical values are also supporting whites' oppression of other minorities, whether immigrants, homosexuals, transgender, and others.

Keeping the crosses burning

Racist is an extremely negative label, perhaps one of the harshest accusations or insults imaginable in our society today. It is so harsh in part because of the memories and images that the traditional, dictionary definition brings to mind – unadulterated white hatred, slavery, the KKK, burning crosses, segregated bathrooms and water fountains, voting restrictions, and the lynching of thousands of black men – all of which seem unimaginable in modern society. These images of racism and racists are kept firmly in our minds, since this ugly part of America's past is still taught in schools, remembered annually, frequently mentioned in the media, and still too frequently displayed by the remaining few white supremacists.

This ugliness is what many white people think of when they hear the term racist. Fortunately, while traditional racism sadly still exists, it has become as unfashionable and socially untenable as child molestation in nearly every segment of the population. Thus, for the vast majority of whites, racism is an ugly part of history that needs to remain just that, history, to be taught for its lessons but never, ever repeated. Wherever it remains, whites, whether Christian, non-Christian, conservative or liberal, will nearly unanimously[iv] agree that it needs to be stamped out.

And therefore, no reasonable white person, Christian or not, likes to be called racist any more than blacks like to be called niggers. Both terms are toxic, their use often leads to an immediate cessation of discourse, dialogue, and most certainly cooperation and collaboration.

Yet, herein lies the problem. The horror of the memory, the ignorance of the thinking, and the resulting insult of the accusation of racism remain in full and even more toxic and venomous than ever. But the new definitions have expanded the application of this toxicity and its insult to nearly all white people, including those who firmly believe that they are without a single racist cell in their bodies. Even as the sting of the word has intensified as society is increasingly repulsed by its ugly historical and current realities, its application has simultaneously spread to more and more whites. Because the power of the traditional definition remains within the modern ones, the term has been given new life and greater power to harm.

In other words, modern racism and the many
variants and versions of the term have simultaneously
kept the terrible connotations of the original term
(e.g. white hoods, slavery, and lynchings) while
extending the scope and breadth of its application to
include any and all whites, particularly Christian whites
and Christian white political conservatives.

Moreover, what is meant when these terms are used may be lost both by the user and accused. The accused may feel nothing but resentment over what appears to be a false accusation and may therefore discount any intellectual or moral authority of the user. The user may mean something other than what the accused infers and may become frustrated and resentful when the accused refuses to engage and listen. And so, the conversation ends.

As these words are used in society like salt in the kitchen, freely and sometimes without forethought or precision, their power to insult increases even as their ability to accurately identify evil is diminished. After all, when everyone is a racist, who is really a racist?

And thus, where progress might be made, it is stalled. Where honest discussions might be had, they are stymied. Friendships and collegiality in the workplace are sometimes replaced with cautious speech, carefully chosen words and deliberate, yet forced, officiousness. Where love might go, mistrust and divisions are the first to arrive.

It is therefore important to understand that these changes in meanings are not just academic exercises. They influence how blacks and whites, both Christian and non-Christian, interact, discuss issues, and solve problems. Without collaboration, effective solutions to issues facing our country will never be found.

Ironically, white sensitivities to racist accusations have resulted in yet another new term.

White Fragility

Coined by Robin DiAngelo in an article and book by the name, White Fragility[lvi] purports that whites live in a society that is deeply separate and unequal by race, wherein they are socialized into a deeply internalized sense of racial superiority and are isolated from racial stress. Having been made secure and comfortable in the cocoon of white supremacy, whites have become intolerable to even minimal amounts of racial stress and are therefore vulnerable to challenges to and discussions of their racism, position, privilege, and power. They have become "fragile."

When confronted or challenged, whites react in typical, predictably defensive ways. Reactions include expressing denial, anger, or frustration, cognitive dissonance, withdrawal, shutting down, ceasing conversations, and even violence. Whites, the author states, "are at a loss for how to respond in constructive ways"[lvii] when their racism and status is challenged. This is because whites "have not had to build the cognitive or affective skills or develop the stamina that would allow for constructive engagement across racial divides."[lviii]

Thus, whites are assumed to be largely incapable of deep discussions of race and racism, much less discussions of any roles whites have historically or currently play in the oppression of others. This fragility is touted as both a cause for the lack of conversations and solutions to racial issues and a reason for the continuation of racism and disparate outcomes. Because whites are too fragile to discuss it, let alone act to stop it, racism continues unabated because it remains unchallenged by those who wield the power to stop it.

Ironically, this sort of label adds to the risks of pushing whites further into their own corners by increasing tensions, creating negative dynamics, and building walls rather than tearing them down. Indeed, it would seem that whites who do anything but agree with the challenges and acquiesce to the accusations risk being tagged with yet another negative moniker. This, of course, increases the likelihood that conversations cease before they are completed and before any progress can be made. In turn, this could set up a self-fulfilling outcome as whites predictably react negatively after being accused of their fragility.

White-only racism

These new definitions isolate the racist emotions and feelings to whites and preclude that other ethnicities could have similar emotions. This is due, in part, to the assumption that the power to dominate others, control the social, political, and economic factors that could lead to freedom, etc., rests solely in the hands of whites. Presumably, this follows from the traditional definition's emphasis on a feeling of racial superiority, since a feeling of white racial superiority could readily flow from social, political, and economic power. Therefore, it could be theorized that without this power, racism could not exist. Indeed, some define racism as prejudice with power. It is said that minorities cannot be racists because they have no power over their white oppressors.

A 2014 movie called "Dear White People" speaks to this now-common notion. The lead character, a black female college student and college radio personality (ironically named Sam White) is known for her passionate views on race. When confronted by the accusation that her radio show was racist, she retorts: "Black people can't be racist ... Racism describes a system of disadvantage based on race. Black people can't be racist since we don't stand to benefit from such a system." So, while keeping the context and negativity of the term, its target is not only expanded but isolated such that only whites can have the emotions of hatred, moral superiority, etc.

Taken to the traditional definition of the term, any and all non-whites are thereby excused from any feelings, no matter how angry or hateful, that might have resulted from any oppression and segregation they suffered. Any reactions to white racism, no matter how ugly or violent, are typically seen as purely defensive and thus completely defensible. And any anger, bitterness and hostility directed towards whites, even for simply being white, becomes readily justified. We see this play out on college campuses where whites are intentionally excluded and taught that their whiteness is something of which they should be ashamed.

Ironically, by the broadening and deepening of the term into a far broader segment of the white population and thus making all whites to be irreparably flawed and inherently unacceptable in their thinking, the new definitions actually beg for blacks to take up the feelings in the original definition. Namely, "a belief that race is the primary determinant of human traits" (in this case, all whites are racists), and "antagonism directed against someone of a different race based on the belief that one's own race is superior." Clearly, it is easy to think less of whites if they are so inherently flawed in their thinking, thereby justifying any sense of moral and intellectual superiority and general indignation against them.

Thus, while many believe that minorities do not have the power to think in certain ways, this does not prevent the risk, if not the manifestation, of negativity and racist thought from those upon whom racism has had such a long, deep and painful impact. This is, in part, one of society's many ways of keeping discord alive and well.

Arguments for singular causality

Some would suggest that the challenges blacks now face are multi-faceted, involving everything from the lingering impacts of historical racism and segregation to the challenges so many of us face in our society, including the breakdown of the family, historical biases against education, the breakdown of traditional moral values and social norms, and the general deterioration of modern American culture, just to name a few.

Yet proponents of these revised socio-racial theories often argue that there is only one source of the tribulations that have and continue to plague blacks – racism. Whether variation in the attainment of home loans or the ability to generate wealth after incarceration, racism is said to be the sole cause of the issues blacks face. Indeed, recent and popular author Ibram X. Kendi writes "racial discrimination is the sole cause for racial disparities in this country and the world at large."[lix] From their perspective, advocates of singular causality suggest that there is a significant risk that the historical context of suffering would be lost if other, non-racial reasons for under-performance were used in explanations of the current events and situations. In other words, if the issues facing black communities are seen to be less affiliated with racism, responsibility for the plight of blacks is increasingly placed on individual blacks themselves and their personal life choices and decisions. (Refer back to the first definitions of modern racism for a good example of this thinking). This, they would argue, diminishes the historical systemic impacts of racism and unduly shifts the emphasis of responsibility away from white racism and onto blacks and black communities.

Thus, there must necessarily be ongoing emphasis on the inherent racism in the system, else individual blacks are left holding a very large and unfair historical bag.

Furthermore, proponents argue that the emphasis of causality must remain primarily if not solely on racism, as any other causes are seen as distantly secondary if not inconsequential. Yes, there may be general societal constraints to progress that many Americans face, but none are as substantive as ongoing and historical racism.

This is actually a relatively easy argument to make, given the history of racism and its continued manifestation in our society. No matter what issues or constraint a given black person faces, racism, whether in the past or the present or both, could be seen as the cause. In other words, a causal line can generally be drawn from nearly any existing outcome to historical and/or current racism. For instance, a lack of career success is linked to a lack of proper education of previous black generations which is linked to racial discrimination in the education system as manifested in a lack of funding, access, etc.

However, by homing in on a single major underlying cause for all related issues, these definitions largely prevent discussions of possible multi-faceted causalities and solutions. Indeed, as we have seen, these definitions have made the traditional attributes necessary for success as well as common Christian social values (e.g. hard work, family unity, sexual morality, and personal responsibility) into hate-filled racist terminology and thus useless for discussion.

Simply put, placing blame on anything other than whites and Christianity is seen as promoting blacks as the root cause of their own issues or diverting attention from the racism inherent in the system. Therefore, a discussion of causes other than racism would be seen as racist in and of itself.

Example of the use of single cause thinking
A Christian black friend used the following example of displaced root causes.

> Due to his upbringing, lack of a stable family, and lack of interest in school, Jamal never learned to read well. His school stopped teaching reading in the third grade, before he was proficient, and Jamal was unable to continue to learn to read once he left that grade. Now, Jamal is in late middle school, and is known to be a problem. Invariably, when it's time to read in class, report on a reading assignment, or turn in homework related to reading, Jamal acts out in school. Jamal is black, but that is not the reason for his behavior. He is not an inherently bad kid because of his race. He is acting out because he cannot read. Of course, there may be myriad issues behind Jamal's inability to read, including teachers, parents, siblings, childhood trauma, mental or physical health, and home environment, just to name a few possibilities.
>
> Yet, by the modern lexicon, he is failing primarily because he is being treated differently because of his race by a white-dominated system, and white teachers and school administrators. The modern definitions would have Jamal mistreated by the school because he is seen as lazy, uninterested in school, and other racially defined negative attributes. Perhaps his white teachers didn't teach him for whatever conscious or subliminal racially motivated reasons. Perhaps they succumbed to their own intrinsic racism and the stereotypes of poor black children. Maybe his school isn't up to a higher standard because his poor black neighborhood is ignored because of racist white politicians who funnel education funds to predominantly white schools.

Alternatively, proponents of singular causality might suggest that Jamal's situation could be linked to historical racism, even if Jamal does not face it himself. For instance, his parents might have remained under-educated by a racist education system, which now prevents them from being able to aid Jamal with homework and reading. And because his parents were not given employment opportunities due to discrimination and racism, they are unable to pay for tutoring or extra materials that might help Jamal do better. Thus, even if Jamal himself does not face racism, the situation in which he is placed makes racism the root cause of his issues.

Whether you agree with this concept in part or in whole, Christian whites need to understand the singular causality argument as they move into dialogues and collaboration with their brothers and sisters. Failure to account for this concept in the definitional discussions may mean coming at a problem from very different perspectives.

Color-sightedness

Ironically, by virtue of the application of the new definitions, whites are no longer allowed to not react to skin color. While the idea of a color-blind society was in many ways physically impossible (if we have eyes, we can obviously see the physical attributes of the person in front of us), the notion that we might not react to skin color was a core hope for the Civil Rights Movement of the last century. But now this notion is thought by some to be inherently racist.

Furthermore, not seeing the race of a non-white person is said to diminish or marginalize that person's heritage, historical suffering, and the current impact of past and current injustices on their life.

Instead, whites must necessarily recognize skin color as a primary attribute of a person, lest we be accused of being racist for ignoring it. Whites can't not care.

Eduardo Bonita-Silva and other academics argue that claiming color-blindness in fact serves to perpetuate the very racism that whites claim to have overcome. Because the aforementioned definitions mean that racism is intrinsic within the fabric of society, unavoidable and self-perpetuating, they feel that ignoring race by claiming color blindness ignores the ongoing racism, bigotry, and discrimination that continues to exist.

Ignoring race thereby means that racism will not be called out and recognized for what it is. Therefore, many sociologists recommend that parents and teachers educate children on race and racism, particularly the modern definitions described herein, and that employers and governments continue to recognize racial attributes as significant to the value of personhood, so as to ensure that external physical attributes can never be forgotten or ignored.

This, in an ironic twist, means that racial equality will never actually be allowed even if attainable, since whites will always be required to see physical attributes first and thereby classify and structure the relationships that they will have with others. Were the races considered equal (as Christians should have always seen them), there would be no need to recognize external attributes or ethnicity. Instead, these remain at the forefront of our relationships, with character and other personal and moral attributes coming into play only after the racial relationships are established and codified.

Racial instability, distrust, and even hate could thereby become built into the general social construct as permanent fixtures.

Loss of specificity

Some of these definitions make racism, in part or in whole, an ethereal entity rather than the actions and thoughts of specific individuals. Thus, one can insist that racism exists without having to point specifically to an individual(s) or institution(s) as racist (though this still happens with great frequency).

For instance, one can say that the judicial system is racist without having to speak about specific judges or prosecutors. Or, one can say that the banking system is racist in its lending practices without having to call out individual bank employees, bank managers, or even specific banks. There is no need of data or other evidence to justify the allegations since racism is said to be ubiquitous within all aspects of society. These broad and sweeping definitions thus lessen the need for proof or evidence of racism while expanding the scope and scale of its existence and impact, whether true or not, in part or in whole.

This does not mean that injustices, unfairness, stereotypes, and/or racism do not exist. Rather, the loss of specificity allows racism to exist as an entity without the opportunity for individuals to quantify it or its impact, admit or deny its existence, or, most importantly, address it directly through remediating action. Racism can, by definition, just be.

This generalization, in turn, silences the voices of those whites who insist that they are not racist by removing the direct causation from individuals and placing it on a largely intangible system. It thereby makes the causality of racism ever-present and very real while removing opportunities to pinpoint and destroy it, make a claim of cleansing from it, or demonstrate any improvements or changes to it.

Racism as an incurable disease

How does one prove that one is not racist? In modern, much broader definitions, it may be nearly impossible for a white person, particularly a Christian white person, to declare oneself to be free of racism.

According to the modern lexicon, whites have little way out of the racist accusation conundrum (rightfully so, some would say!). Whites are inherently racist, whether they know it or not. Therefore, denying one's racism actually proves that one is a racist. Indeed, it is said that any white person who starts a sentence or answers an accusation of racism with "I am not a racist" is simply proving the accusation. After all, it is thought, why else would you be accused in the first place were the accusation no true? Denying it only makes you either completely unaware of your inherent racist thoughts and attitudes or a blatant liar.

Adding a "but" to the end of the "I am not a racist ..." statement is even worse, since it is assumed that whatever comes from one's lips next will be a racist statement. So, a white person who says, "I am not a racist, but" is only denying their racism in their own heads, since anything that follows the "but" will very likely be, or be interpreted as, racist words and thoughts. Whites, in a sense, are only fooling themselves and trying to justify away what they cannot extract from their existence.

Similarly, denying that others are racists, such as, Christian whites, your church group or civic club, and/or certain white politicians and political conservatives, will certainly earn you the racist moniker. This is because it is difficult, if not impossible, to disprove the accusation.

In dialectics and the fine art of debate, this is what is known as argumentum ad ignorantiam or argument from ignorance (where the term ignorance is defined as "lack of evidence to the contrary," not as a reference to the intelligence of the arguer). Essentially, a proposition is held to be true because it hasn't yet been proven false (or vice versa).

For instance, the world is deemed flat if there is no evidence to prove that it is round. Taken to an extreme, if a man cannot prove that he is not cheating on his wife, then he must be cheating on his wife.

For the sake of this discussion, if one cannot prove that one is not a racist, it is assumed that an accusation of racism is true. And since, for example, I cannot prove as fact my emotions, thoughts or feelings on race, I am therefore deemed by the proposition to be racist.

Likewise, if a politician's motives for promoting a given social policy cannot be proven to be based on something other than race, then that policy must be based on race if someone deems it so. Similarly, the economy, social structures, the justice system, and society in general are all racist if whites cannot prove otherwise.

And since that proof, such that it can be found, is sometimes ethereal and thus can nearly always be called into question, there is little way to make a counterargument, no matter now nonsensical the supposition may seem to be.

This means that the evidence of racism need not be present for the accusation to be made, since the weight of proof is on the accused. It is up to the accused to prove what may be unprovable, leaving the accuser with the freedom to hurl accusations without the need for actual evidence.

And as we have already seen in the previous sections of this chapter, the very act of trying to refute an accusation of racism yields an affirmation of the accusation. Simply put, if a white person denies being a racist, surely they are one, based on the allegation alone if nothing else.

Furthermore, a given outcome can be deemed to have a primary or singular root cause even if multiple variables might be in play. For instance, the justice system can be deemed to be racist if an outcome (e.g. black male incarceration rates) cannot be directly and completely tied back to other specific variables. Even the clear evidence of other tangible variables cannot completely disprove the presence of a proposed variable if that variable cannot be completely disproved. Thus, even though argumentum ad ignorantiam may only apply to one element (race) of a broader causality there may as well be only that singular cause since it invariably becomes the point of focus.

And due to the toxic negative power of the term racism, once the accusation is made, the damage may have been done, regardless of whether actual evidence to the contrary is later produced. By these definitions, no matter which way a white person turns, no matter what he/she does or does not do, he/she is a white racist if they cannot prove otherwise.

This, of course, creates tremendous resentment among those whites who consider themselves to be far more intelligent and sophisticated than the few remaining white supremacists.

Small wonder, then, that the easiest way to shut down dialogue with many white people is to hurl the "r word." The word itself, especially when used inappropriately, causes either an immediate defense response and/or anger. This gives the word far more negative power than it would have had otherwise, as it makes whites even more defensive and resentful. Thus, the danger in the expanded definitions is the continued and exacerbated divisions they create.

Racism and zero-sum opportunities

Definitions such as white privilege also create the notion that there is a limited amount of opportunity within our society, a single pie of a given size that must be divided among our people. This creates the notion that there is a zero-sum scenario[ix] to the distribution of opportunities. That is, if a white person is to gain, a black person must lose, and vice versa. This, in turn, tees up fights over what is assumed to be a fixed, limited, and presumably undersized pie. Whites must therefore give up their privilege, opportunities, wealth, etc., in order that blacks can attain their due privilege, opportunities, wealth, etc. In most of these racial constructs, there is no way for whites to prosper while blacks simultaneously prosper. The former simply does not allow the latter. Therefore, whites must give up some of theirs so that others can have more.

That said, it is quite clear that blacks, as a group, have and too often continue to start life's race from a different position on the track. As a later chapter explains, socio-economic constraints such as a lack of generational wealth and important social constructs puts many blacks at a relative disadvantage.

The question for whites therefore becomes, "How do whites give up privilege?" Indeed, some of the white frustration with the white privilege concept is that there is no way to redistribute whatever "it" is, because "it" isn't something tangible. Furthermore, how would whites know when they have denied themselves enough privilege or opportunities to allow for a sufficient amount of success within the black community, by whatever measure chosen?

Moreover, some would argue that even if there is a single cause of all black inequality (i.e. racism), how does replacing one form of subjugation with another make society a better place? Would not society be a better place if all could pursue their dreams and visions and use the gifts with which God has blessed them? Indeed, society as a whole would be harmed if any of us, whether black or white or Asian or Hispanic, were not allowed to use our talents to pursue whatever we feel called and passionate to do. If one is held back for the sake of another, well, we have already seen what happens!

Thus, if the opportunities for all are to be optimized, and we are to generate as much well-being as possible within our nation and our world, ALL citizens must participate, ALL citizens must have open opportunities, and ALL citizens must work to achieve their own life goals. Christians, united in action, could help solve this dilemma in a God-focused way.

Christians could and should unite to ensure that barriers to the use of God's gifts are torn down, such that all can use their God-given talents and abilities as they choose to do. This is one reason why I chose healthcare, justice, education, and race as the four focal areas of the proposed unity in action. Fixing these four areas will ensure that all our people will be able to achieve their own God-given purposes.

IMPACTS ON FUTURE GENERATIONS

Perhaps the greatest danger of these new definitions is the impact the messages in these concepts have on our youth. Specifically, what does it mean to our Christian youth to say, "God has a plan for your life greater than you have for yourself" (as I have heard black pastors preach) followed by, "There are powerful, unseen, and immutable forces that will keep you down, oppress you, and prevent you from achieving your dreams!" The precepts within institutional and systemic racism and white privilege present a world that is insidiously created, self-perpetuating, and hard-wired to suppress future success for any and all blacks, young and old alike.

Thus, our youth are taught one or more of the following.

- Blacks cannot succeed because of the systems that have been created to keep them from success. Therefore, why bother? They can't get ahead anyway because the white power structures, built on the strong foundations of generations of racism, won't let them.
- Christianity, whether in whites or blacks, is at least partly responsible for the racism that infects American society and culture. Christian whites have racism built into every fiber of their being, and Christian blacks unknowingly support racism and its many institutions by teaching the Christian values that give life and sustenance to modern-day racism.
- Since blacks cannot achieve their own success using their God-given talents, they must take the pie pieces of others through whatever means necessary. Only through taking from others can they have what they want and need. And since such an unjust system has been nefariously created by white power, it is justifiable to take from those who have white power what was taken from you and your ancestors.

This can have the simultaneous impact of sucking the inspiration and passion out of black youth while enraging them to resent and even hate white people, Christian whites, and/or Christianity. It certainly doesn't support the notion, "Unite with your Christian white brothers and sisters to change the world for the glory of God!" Perhaps this now-justified animosity will go on with them to their college campuses, where secular thought thrives and animosity, resentment and hatred finds an intellectual life-support system.

Will this impact how they approach life as adults? Certainly, one can see where this might lead, and where it would likely not lead. We are already seeing this kind of thinking broadly applied on our college campuses where deeper thinking has given way to an unusual desire for the very segregation we once deplored. Black-only dorms are popping up at universities all over the country, while white youth are being shamed and shunned merely for their skin color.

More specifically, think about what these messages say to Christian black youth:

- God is not in control. White racists and uncontrollable racists systems are.
- God may have given you gifts, talents, abilities, and desires, but He has no power to let you use these for His glory and your own well-being.
- You cannot overcome and are doomed to failure because you face a system that is, at its core, against everything you are as a human being.
- This problem is largely insurmountable, since it cannot be seen but is ever-present, ever dangerous, and will impact your life henceforth just as it did the lives of your forefathers.
- You can only succeed by taking from others, not through the talents and gifts a loving God has given to you.

Think, too, of the challenges this presents to attaining a joyful Christian life. If our kids are raised and steeped in the belief that they are hated and maligned, how much more difficult will it be to find the joy of a life in Christ? Society's preferred responses to its messaging ... hate, resentment, and blame ... all serve to constrain our youth from seeking out the joy of knowing Christ. By creating a fertile field for rage, animosity, and resentment, society is making more difficult the path to the joy and contentment of a Christ-filled life.

These divisions also reduce the likelihood that our next generation will solve the issues that our white forefathers caused. Animosity and ongoing hate are self-spawning if given an environment in which to reproduce. It takes conscious effort to bring Christ to this world, whereas bringing hate is relatively easy.

And since Christian whites are more commonly singled out in these definitions as having racist characteristics, the likelihood that black youth in black churches will go on to see their white brothers and sisters as future allies is diminished if not eliminated. It may even cause some to become disgruntled with Christianity, since if Christians are the root cause of racial divisions in our current society, with their micro-hatreds and hidden oppressive machinery, why should they worship their same God? Certainly, Christian blacks' alleged tacit support for racism's core theological foundations does not support ongoing faithfulness to Christ's teachings.

Moreover, if society, schools, parents, and influencers are constantly telling our kids to see the differences between people, how much more difficult will it be to look beyond the superficial to what God sees? How difficult will it be to stop seeing what society tells them to see every day … skin color, income, possessions, power, sexuality … and see all others as individual children of God, created and loved by Him? Instead, how easy will it be to adopt society's identifiers for everyone they know and meet that are based on everything but that which eternally matters? How difficult will it be to see brothers and sisters in Christ as just that, and only that?

Remember, our God knows no racial preferences. But neither does Satan. If allowed, the latter and our society will happily use the racial divisions of our current and past generations to help keep future generations from the joy and fruits of a Christ-filled life.

These are not the outcomes that forward-thinking Christian whites would have hoped for, as the progress towards unification seems as far away as it ever has.

Thus, while black children certainly need to be educated about the history and current status of racism, slavery, and bigotry in America and the world, we should consider the message that concepts such as institutional and systemic racism speak to our young people. These concepts are far more easily translated into animosity and resentment than Christian love, forgiveness, and unity.

Therefore, the impact of these new definitions and their implications on America's young is perhaps the most troubling.

CHRISTIANITY AND FRIENDLY FIRE

There are some insidious, underlying meanings and impacts to this evolution of the definitions that are specific to our efforts as the body of Christ. Because these new definitions impact our society and its ability to discuss, interact, and create solutions for ongoing and new social issues, so too do they influence our churches and our ability to unite across racial boundaries to become the voice and feet of Christ.

And since Christian whites are specifically called out as racist due to the morality and values that we purport our Bible to teach, the new definitions have turned personal traits that were heretofore positive into racist attributes and thoughts, further separating the Christian races.

Cleverly, this subtle, yet highly effective, tactic has split Christians into separate warring factions, which provides anti-Christian forces a dual benefit. That is:

By aiming for all of Christianity and Christ's teachings via the targeting of Christian whites, the attackers both keep the Christian races split and simultaneously work to neuter the power and role of Christianity in both the black and white communities and society writ large.

This strategy is supported by the aforementioned sociologists and academics who have already concocted a direct linkage between white racism and Christian values and social standards. The unattractive linkage is further aided by the alterations to the definitions of key racial terminology which have kept racism's toxic Bull Conner imagery intact while expanding its application specifically to all Christian whites. This means that the integral relationship between racism and Christianity has become more and more formalized in the modern social lexicon. Hence the negative image of the allegedly racist Christian white male.

Moreover, there is a growing chorus of Christian authors, pundits, pastors, and professors who are using the tainted history of the American white Christian church to demonize both past generations and modern-day Christian whites. Their messages often include calls for not only the acknowledgement of the racist sins of the past but acknowledgement of rampant current racism within the Christian white community as well as monetary, social, and emotional compensation from white churches. Recommendations typically include reparations from whites churches, the funding of black church plants, etc. Yet, while their hearts may be in the right place and their desire for solutions may be genuine, the demonization of Christianity's history and Christian whites nonetheless serves to support society's general anti-Christian messaging and the racial divisions within the faith.

And so as Christian blacks fight against present-day racism, they align with those who fight against Christian whites and traditional Christian morality and behaviors, whether intentionally or not. It doesn't matter whether Christian blacks might consider some or all of their Christian white brethren to be racists. Even if Christian blacks do not mean to include their white brothers and sisters as targets in their struggle against racial disparities, society has already aimed the gun for them. Their fight against racism pulls the trigger against what might be an inadvertent target. And so, as society has constructed its stereotypes and misrepresentations, attacks on racism are simultaneously attacks on Christianity and Christian whites. If nothing else, open support for Christian values can paint Christian blacks as hypocrites and mere unwitting pawns in the Christian white game of dominion and oppression. Thus, from the viewpoint of Christianity's most strident opposition, Christian blacks either fight against their own or appear to support the very structures that keep their own people down, or both.

Thus, for Christianity's opposition in society, having Christian blacks in the fight is advantageous, particularly as long as only racial issues are highlighted and maintained, Christianity remains hidden, and certain social and sexual causes go unchallenged. In other words, as long as Christian blacks are black first and foremost, and only Christians secondarily, they can be made useful by unknowingly aiding in the fight against their own. Christian blacks are thus pressured to be part of their own race first and foremost and part of any cross-racial body of Christ subjacently. They are further pressured to openly or tacitly support and espouse the white racist narrative as they try to solve for the ongoing injustices in our nation. By focusing on white Christianity's alleged ongoing role in racial oppression, society draws Christian blacks into the fight against their white brothers and sisters and even the social values that all Christians should share.

As if shooting at an enemy on a smoke-engulfed battlefield, society thereby has us shooting at one another. All the while we think we're winning, yet we don't even see the damage we are doing to our own troops.

All Christians are alike

Even if only by virtue of the association with Christianity in general, which society views as racist, homophobic, and generally anti-everything, it is harder for black churches to promote Christianity to their youth, promote Christian values in the culture, and generally impact society. It is also far more difficult for Christian blacks to unite with Christian whites to impact our society. Moreover, it is easier to keep black churches and their congregations isolated and siloed from their white brethren, reducing the chance for broad and deep societal impacts.

Society has thereby determined a way to reduce the influence of both groups while only needing to openly attack one. The opposition can thereby malign many Christian moral and behavioral standards and reduce the influence and strength of Christianity within both society and the African American community, particularly among the black youth who increasingly see Christianity through the lens of society's portrayals of Christian white men.

Watering down

And as this occurs, there is greater risk that the tenets of our faith and the essential teachings of Christ will be diluted. We can already see how churches, eager to be politically and socially correct, have quickly moved away from teaching Christ towards trying to appease society by "going along to get along."

Many Christians have already become "secret agents" rather than proud purveyors of our faith. At work and in society, Christians are less willing to speak out about their faith, fearing a backlash that society has been eager to generate. The result is that too many of us intentionally or unintentionally place our faith fourth or fifth on the list of attributes for which we are or want to be known. Whereas common questions in a conversation with a stranger once might have included "Where do you go to church?" this is now left unspoken for fear of offending or causing disagreement and rejection. Indeed, sometimes we don't want others to know we are Christians, fearing the isolation and negative judgments that society has and will place on us.

This is, of course, self-inflicted to some degree. As Christians, we often fail to acknowledge of our humanity and let society presume us to be "holier than thou" such that we are mocked for our hypocrisy. Rather than speak truth to our failings and the foolishness of our past, we instead hide our faith as if ashamed of the God of our fathers. It is easier to stay silent and acquiesce than to have deeper conversations.

Simply put, we defer rather than defend.

Examples

We see this displayed each day in the news. Some politicians will claim Christianity but behave, speak, and vote in ways that seem to be anything but Christian. They use Christianity when it's convenient or makes them seem somehow purer, but then malign the faith with their words and actions. Naturally, this does nothing for the reputation of Christians and Christianity, making more and more of us disgruntled and even ashamed of what our faith has become. We become less engaged, less evangelistic, and less willing to share what God has given us through Christ.

Likewise, there is the example of the commonly stereotypical Christian in the workplace who is known to lie, deceive, and backstab while the non-Christians are known to be honest and kind. I have personally known both men and women in the workplace who, if asked directly, will profess to be Christians but whose words and actions are an embarrassment to the faith. They are loyal to their careers, money, power, and company growth first and the God who created them only when it's convenient or beneficial to their personal or business goals. When this is seen by subordinates and the young adults in the office, it is no small wonder that they are seen as hypocrites and their faith as a meaningless badge, used only as needed.

Thus, the ongoing battle against our faith is showing signs of success. This cannot go on, else our faith will continue to suffer and our opportunities to impact society will continue to slip away.

WHAT SHOULD CHRISTIAN WHITES DO WITH THIS?

Now that at least some of the definitions and their implications have been explained, what should Christian whites do with what might be new information and perspectives? The natural tendency might be to become angry, defensive, and defiant. I have heard Christian white leaders insist "No one can ever call me a racist!" (though, in truth, that began decades ago).

Likewise, you might demand a fair and complete assessment of your attitudes, feelings, and thoughts. Or, you might insist that there are indeed multiple causes for the myriad problems your black brothers and sisters face, whether racism is a large or small component.

Alternatively, you might agree with many or all of these characterizations, believing that racism has and continues to play a significant and highly corrosive role in our society. You may agree that racism is institutionalized and therefore seek to partner with your Christian black brothers and sisters to eradicate racism wherever it is found or even suspected.

Regardless of your reactions to what has been written, I would urge my Christian white brethren to step back, ponder deeply, pray diligently, and objectively evaluate both your own attitudes and feelings and those of the people around you. Evaluate how you, your co-workers, and members of your church and community interact with others, particularly minorities. Look at the systems, institutions, and organizations that are said to be racist, and objectively evaluate how blacks were and are treated. Objectively search your soul, seek Godly wisdom in how to manage what you have read, and change whatever and as much as God calls you to.

Importantly, in order to begin bridging the gaps that divide us, I highly recommend that you do all this within the context of conversations with Christian blacks. As you'll see in coming chapters, there are definitive and uniquely Christian approaches to these conversations. Indeed, only Christians are called to have the conversations in the manner described. To be clear … we cannot rely on society to lead the way!

Whether you agree or disagree, in part or in whole, with the definitions and their implications as I have described them, it is quite clear that Christian whites must necessarily deal with this issue. Christian whites do not have the luxury of ignoring the issues, disengaging, or refusing to participate in painful discussions. If God's glory is to be shown, and Christ and Christianity are to be seen in a better and more realistic light Christian whites simply cannot ignore what society is teaching. If for no other reason than to bridge gaps in your own community, you must engage in what might be wrenching conversations with people who have and may again say things about you that you might consider false, offensive, and hurtful. Perhaps this is the price we must pay for the sins of our past.

Thus, it is critical that you avoid isolation and instead boldly embrace the challenge of creating a different society one that is led by rather than arrayed against Christians. In the chapters to come, you will read about the importance of uprightness in these conversations, and the tasks that both Christian whites and Christian blacks need to do in order to unify the faithful, create unity in action, and bring glory to God.

Having difficult but important conversations is only a start.

WHAT SHOULD CHRISTIAN BLACKS DO WITH THIS?

Just as Christian whites need to understand the perspectives of the black community (such that this is possible), Christian blacks need to understand how these definitions may have served to stop conversations and create divisions. Even if 100% accurate, society's harsh, often anti-Christian presentation of these definitions leaves plenty of room for defensiveness, denial, and deflection.

Furthermore, regardless of whether you believe that racism is partially or wholly responsible for the current plight of blacks in America, it behooves us all to consider the impacts our disagreements are having on the faith. It is therefore critical that Christian blacks take a role in opening dialogue and creating space for what might be difficult conversations. Doing this as brothers and sisters in Christ will break down barriers that might otherwise be fortified and bridge gaps that would otherwise remain wide.

In the chapters to come, you will read about the importance of uprightness in these conversations, and the tasks that both Christian whites and Christian blacks need to do in order to unify the faithful, create unity in action, and bring glory to God.

Having difficult but important conversations is only a start.

SUMMARY: WHAT IS TO BE DONE?

This chapter is meant to help both Christian black and Christian white readers understand the contexts within which racial terminology is used, how terms are interpreted in today's society and the significance of their impacts on both racial unity and God's role in our society. The current negative and hostile environment is being spurred by genuine and deep gaps in communication, caused in part by changes in definitions of key terms that simultaneously perpetuate the horror of the past while blaming more and more for its alleged continuation. A definition meant to explain the current state of affairs becomes a hateful and harsh accusation that eliminates dialogue and heightens sensitivities and malice.

Even if the new definitions weren't meant to divide, they have nonetheless done so. Yes, the new broader applications may have opened some eyes to the ongoing plight of blacks and the struggles that they continue to face in aftermath of blatant segregation, injustice, and mistreatment. But this might have been done by other, less divisive means. One can remove a cancerous tumor with a hammer and a fork, but the patient is left in far worse shape.

By spreading the term racist to include more and more whites, particularly Christian whites, the new definitions have served to increase the tension between the races as otherwise loving and caring people are maligned and labeled with attributes they do not possess. Thus, the underlying messages of these new definitions of racism may serve to continue to divide Americans, particularly Christians, into bitter racial rivalries.

Of course, this is precisely why God's church needs to step firmly and boldly into the vacuum. God's church, united in action, can step into the fray with Godly attitudes and actions to show a better way. By showing God's church to be different from our society, we can differentiate Christianity and its message from the politics that swirl around us. Through thoughts, words, and deeds, unity in action will impact society in ways heretofore unimaginable.

As Christian blacks and whites, we must seek to interact with each other in a very different way than the world now sees. America's churches, united by causes and goals, need to continue to work to change the systems, structures, and errant beliefs that keep anyone, not matter what race or creed, from reaching the potential which God has given them.

And to do this, we must begin to show ourselves to be "upright," living and speaking with a purity of honesty, objectivity, and integrity as we seek to influence all those around us. In doing so, God's glory will shine through the Christian American church to show an increasingly secular society a better way to live, interact, and love one another.

THE CALL TO UPRIGHTNESS

"Whoever would love life and see good days must keep their tongue from evil and their lips from deceitful speech." (1 Peter 3:10, Psalms 34:12-13)

A VOID TO BE FILLED

It is said that nature hates a vacuum. That is, into any void, something will flow. When our politics, our culture and our society is as divided as it is, there is a void in the middle where civility, love, honesty, integrity, and objectivity once lived. And something or someone, at some point, will fill that void.

Our society has always been divided, to some degree, by various combinations of politics, race, class, gender, and other factors. But in recent years, our politics and social divisions seem to have become increasingly, nearly exponentially more visceral and hateful. Consider any relevant political or social issue of our day, whether incarceration of the mentally ill, discipline in our schools, public prayer, legal and illegal immigration, school performance deficits, abortion, gaps in health care and wellness, the ongoing existence of racist groups, the redefinition and redirection of hatred, the justification of violence, etc. Any of these topics and troubles will likely have at least two sides to them, whether we call them red or blue, left or right, evil or good, right or wrong.

But as our society becomes increasingly divided and filled with anger, rage, and bitter hatred, debate and the finding of mutually beneficial solutions becomes increasingly difficult, if not impossible. Gone are the days of friendly "Firing Line"[lxi] debates over important issues of the day. We no longer allow the "other side" any credence or even legitimacy, and wholly discount anything and everything that comes forth from there. Hate and rage have taken over as a reasonable and acceptable means to express opinion. Discussion has been replaced with disdain. Reasonable, educated dialogue has been replaced by visceral demagoguery. Pure integrity has been shown the door in favor of spin, hyperbole, and half-truths.

Indeed, Americans are often more concerned about which side wins than what is actually right and wrong. We look first at who developed the idea or solution rather than at its merits. And in politics, errors and mistakes are simply not allowed by the "other side," as any sign of error is seen as a sign of weakness to be pounced upon. Even when we see the error of our own thinking, we are often forced into defense of, or at least justification for, our side, even if our side is clearly in the wrong, in part or in whole.

We thereby build our "war camps" from which we regularly launch attacks on the "enemy," even when that enemy has the best of intentions if not better options and ideas. As the ability to peacefully disagree wanes, so too does our willingness to be objective and honest.

So, as a nation, the void left by the loss of love, honesty, integrity, and objectivity in the public space has created a vacuum. If Christians do not fill it with our own love, honesty, integrity, and objectivity, this void will most likely be filled with something or by someone who does not share our beliefs. Instead, it will likely be whoever or whatever is the most powerful and influential, even if that power is based on deceptions, lies, hate, or unjust authority.

It is into this gap, this increasingly widening chasm between and among Americans, that the Christian American church must dive. Headfirst, eyes wide open, and fearless. We must enter this gap for the many reasons outlined herein already – to bring glory to God and God's church, to unite Christians around common causes, and to impact American society in profound and deep ways. Only through our example will society see the power of Christ in a new way.

CALLED TO BE DIFFERENT

If indeed we are to step into this void; if we are to unite as Christian brothers and sisters to act on behalf of our God in our nation; if we are to impact our society in the name of the God we proudly worship; then we must necessarily be wildly different from the world around us. Of course, we all know that we are called to be different from the world. As the commonly cited Romans 12:2 puts it, "Do not conform to the pattern of this world but be transformed by the renewing of your mind. Then you will be able to test and approve what God's will is—his good, pleasing and perfect will."

The Living Bible translation states the same verse this way, "Don't copy the behavior and customs of this world but be a new and different person with a fresh newness in all you do and think. Then you will learn from your own experience how His ways will really satisfy you."

Likewise, 1 Corinthians 3:18-19 tells us, "Do not deceive yourselves. If any of you think you are wise by the standards of this age, you should become 'fools' so that you may become wise. [19] For the wisdom of this world is foolishness in God's sight."

Given the toxicity of our politics, and the lack of integrity, honesty, and objectivity in our dialogue, it is pretty clear that if Christians want to be different than the rest of the world and our society, all we need do is be honest and objective, and display a deep sense of integrity. Poof! Like magic, we're different! Having a deep, indwelling sense of honesty, integrity, and objectivity would make anyone seem quite strange in today's world!

Indeed, the Bible tees us up for this new "different" role in society by calling us to take on several other important attributes that will be critical for our unity in action.

A LITTLE A.D.D.

Society, technology, media, the pace of modern life, and the "instant gratification" culture has made us all a little bit A.D.D., particularly when it comes to our interactions with the world and those around us. How many of us really stop and think hard about what we hear and see? How many simply regurgitate what we hear on a snippet on the news or read the headline as if it's the entire story or repeat what we heard through the grapevine as if it were gospel. We are too often quick to judge and slow to think.

WHAT ARE YOU THINKING?

Author and social psychologist Timothy Wilson has written about the strength and power of what he calls the "adaptive unconscious" mind. In Strangers to Ourselves: Discovering the Adaptive Unconscious,[lxii] Wilson explains that only a very small percentage of our brain's power is used for "conscious thought," and that the unconscious mind is far more active and influential, with a higher degree of "thinking" capacity, than we previously understood. He describes the adaptive unconscious mind as being capable of problem solving, prediction, emotional reaction, and the construction of broad narratives without the intervention of the conscious mind.

Thus, he posits, the adaptive unconscious mind may be the primary element in our personalities by controlling our judgement, actions and reactions, motivations and fears without us really knowing it. This would suggest that we mold our reality based on how we unconsciously view the world around us. We react without conscious thought to the many stimuli, as our subconscious mind quickly categorizes things for us to keep us moving forward with life.

Whether this theory is true in part or in whole, it is clear that we all come to conclusions without deep thought. The pace of life encourages this rapid-fire approach to decisioning by casting more and more decisions into the realm of the quick and expedient, regardless of the "whole truth." A part truth, or at least something that resonates positively or negatively with us, is enough for our speedy decisions.

The new speed to judgment

Ironically, the internet and the overwhelming speed and availability of data, information, and opinion may be serving to reduce our willingness to actively and consciously pursue truth. I have noted that, particularly among our younger generations (e.g. Millennials), there is an increasing quickness to judgment despite the ease and speed of access to a wealth of information from myriad sources, including and especially the internet. The challenge no longer seems to be a deep and objective search for truth but rather the speed with which one can find an opinion that matches preconceived, socially favored, perhaps unconscious, ideas. Questions that once took time and effort to research, ponder, and challenge are now immediately answered, whether rightly, wrongly, or completely, by a tweet, blog, or YouTube video. And the vastness of the internet makes finding opinions that match one's own quick and easy, leading to an exponentially faster confirmation of opinion and a corresponding quickness to dismiss opposing viewpoints or challenges. Echo chambers are everywhere and stand ready to please and support the like-minded.

Quick access has also made deeper thought and intellectual challenge seemingly less necessary. Since there is such a plethora of existing thought available for the taking, it is far easier to adopt what is quickly accessible than to delve deeply and ask time-consuming questions in order to form one's own intellectual foundations. The voluminous support of an idea or supposition in the blogosphere may not be indicative of its actual validity, but rather only its popularity. And since the deluge of conforming opinion feeds on itself, it can quickly become overwhelming.

This also means that any effort to delve into a subject, theory, or question might likely be met with unilateral support rather than dispute or refutation. Importantly, the result is that offering or harboring a dissenting view or even questioning the thoughts of the masses can feel like swimming against a hurricane's force.

Moreover, the vehemence with which some support their ideas and beliefs online makes dissention socially risky. Even questioning the prevailing viewpoint often leads to online bullying, shaming, ostracization, hateful accusations, and even threats of violence. The incentive to inquire deeply and challenge ideas is thereby greatly diminished, making sheepishness far less painful than inquiry.

Thus, the speed to decision is made quicker while the research and analysis used to support those decisions are being minimized. This makes a race out of being informed enough to have an opinion but not deeply knowledgeable enough in matters and issues about which so many passions erupt.

So, even though counterpoints for our thoughts and ideas are as readily available as the support, too many opt for a quick affirmation rather than dig deeper to challenge what is socially acceptable or a personal bias. Access and speed are thereby making us intellectually lazy and unduly self-assured, as we take in only what is required to form or support an existing thought, supposition, or theory. Put another way, Twitter has taken the place of the library.

Thus, what is superficial and comfortably agreeable becomes iron-clad dogma, increasingly accepted as truth since fewer and fewer choose to challenge it. This makes facts out of half-truths, turns bias into objectivity, makes news out of mere headlines, and creates intransigence where stimulating debate once thrived.

Being wrong

Importantly, these theories posit that the unconscious mind can get things wrong. For example, if the truth is somehow damaging, threatening, unpleasant, or goes against some internal, subconscious grain, the unconscious mind will make a sort of "protective judgment" without using all the available information. For nothing says that the unconscious mind slowly and objectively analyzes and evaluates stimuli behind the scenes before offering the conscious mind its feedback and "wisdom."

Rather, the unconscious mind might be shaped and molded as is necessary to ensure self-interests, survival and sustainability. This could include protecting us from suffering insult or injury to our ego, pride or positions. Thus, tightly held beliefs go unchallenged as the unconscious mind molds our interpretations to fit an historical or acceptable narrative or belief system. Past events, interactions, education, and thoughts could combine to taint the unconscious with its own preconceived notions, which it then passes along as skewed interpretations to the conscious mind, our personalities, actions, and thoughts.

If the unconscious mind is as powerful, controlling and potentially incorrect as Wilson and others suggest, then we likely have some rather incorrect views and presumptions of the people, places, and things we encounter in day to day life. And this, in turn, is reflected in our stereotypes, assumptions, and quick judgments that we rely on in daily living.

And even if the Adaptive Unconscious mind is only an interesting theory for academics and psychologists, we should nonetheless consider how we make judgements about those around us, the events that we see, and the world as we encounter it because those judgments may not always be correct. Just how quickly do we make our judgments, and what influence does that have on their accuracy and legitimacy?

Creating an open mind

By whatever explanation we choose, we must prevent our unconscious mind, adaptive or otherwise, from making judgments before our conscious mind slows down long enough to evaluate, assess, and decide with full integrity and objectivity. You might believe in the unconscious mind or simply believe that we are just so busy and harried in our day to day lives that speedy judgments are simply part of the way we have to live to survive. Or, that we are just mentally lazy and quick to judge. Or perhaps that society's dialogue has become so toxic that it has made us less apt to ask questions and delve, for fear of the repercussions.

Regardless, we constantly miss opportunities to consider more deeply the scale and breadth of the issues, problems, and solutions with which we are presented. Furthermore, we miss opportunities to better know the people we encounter, help those who might need it, and solve for the issues our fellow Christians and non-Christians face.

This all points to the central theme of this chapter. That is, we, as Christians, must be able to step back and think differently about the world around us, how our actions and the actions of others intersect, and the multi-faceted causes of the circumstances in which we and others live. It simply means that all Christians must take on a new and difficult role and make an example from our thoughts, words, and actions to a world that has seemingly lost its ability to think, speak, and act with love, honesty, integrity, and objectivity.

Only by doing so can we more effectively address the issues faced by all our communities across our nation.

CALLED TO BE UPRIGHT

Biblically, integrity and honesty seem to be blended into the term "uprightness." God uses the term "upright" around 75 times (specifically in reference to personality traits and intellectual characteristics)[lxiii]. Used in this context, the word refers to a person able to stand straight and tall with the knowledge of their integrity and ongoing efforts to be Christ-like, walking humbly with God against the destructive ways and temptations of the world. It could be contrasted with the diminished stature or standing of a liar or thief, or one whose guilt and shame keep them from standing tall before honorable men.

The word is commonly used in conjunction with other adjectives further describing a person's character, such as "blameless and upright" (Job 1:1), "good and upright" (Psalms 25:8), "faithfulness and uprightness" (Psalms 111:8), "integrity and uprightness" (Psalms 25:21), and "the integrity of the upright" (Proverbs 11:3). Indeed, "upright" and "integrity" are used together five times in the Bible.

In Proverbs, "uprightness" is commonly juxtaposed against some other negative attribute or type of person, such as "the unfaithful" (Proverbs 11:3), "wicked" (Proverbs 12:6), "fools" (Proverbs 14:9), "the guilty" (Proverbs 21:8), and "those who despise [the Lord]" (Proverbs 14:2).

Uprightness, then, is a sort of an overarching term used to describe those who walk, speak, act, and worship with integrity, honesty, and objectivity. As Christians, we are called to be upright in our pursuit of faithful service and Christ's righteousness as a counter to the wicked ways of the world and our society. I will therefore use the term "uprightness" to apply to several other terms that fit under its umbrella.

The Christian need for uprightness

Uprightness will allow us better dialogue between Christians, particularly related to the issues we seek to influence. Without this key attribute, we will speak, act, and think no differently than the rest of society. As a result, we will rightfully be called hypocrites and fools for speaking, acting, and thinking just as the world does, even as we preach against it and its ways. Furthermore, our words will capture little attention, as they will be no different than the words of any other worldly group or entity.

To be clear, this is not easy. Indeed, most people would consider themselves to be upright, exhibiting the purest of honesty, integrity, and objectivity in most situations. And they would be wrong. Not because they are dishonest or disingenuous, or because they do not seek integrity.

Rather, we all tend to work from limited and incomplete data, use headlines as facts, jump to conclusions, fail to see the complete picture, or use preconceived notions to make important decisions. We are thereby all guilty of a lack of uprightness, to some degree and at least some of the time.

Furthermore, being upright is simply difficult work requiring ongoing effort. Indeed, uprightness requires the same kind of attention, conscious effort, and ongoing awareness of a true prayer warrior. Constant introspection, constant study, and constant questioning, with a lot help from the Holy Spirit.

Thus, prayer and uprightness should go well together, since both require contact with the Almighty and an ongoing, conscious intensity. And since God has given us both the calling to it and the means to achieve it, Christians are uniquely qualified to seek it out, acquire, maintain, and exhibit this uniquely difficult yet differentiating quality.

We must therefore be constantly vigilant to ensure that we are being upright, especially in the kinds of discussions and decisions suggested in this book. Doing so will allow us to achieve the very difficult tasks suggested herein. Not doing so will surely lead to failure.

The next step in the discussion is to explore some of the terms that are wrapped up in the broader definition of "uprightness" to understand what they mean in this context. These are honesty, integrity, and objectivity.

THE ATTRIBUTES OF UPRIGHTNESS

Honesty and integrity

How many times does the Bible tell us to avoid lying? Leviticus 19:11, "Do not lie." That's pretty plain, eh? Ephesians 4:25, "Therefore each of you must put off falsehood and speak truthfully to your neighbor, for we are all members of one body." Then, of course, there is Commandment #8.

God uses the words integrity, honest, honesty, and upright roughly 123 times (depending on the translation you use). Obviously, these traits are important to Him! Indeed, Jesus Himself is referred to as a "man of integrity" (Mark 12:14, Matthew 22:16). If we are to be like Jesus, then surely we are to have the utmost integrity within us. We are thereby called, by example and fiat, to display pure integrity.

By contrast, in today's politics and social issues, "spin" is more likely to be used in a sort of Orwellian fashion to define a specific version of the truth used by one side or the other of an argument. Yet, spin is rarely the "whole truth and nothing but the truth" and might be just the opposite.

Indeed, as our politics becomes more and more toxic, displaying pure honesty and deep integrity will very likely have one shunned by both sides of the political aisle, perhaps especially on 's own. The common phase uttered by politicians on a regular basis, "What Americans want ..." is only half true on the best of days.

Just consider how often we hear something other than the pure truth. How many times have you heard one story only to find the truth was the exact opposite, as if told by your toddler? How many times have you been told something by a source you thought you could trust, only to find the flagrant and intentional use of lies, deceptions, and bias? Look at how churches are torn apart and members turned into cynics when deceptions are invented and deployed like weapons. Whether to uphold a personal belief, support a personal endeavor or deeply held theory, or create a false impression of someone or something else, two plus two can equal just about anything when honesty falters.

Moreover, we may often feel that we are being totally honest when we are instead relying on preconceived notions, personal opinions, internal biases, or limited knowledge. We may think that we are being honest when we don't yet know or haven't bothered to get all the details or haven't yet considered all the relevant facts and perspectives on a given topic or haven't taken the time to investigate it fully. To use modern vernacular, we use Twitter for our information instead of an Encyclopedia. We thereby think we are being honest, yet we might be ill-informed and too quick to judge.

Of course, nowhere does the Bible tell us to use our own personal viewpoints and opinions, political stances, limited information, or our own understanding and experiences to develop our own personalized version of truth. Rather, God specifically calls us to be totally and fully honest. Period. No if's, and's, or but's.

Therefore, we must often pursue the truth at a deeper level, with a more open mind, than we are often accustomed to and society recommends. We must leave no stone unturned as we pursue an understanding of truth that God Himself would respect. Only then will we serve as examples for our society, speaking, acting, and thinking with an integrity that reflects the purity of God.

This means that we must sometimes, and even constantly, put aside the things we know, or think we know, in the pursuit of the kind of action called for here. For without purity in thought, we cannot come to what is right and good, and thus run the risk of errant solutions that will harm rather than help God's intentions.

We must constantly challenge the preconceptions and prejudicial judgments that we always carry with us. We must also be willing to freely and openly admit error in our pursuit of honesty and integrity. This is rarely if ever done in our society, as it is seen as a weakness rather than a positive attribute. But only by admitting error, in part or in whole, are we free to learn from both our own mistakes and those of others. Without the free and open willingness to admit error and forgive the errors of others, we are left to harbor and nurture falsehoods and ill feelings. This only serves to diminish relationships and reduce the chances for new solutions and ideas.

Furthermore, the ongoing pursuit of honesty and integrity and the admission that, at least on occasion, we fail to achieve them, should push us to humility before God. All are fallen, but when we fail to see the error of our ways and fail to genuinely pursue these important traits, we take on a sort of hubris that is antithetical to God's word and His commands.

Lastly, and importantly, only through this relentless, prayerful pursuit of truth and integrity will we will be able to bring together our disparate Christian groups to address the root causes of the issues of our day as unified brothers and sisters. We certainly will not be able to heal the breaches between Christian blacks and Christian whites using the spin, lies, half-truths, and devotion to personal agendas and self-serving opinions that society uses. Rather, unity requires us to answer God's call to be honest and value integrity. Without these attributes, we may never be able to solve for the breaches between us.

Intellectual honesty

As a distinctly non-biblical term, "intellectual honesty" simply means that one's intellect does not interfere with one's pursuit of the pure truth. Rather, one who adheres to this level of honesty refuses to use their God-given intellect to misuse information or allow facts to be disregarded simply because they run counter to a held position or belief system. Intellectual honesty demands that the pursuer present facts in an unbiased, unambiguous way, even if those facts upend deeply held beliefs, age-old theories or cause personal embarrassment. As Dragnet's Joe Friday was famous for saying, "Just the facts, ma'am." Or, think of Spock of Star Trek fame.

This might seem like an odd thing to have to clarify, but clearly the smartest people will often use their intelligence to spin lies and develop the most devious of deceptions. For instance, "research" is not all as pure as we like to think. It is not uncommon for contracted medical or scientific researchers to be quite biased, publishing studies that are based more on who paid for the research or some preconceived expectation of the outcomes than on the actual results of the research process.

Likewise, just look at many of our elected officials, many of whom are intelligent people, to see how facts are twisted and abused for the sake of position, power, influence, prestige, and "self-righteousness." Small wonder that Americans have lost trust in their elected leaders and Congressional approval ratings have been as low as 13% in recent years.[lxiv] This lack of honesty is exhibited throughout our society, leading to general cynicism and mistrust of many of our once respected institutions.

Consider, too, the opposite of this term, which would be "intellectual dishonesty." This might be the stereotypical genius who uses his intelligence to steal, hurt, and create injustice. Think of stereotypical greedy trial lawyers who use misfortune and their own cleverness for their own ill-gained riches; or a politician who deliberately misuses information and statistics to advance a cause or damage political opponents; or hackers who use their computer skills to steal and wreak havoc.

But because God has blessed us with education and intelligence, we must be cautious to avoid using our gifts for wrongdoing. Thus "Intellectual honesty" is another form of the same sort of honesty that is required of Christians. We are called by God to use our God-given intellects and talents to pursue the truth, just as we pursue Him and Christlike behavior.

Indeed, because we have God-given intelligence, we are thereby required to use it to delve deeply, inquire honestly, and evaluate both questions and answers with pure integrity. Nothing about Christ said "bias." Nothing about His words were meant for political enrichment or personal gain. Likewise, we are to pursue the truth as He did ... for the sake of the salvation and betterment of our fellow man.

We must always remember that, as we pursue action in our society, we represent His name, His church, and His glory. And we should always use His gifts for their intended purposes.

Objectivity: The hardest of them all

As a similar term under the "upright" umbrella, objectivity is the twin brother of intellectual honesty. Objectivity is perhaps the most difficult of human traits to obtain and sustain. As with integrity, objectivity is made even harder to achieve when others refuse to use it, which perhaps is why so many of us fall prey to the easy way out ... our preconceived notions, stereotypes, and prejudices. This is particularly true when we think about our assumptions about the problems society faces and the solutions, leaders, and political parties we tend to lean towards.

Objectivity demands that we examine each situation, circumstance, and person anew. We must necessarily be objective if we are to see beyond our stereotypes, preconceived notions, and personal biases to get to the truth and to truly think, speak and act uprightly. If for no other reason, people, circumstances, knowledge, and situations change over time, thus requiring a constant vigilance over our thoughts.

But a lack of objectivity comes as we are influenced, taught or learn to believe certain things or think in certain ways. We tend to observe the world through the various lenses that are carved and shaped throughout our lifetimes by our experiences, interests and education, similar to the way in which Wilson suggests our unconscious minds are used.

This yields the perspectives, attitudes, and beliefs about what we see around us, the way we interact and live, and the means by which we solve problems. Some are learned the hard way through personal experiences. Others come from what we learn from others whose opinions we trust.

Thus, there is a natural tendency to learn from our past, the past of others, and our own personal belief systems and use these lessons to create stereotypes, preconceived notions and prejudices about a great many issues, people, systems, objects, and events around us.

These are then used by our conscious and unconscious minds to create narratives and weave together acceptable storylines that align with what we already think rather than what might actually be true. Our "research" and "facts" are commonly only those we have collected in support of the positions we started with rather than any that might challenge or defy our core beliefs.

These prejudicial constructs are not always bad, mind you. If you see a large dog without a leash running towards you, you might not wait to discover whether it simply wants to be petted before seeking safety. Perhaps you've never been attacked by a large dog, but you've heard of plenty of people who have been, so you don't delay in acting to prevent a bad situation.

Likewise, a group of men walking towards you as you walk alone in a dark alley late at night might automatically give you pause. Maybe you've watched just a few too many horror movies and detective shows to feel peace when you encounter strangers in a dark alley late at night. Or maybe your city is known for its crime rates. Regardless, your brain might quickly lead you to fear and take steps to prevent a harmful event.

Of course, the complete reliance on stereotypes keeps us from questioning the current scenario we face. While we might not take time to question the intentions of men in a dark alley, we might take a moment to question our current beliefs about other, less immediately frightening things. Think of the generalizations we place on groups of people by their characteristics, whether by age, dress, race, appearance, and/or mannerisms. Think of the assumptions we make about our existing beliefs, such as the fairness of the justice system, the existence of man-made global warming, or the integrity of short-term lenders.

Consider your own need for objectivity as you interact with people, evaluate problems, watch the news, and go about your daily life. For example:

- What if you saw a group of rough-looking, cigarette smoking bikers hanging out in a bar on a Sunday morning? You might think, "Wow, either those guys don't waste any time getting the party started or last night's party is still going on!" only to find out that they are a group of Christian bikers holding a church service. "God's Rolling Thunder," a "biker church" in Georgia, has some of the kindest, most loving and communally active Christians you could ever met and got its start meeting in a smoke bar on Sunday mornings before the place opened for business.
- What if you met a middle-aged white man with what some might describe as an "effeminate voice and mannerisms," dressed in bright colors, singing at the top of his lungs? "He's gay!" perhaps? Well, instead, he might be the Minister of Music at a Baptist church, a father of three, and devoted husband.
- What if you met a young black man with dreadlocks in shabby clothes with a basketball under his arm? You might sooner think something negative than think of him as a dedicated leader of a ministry for at-risk middle-school kids.

And those are just examples of people. Think of all the social problems we face, from crime to justice, education, healthcare, and race. What are your preconceived notions about these issues? How might the perspectives of people in a different community impact your viewpoint? Might you be harboring opinions and prejudicial judgments that you refuse to challenge?

For instance:

- What if American culture dictated actions and beliefs to our kids that exacerbated negative stereotypes, personal habits, and social norms that were counter to God's teaching and bad for their long-term success?
- What if well-meaning politicians, power brokers, and government institutions supported economic, education, and social policies that are meant to help but in fact hurt the poorest among us?
- What if well-meaning Christian whites are incorrectly pegged as racists due to their adherence to Biblical principles?
- What if culture and personal choices had more to do with a negative social situation than racism or hidden biases?
- What if your favored political party supported actions and policies that ran counter to the will of God?

Importantly for this discussion, Christians will need deep-seated and ever-present objectivity to delve deeper into the intractable issues of our communities.

Let's face it … intractable issues aren't easily solved, largely because they are so complex in origin. We can't fix education just by increasing teacher pay or getting rid of teachers' unions. We can't improve health by simply opening up a new clinic or offering free insurance. And we can't address crime and justice without accounting for mental illness and drug and alcohol dependency.

And the more complex the issue, the more we need intellectual honestly and objectivity throughout our analytical process to prevent us from developing solutions too quickly, relying on preconceived notions, jumping to conclusions, and failing to get to the real issues at hand. For some, jumping to conclusions is their only exercise! Fighting this tendency is hard, just as hard as resisting the defense impulse when you see the big dog coming at you.

Therefore, objectivity is a key required trait of the active Christian, for without it we cannot continue to seek the truth and constantly seek out new solutions to our most perplexing issues. If we settle too quickly, the solutions we've developed may not be effective. And if we fail to be objective, we may miss great opportunities right in front of us. And this, of course, is why these attributes are so important for unity in action with other Christians!

If we are to be active Christians, if we are to fill the void left by the demise of uprightness in our society, and if we are to create a better image of God and

God's church in America for the sake of God's glory and the increase in His flock, we must necessarily rise above the world and its overwhelming use of lies, little white lies, deceptions, and "spin." We must be upright. Honest. Full of integrity, with complete objectivity. Only then will we set ourselves apart from the world, and thereby be able to do the work of God in our society as a unified Christian church. And yet this is remarkably difficult to do, even for the prayerful Christian.

HOLY CONVERSATIONS

"Holy Conversations" have been described as having several attributes, including uprightness and its underlying attributes ... [intellectual] honesty, integrity, and objectivity. Indeed, these are absolutely necessary for these Holy Conversation to take place.

The four attributes of Holy Conversations are:

1. They make us vulnerable. And in so many ways. Think about opening a dialogue with the congregation and pastors of a nearby church of another race. Think about what internal walls you will have to tear down, the scars you might have to expose, the personal baggage, animosity, suspicion, and preconceived notions that everyone will have to leave behind. Think too of the caution, suspicion, and skepticism with which you might automatically approach a given situation. Think about your past experiences with other similar meetings and situations and what they would tell you about what is about to happen. Then, think about throwing all that away, thereby coming with the innocence of a child, without preconceived anything, without any prejudicial judgments, biases, or thoughts. That's vulnerability! If many, if not all of us, do not feel a little vulnerable as we start these cross-racial discussions, we aren't doing it right. For every situation, there may be dozens of preconceived biases that will have to be forcibly removed from our minds. We haven't quite let go of enough of our own "stuff" and are keeping too much of our history, biases, preconceived notions, and unconscious and conscious stereotypes around. It will take a LOT of effort, but it is crucial that we all lose them.

2. They are time-consuming. Yes, these conversations and the subsequent planning and activation of our unity in action will take time. Not just months, but perhaps years. And throughout this time, we must necessarily continue our upright dialogues. Our

conversations will morph over time, as relationships are built, projects and targets change, the situations in our communities change, and people grow together as Christian brothers and sisters.

3. They require big questions. Certainly, we are addressing some of the biggest questions in American church history while trying to address some of the biggest issues in society. Of course, this is why uprightness is so absolutely critical, and why objectivity and intellectual honesty require us to constantly challenge any and all preconceived notions and ideas. We should be asking God-sized questions, because we have a very big God who is capable of very big things if we allow Him to work through our very big faith! God-sized questions will likely require God-sized solutions.

4. They bring big surprises. Indeed, as we venture down this path, break outside our siloed efforts in our communities to join with others in a holy collaboration, we may find that God opens some big doors, breaks down some persistent barriers and allows us to do great works!

Even better, we will be able to show our society that being a Christian isn't about damning people to hell from a street-corner bullhorn, leaving salvation literature in a public toilet, or sitting in our sanctified ivory towers preaching to our choirs. Through our unity in action, we will show what we have been doing in the centuries since Christ was a carpenter: helping people, displaying love, loving mercy, and doing justice.

But, even more, we will show our society what living uprightly can do for the most difficult issues they face. That, in and of itself, will be a big enough surprise for the world! And we might in turn be surprised by the impact that has on folks who want to know a little more about what this Christian thing is all about.

These Holy Conversations are essentially what we will be required to have as we delve into the difficult barriers that divide Christians, particularly along racial lines.

For the sake of our unity in action, we needn't use these Holy Conversations to settle doctrinal or ecumenical difference, for these do not impact our ability to act in our communities. Indeed, those discussions will only serve to keep us in silos and unable to unify.

Rather, we need to reserve Holy Conversations for those issues that unnecessarily keep us from becoming active bodies of Christ in our communities.

BIG ONIONS

Education, justice, race, and health are four of the top issues facing our nation. Just look at the headlines in any newspaper or news website today, and you'll likely find at least one of the four mentioned. They are difficult issues because, like big onions, they have lots and lots of layers. Peel back one layer and you'll find more.

The complexity of these problems requires more than talking points and headlines for solutions. All too often, however, we decide on a solution to a problem that is politically expedient, looks good on paper, is "tangible" (e.g. something that a politician can point to, like a "blue ribbon panel" or a nice new building), or is easy enough to do without full consideration of the depth and breadth of the problem. Moreover, complex problems require complex solutions, the results of which are commonly unpredictable and politically difficult.

For instance, if we reduce incarceration rates for petty crimes to reduce the population in local jails, there may be negative "downstream" outcomes to some neighborhoods that we don't predict. If we open a free health clinic in a poor neighborhood, we may not see an increase in overall health status that we hope to see if other variables to health and wellness, such as food and housing, are not addressed.

Thinking about these "interdependencies" is often the hardest part of the development of solutions to complex issues. Yet it is these interdependencies that can keep our solutions from working effectively or completely. And it is these interdependencies that often cause the most intransigence and undue loyalty to preconceived notions to pop up. Thus, as mentioned, it is critical to prevent "conclusion jumping" as we seek solutions to these large, onerous problems. Only through ongoing introspection, continuous analysis, and objectivity about our ideas will we achieve the results we seek.

And because anyone taking on the challenge of walking uprightly has to be a very special and committed person, the Christian church is the only entity realistically capable of developing appropriate, lasting, and workable solutions to these most intractable problems.

Politicians, political parties, special interest groups and even the best minds in the country often lack our divine, unifying call to act on behalf of our fellow citizens in an upright, Christ-like manner.

However, if we act as Christians, thinking, speaking, and working with uprightness and God's love within us, we can help solve these problems within race, education, justice, and healthcare while bringing great glory to God and people to the light of Christ.

SUMMARY

There is a growing void as honesty, integrity, and objectivity are being extracted from today's society. With these go trust, collaboration, cooperation, and constructive dialogue, which are rapidly being replaced by anger, harsh, and often false accusations, lies and discord. Our churches need to step forward into this vacuum left by our society. Walking uprightly, united by our passion for Christ and our goal to act and speak like Him, we must go hand in hand, arm in arm into the fray. It won't be easy, pretty, or even fun. It will require conscious effort and the ongoing prayerful tenacity of a true prayer warrior. We must constantly challenge what we think we know so that we can discover what we don't know. But through prayer and constant contact with the Holy Spirit and the communion with other brothers and sisters in Christ, we can break down even centuries old barriers, come together and create solutions for our society.

And this will offer God's church the opportunity to show our broken society what can be done when Christ is deep within the hearts and minds of a group of people. United across racial boundaries, and with the scars of open dialogue to show for it, we can do great things for our society and God's Kingdom in America. We can have Holy Conversations and dive headfirst into the deep layers of society's biggest onions.

Through our unity in action and the glory our efforts will bring to God, we can bring new people to Christ and an awakening to the next generations of Americans.

SILOS

PERSPECTIVES

The church was founded in 181 . It is the oldest African Methodist Episcopal church in the South and s therefore often fondly referred to as "Mother Emanuel." Throughout s history, the Emanuel A.M.E. church has seen the harsh realities of our troubled, racially divided past.

In 1822, it was burned to the ground by a group of angry whites after one of its founders, Denmark Vessey, was implicated in a slave revolt plot. He and more than thirty other men were executed, most by lynching, some as the result of secret trials. The church was not rebuilt until after the Civil War ended, after which it was rebuilt twice, with its current edifice completed in 1892.

The relevance and history of this great church continued into the modern era and the Civil Rights movement, with great leaders including Dr. Rev. Martin Luther King, Jr. and Rev. Wyatt T. Walker visiting its historic location. Sadly, its history with the violence of racism did not end there.

On the night of June 15th, 2015, a self-professed white supremacist named Dylann Storm Roof came to the Wednesday night prayer meeting at Mother Emanuel A.M.E in Charleston, S.C. After engaging with the small group of congregants, at approximately 9 p.m., he pulled a .45 caliber Glock from his fanny-pack. Beginning with the nephew of an 87-year-old woman who tried to shield his aunt's body, he proceeded to systematically and methodically murder Christian black men and women. Within minutes, six Christian women and three Christian men lay dead.

The horror of the incident spread throughout the nation in the few next days. I was particularly touched, given how many of these churches I'd visited over the years. I could vividly see in my mind how this crazed man might have been warmly received by the unknowing congregants, with hugs and God Bless You's all-around before their execution began.

As I tried to wrestle with this act of pure evil, I immediately felt that this was an opportunity to show Christian solidarity. There, in this act of pure and vile hatred, was a chance to turn evil into good in communities throughout the southeast.

So, I began phoning the offices of state and regional associations of the largely white Protestant denominations. After many attempts to reach someone, I finally heard back from a gentleman in a state Baptist association. After exchanging our mutual horror at the situation in Charleston, I explained why I was calling. He quickly said, "We honestly have no idea what to do. Do you have any ideas?"

"It's actually rather easy," I said. "Tell the pastors throughout your association to close their doors on Sunday. Tell them to cancel the usual Sunday worship service immediately. Instead, have them tell their congregants to disperse into their communities, find black churches, and lock arms and pray with their fellow Christians. Show solidarity. Show love. Show that we are all Christians first and foremost, and when any of us die, we all mourn together."

I continued, "At least get them to have some of their congregants to go into those churches, a delegation of sorts, and show that we feel their pain, as fellow followers, and support them in their grieving."

For a few moments, all I could hear on the other end of the phone was silence. The idea clearly had not crossed his mind. I guessed that he was immediately grappling with the concept of the logistics of such a request, and the administrative and bureaucratic hurdles he would have to jump over to even suggest such as act, no matter how noble. And I'm sure he knew the financial risk associated with fully closing a church, if only for one Sunday, since missing even a single week's offerings can yield a tremendous financial burden in many churches. At least, I hoped that's what he was thinking.

Finally, he said. "Well. That would be very difficult. Very difficult indeed." After some additional pleading, we ended our discussion with a cursory and ironic "Good luck." I knew without much doubt that my suggestion would not be tried, even in part. For whatever reason, this was too much to ask. For whatever reason, whether financial, logistical, or other, there was simply no fervor to disrupt the normal routines of Sunday morning corporate worship for the sake of Christian solidarity, or to even go through the effort of trying to create that disruption. While I do not believe the objection to this action to be racism, for whatever reason or reasons, our churches simply aren't wired this way. This was an idea too strange to consider.

A hundred questions rattled through my brain after that initial conversation, particularly since the other emails I sent and voice messages I left never saw responses. Would these entourages even be accepted if they went? Would such an act have its intended result? Would it be interpreted as an act of solidarity or taken incorrectly as patronization? How would the logistics work out? And would black churches in distant cities even mourn the event within their own congregations and services on the following Sunday morning? Even if Christian whites went forth, would there be something to join in on?

Perhaps hundreds or thousands of church congregations did exactly what I'd imagined. Perhaps bridges were crossed of which I am not aware. Still, there was something less than automatically and naturally positive about the reaction I received.

But the biggest question I kept coming back to was the simplest of all. "Why is this simple act of solidarity so hard?"

INTRODUCTION

Before unity can occur, it will be critical for each church to evaluate its position within its community and its feelings and proclivities towards integration with the larger body of Christ, both within its local area and the American Christian community.

This means an examination, often a deep and critical examination, of the congregation's willingness to step across deep and scarred racial boundaries to create new and constructive relationships. This and the following chapter are intended to outline some of the many difficulties of and opportunities for unity within the American Christian church. This chapter on Silos describes the various reasons that our churches are separated from one another and how these divisions are driven by factors other than doctrine. Some of these reasons, though legitimate, become excuses for failing to step outside our walls and engage with other Christians. Others are simply more about pride, ego, self-righteousness, and other worldly factors.

Therefore, the following chapter on Synergies deals specifically with ways in which these silos can not only be breached but torn down.

350,000 REASONS

Geese fly in flocks. Wolves travel in packs. Buffalo run in herds. Christians go to churches. Of course, none of these things are inherently bad. For geese, the flock helps efficiency in flight. For wolves, there is power in numbers. For the buffalo, there is security and strength within the herd. For the Christian, there is all that and more. Indeed, the Bible specifically calls us to join others in communion with other believers (lest you are one of those who thinks you can get what you need from your couch and the internet).

But when people join groups, whether sororities, Rotary, professional organizations, or churches, natural allegiances are formed. Like geese in a flock, we tend to stay together, forming friendships and loyalties all along the way.

For congregations, these synergies, friendships, and loyalties are often what keep us coming back to our churches after a beloved pastor retires, a loved one passes, a daughter gets married, cancer strikes, a child is born, or a career unexpectedly ends. Our fellow congregants are not only a great source of spiritual strength in times of troubles, but also friends with whom we share God's blessings, allies in service opportunities, and a means to feel comfortable being a Christian in a society that is distinctly and increasingly anti-Christian.

Furthermore, loyalties are built based on the pastor whose message and style you like, the proud and long history of the church in your community, the church where you were saved and in which you may have grown up, the doctrine of your denomination, the work the church is doing for your favorite charity, the friends you have, and the services you perform through and in your church. After all, we like where we are, else we wouldn't be there.

And with those loyalties naturally comes a sense of commitment and belonging. This is reflected in ongoing support for fellow congregants, the ministerial staff, doctrinal positions, a willingness to lend additional help in times of trouble, rallying to support causes the church supports, and a general sense that going anywhere else is simply not an option. You love your church, and you support its sustenance.

Thus, critical roles that our churches play in the lives of their members include:

- Ensuring both adults and children are properly spiritually nurtured
- Serving as a place of Christian communion, friendship, bonding, and love of one another
- Enabling a place where congregants come to worship God, give thanks, and offer blessings to each other
- Offering solace, love, and a helping hand when needed
- Serving as a locus for the work of missions and community service activities
- Generally serving to build, grow, and support the congregation as part of the larger body of Christ

All these and more are reasonable functions of the church and include the expectations of most congregants. And as individual congregations, we routinely serve the poor, clothe the naked, and offer shelter to the homeless. We may send missionaries overseas or across the nation, send our youth to work in poor communities, help at-risk kids read and write, and regularly open our doors to newcomers.

Yet, even as we become the mortar that keeps the walls of our churches standing strong against the harsh, ever present winds of society, those same walls can isolate us from other congregations in our community. Our fellowship can keep us in individual church silos.

As an example of this thinking, one of my favorite radio ministry pastors and leader of a California mega-church recently stated, "I don't care what other churches around here are doing. I don't know and I don't care. I only care about what WE are doing! I only care that WE are serving God!"

Thus, the place where we find some of our greatest blessings can also keep us from being an integral part of the larger body of Christ, since some of the constraints to broader collaboration lie in the loyalty, commitment, and sense of belonging to an individual church, pastor, and congregation. If only because the work within our church and its many ministries is already nearly too much to bear, the idea of collaboration with other congregations is often not even considered.

This can be particularly true if collaboration means letting another church take charge and lead an effort, or if collaboration outside our denomination or local community is involved. Thus, there are myriad excuses for keeping our Godly charities, community work, and outreach efforts within our own congregations.

Indeed, some will no doubt argue that it's plenty hard enough to wrangle their own congregants to get and stay involved in ministries. Work, kids, distance, and life get in the way of our efforts to do God's work in our churches and our communities. The ongoing work of God requires our time, energy, precious weekends, and already packed evenings.

Some would therefore argue that just getting their own church members involved and engaged is hard enough without trying to deal with communications, scheduling and coordination with other Christians we don't even know and with whom we do not regularly associate. This is no doubt particularly true when it comes to crossing over age-old racial barriers and collaborating with communities we may know very little about.

Others might argue, "Why should another church lead when we have leaders here in our church? We have a vision for satisfying the spiritual needs of our community, and we don't need others telling us how, when, and where to do that. Our pastor knows what he is doing and is perfectly capable of leading us where we need to go. We have our goals, so let other churches have theirs."

Competition and other silos

There is also an inherent bit of competition and self-interest amongst churches of the same geography, reflected in the need to sustain and grow members and contributions in support of the church functions, infrastructure, pastor(s), and staff. Churches compete for not only the hearts, minds, and contributions of existing members but those of potential new Christians and new members who can fill both pews and coffers.

Indeed, studies show that the growth of "mega-churches" and recently established churches comes not from new believers and the expansion of God's Kingdom but from current Christians of other churches who simply move their memberships.

These sentiments are reflected in comments that would typically go something like, "We need to stay focused on our own flock and growing our membership, so why should we help another church grow theirs? Why should we help them become stronger and more influential when we need to grow and be stronger, too?" It can even come down to a question of marketing strength within a local community. Let's face it ... we often assume that the stronger our presence, the faster our growth, and the more influential our members, the more likely we are to be around to preach the word in the future.

Moreover, the challenge for many churches is simple survival as changes in demographics, ethnicities, neighborhoods, the society and culture, and economic trends shift to make sustenance and growth more difficult. After all, a dying church with diminishing membership, empty pews, and growing budget constraints may not be as attractive to current and potential new members. In many smaller towns, demographic shifts have left more senior congregations without long-term strategies for sustainability. In growing metropolitan and suburban areas, established churches struggle against the growth of new churches, mega-churches, and shifts in "church consumer" preferences that can sometimes dilute Christ's message.

Then of course there are the doctrinal differences that can get in the way of the larger cause. "They aren't even going to Heaven ... they don't dunk! Why should we promote an incorrect reading of the Word by working with THAT church?!"

Likewise, there are "church personalities" to be overcome. "I don't like that preacher's 'feel good' message or his style. They don't even have enough respect for God to dress nicely for services!" Thus, Christians can quickly and readily get mired in the "non-essentials" and distance themselves unnecessarily from one another.

This all leads to an inward focus as the fear of loss of influence, denominational boundaries, geography, and other issues keep churches from collaboration.

IMPACTS OF RACIAL SILOS

Importantly for this book, getting traditionally and historically black and white churches to come together may be an even higher hurdle. Depending on the community, it is these racial silos that may be the most historically fortified, the most rigid, and the most protected. Therefore, this book is primarily focused on the racially derived gaps that exist between black and white churches and the impact our silos have on our abilities to be more effective in doing God's work.

These divisions were created largely as a result of racism, but remain as a result of more benign reasons, such as worship style preferences, familial history, geography, race loyalty, a desire to be with those who have shared similar life experiences, a near complete lack of knowledge of other cultures and peoples, and political differences, just to name a few. Regardless of the reason, these silos keep our power diluted and unplugged from the rest of God's children.

Of course, this doesn't mean that white folks don't go to black churches, and vice versa. It happens every Sunday in churches all over the nation. Indeed, there are tens of thousands of multi-cultural, multi-racial churches throughout the country, even in the Deep South.

Yet, this in no way means that the racial divisions within the Christian American church are healed. Nor does it mean that Christians are leading the way in our racially divided society by showing a better way to interact, work together, and love one another. Nor do these "integrated" churches have any higher propensity to collaborate with other churches to impact society than the more common racially segregated churches.

And even if there are excellent examples of multi-cultural churches, our historical, racially motivated divisions still maintain completely racially separated church organizations, denominations, organizations, charities, and communities. While God has and continues to use these silos for good in His own way, they also now inhibit our ability to impact society's major issues and thereby bring glory to God and more people to Christ.

Therefore, it is critical that Christians address any and all racial silos that keep us apart. Of course, this does not mean we must all attend racially integrated churches. To the contrary! We can and should keep our congregations and worship as we feel comfortable and yet still uprightly collaborate across our racial boundaries so as to break down our silos. However, we choose to do it in our own communities, break them down we must, else we cannot and will not have the impact on society that we should. And as shown in previous chapters, failure to unite may serve to aid our detractors and enemies in their fight against us.

Fortunately, even in isolation from other Christians in churches around the corner or across town, we occasionally prove that we can come together to do great things for our communities. At Thanksgiving and Christmas, we might align to distribute Thanksgiving turkeys to low-income families or Christmas toys to poor children and orphans. During natural disasters or emergency situations, Christians will unite without blinking to provide for the immediate needs of an injured community nearby or on the other side of the country.

But yet even as we do great things for our communities, rarely do we collaborate, intentionally and on an ongoing basis, across denominational, racial, socio-economic, and geographic lines. When it happens, great things can occur. When it doesn't, or when there is resistance to it, sub-optimal outcomes can occur.

OVERLAPS

In our zeal to serve, our silos create situations in which various siloed church ministries overlap one another. Indeed, it has been said that only the many agencies and divisions of the Federal government have more overlapping efforts than churches. Of course, it is never a bad thing to do good things, even if others are doing those same good things. But it may be inefficient and costly, using precious resources to deliver less than optimal results.

Take the example of a recent church-sponsored school backpack giveaway. Each backpack had been filled with various donated school supplies, from pencil to paper, and was meant to go to "under-privileged" kids. As the mothers stood outside the church fellowship hall waiting to get bags for their kids, I overheard two discussing their next stops.

As it so happened, these mothers knew of two other similar backpack giveaways at nearby churches, and they were plotting where they would go next. One even commented on the relative quality of bags she'd seen in years past at the various churches where they were given freely.

Was this abuse of the giver? Maybe. Is it bad that more than one church gave away backpacks on a single Saturday before the school year started? Your call. But could there have been a better coordination of efforts, perhaps such that more families could have been touched by a single, larger effort? Likely!

Now, think more broadly about the areas of focus suggested in this book. Education, justice, healthcare, and race. How much can any single church, no matter how large or influential, do to impact these issues? Yes, we can send congregants to help kids read better. Yes, we can send our faithful out to help conduct health fairs. But education and health are far larger and more intractable problems than one church can fix. There simply aren't enough resources in any single church to wield the kind of power, influence and resources to change these issues for an entire community, much less the nation. Alternatively, we are more likely to have greater influence as a group of churches, all pursuing the same goals, than as individual congregations.

Thus, as church members "fly with own our flock," we may miss opportunities to serve our communities better, particularly if these issues are large in scope, scale, and depth. Importantly for this book, we simply don't collaborate on the key social issues facing our society. And this, in part, is why the church has lost influence in society.

Christians must therefore learn to drop their loyalties and accept their roles within the larger, community-wide and nationwide body of Christ.

CELLS AND BODY PARTS

Let's face it, given a choice, few want to be the little toe in the body of Christ. The little toe doesn't really do much and doesn't really have that much influence over the functionality of the rest of the body. We would all prefer to be the brain. After all, that is where the action is. Or perhaps the heart, since this is one of the key body organs without which the entire body would die. Indeed, we would all prefer to play a vital role in the body rather than be a part of the ancillary "support systems."

Of course, each church cannot be the center of community power, the hub of community activity, or the go-to place for community-wide leadership. That is what we're trying to do now.

But even the largest churches, whether black or white, lack the manpower and spiritual strength to change critical flaws in our society on their own. And even the smallest congregations have within them passionate members who can take on great responsibilities if given the opportunity.

Moreover, all brothers and sisters can bring their own God-given, unique and valuable perspectives, power, abilities, and passions to the many issues our society faces. If unleashed, this collective power will yield greater creativity and strength in the creation of sustainable solutions.

Just as cells are part of organs, they are also part of the entire body. Without each cell supporting the function of each organ, the organs cannot support the body and the body is at least less functional if not entirely dead.

Likewise, individual congregants are part of individual churches that are part of a larger American body of Christ, which is part of the worldwide body of Christ. As such, each of us plays a part that must not be rejected. But if we are separate from one another, as disconnected organs of the body, we are no more than the pieces of a butchered carcass on the butcher's block.

Therefore, we must all accept our respective roles as individual Christians and as congregations in the larger body of Christ. To truly be collaborative and unite in action requires us to put aside our loyalties to both our own churches and our races for the greater good of God's earthly mission and our society.

Needless to say, we must still love and support our churches, our pastors, and fellow congregants and support them with our tithes and offerings. And within our own congregations, we must be part of our congregation's body of Christ, playing our roles as God calls us to do.

But beyond these, there is also another body to be served ... that group of collaborative local churches in the community's body of Christ. These are as important as individual congregants and churches to having the kind of societal impact we all want God to have. By using our skills, talents, and our many resources wisely and efficiently, we can indeed serve them all.

SUMMARY

The goal of this book is to bring historically siloed groups together. Through thinking, speaking, and acting "uprightly," true and full collaboration on key social issues, and showing the world a better way to live, interact, and solve problems, we can and will drive our nation towards what might eventually be called the Next Great Awakening.

But until all black and white churches come together to impact the intractable social issues within their local communities, I will continue to say that we are not as effective and efficient as we could and should be.

To shed some light on what this requires, the next chapter covers the synergies that exist and how churches need to approach their communities in order to make collaboration possible.

SYNERGIES

"¹Therefore if you have any encouragement from being united with Christ, if any comfort from his love, if any common sharing in the Spirit, if any tenderness and compassion, ²then make my joy complete by being like-minded, having the same love, being one in spirit and of one mind. ³Do nothing out of selfish ambition or vain conceit. Rather, in humility value others above yourselves, ⁴not looking to your own interests but each of you to the interests of the others. ⁵In your relationships with one another, have the same mindset as Christ Jesus." (Philippians 2:1-5)

INTRODUCTION

You've already read a lot about the history and current status of the various divisions within the American body of Christ. But how would churches change their focus to include cross-denominational and cross-racial collaboration? What would the American body of Christ need to look like so as to make it more influential in our society, bring glory to God and solutions to the intractable issues facing our country?

The image below present one option, a sketch of what the individual churches, as parts of the bodies of Christ, might look like and how they might relate to one another.

CHURCH CONGREGANTS

The circular image depicts the various components of the larger communal body of Christ, starting at the "one o'clock" position with the individual church congregants. These are individual Christians who need or can help provide nurturing, spiritual, and emotional growth, guidance and mentoring, and other support. They may need help finding their own passions for work in the

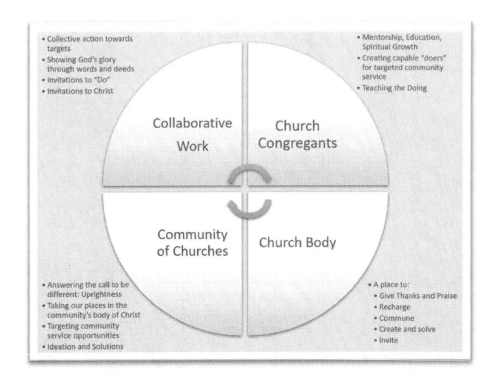

- Collective action towards targets
- Showing God's glory through words and deeds
- Invitations to "Do"
- Invitations to Christ

- Mentorship, Education, Spiritual Growth
- Creating capable "doers" for targeted community service
- Teaching the Doing

Collaborative Work

Church Congregants

Community of Churches

Church Body

- Answering the call to be different: Uprightness
- Taking our places in the community's body of Christ
- Targeting community service opportunities
- Ideation and Solutions

- A place to:
  - Give Thanks and Praise
  - Recharge
  - Commune
  - Create and solve
  - Invite

Kingdom or may bring a new passion to the congregation. They may be able to support their fellow congregants in dealing with a personal crisis or painful situation and help celebrate God's blessings as they pour forth. Some will need to grow their faith; others will serve as mentors to new and growing Christians. Indeed, some will have spent a lifetime in the study and application of the Word, yet some won't know enough to bear up against even the slightest scrutiny from co-workers and neighbors.

To achieve this, there needs to be an assessment of individual and aggregate gifts and passions within each congregation in order to assess the individual and aggregate capacity to serve. The idea, of course, is to facilitate the creation of capable "doers" for work within the church, the community, and the body of Christ. This would include a self-assessment of the knowledge and understanding of the essentials of the faith, as is necessary to support each person as they venture forth into the various activities to which they are called.

Naturally, there will inevitably be many gifts and talents under one church roof. Congregants should be encouraged to discover their God-given gifts and passions and mentored as they put them to work within the congregation and the larger communal body of Christ.

As individuals, some will be further along the path towards discovering and using their talents and passions than others, just as some are further down the path of understanding scripture and sanctification. Some will need encouragement to discover theirs. Still others will be new to their faith and in need of both mentoring and gift/passion discovery.

But, regardless of their current status, each person must play a role, regardless of how seemingly small or large some roles might seem. So, within each congregation, there should be the means and the will to grow every congregant in the discovery of the passions and gifts that will be used for the Lord's work. Relationships, mentoring and coaching are therefore critical elements of any church or church sub-group, as they allow each congregant to help both themselves and others, no matter where they are in their walk with God and the use of their gifts.

Latent Capacity

It should be a goal of any pastoral staff to fully understand the applied and latent "capacity to serve" that is in each church via its congregants. That is, there is a total capacity for action within the church that can be measured. As each member's gifts and passions are catalogued, their availability and constraints to service listed, and their current need for or capacity to offer spiritual mentoring quantified, the collective "capacity to serve" becomes known. Regardless of the average age, socio-economic make-up and location of your church, the gifts and passions of members add up to a certain amount of potential energy, capacity and capability for action. Some churches will be using a high percentage of their "capacity to serve," some very little. As you quantify this, you will learn what your church can do, where its greatest strengths are, and in what areas the most passion lies. As you grasp the capacity of your congregation, focus on the strengths you see in your congregants rather than try to fill empty holes in the long list of possible activities. For instance, if your congregation happens to have an energy and passion for youth, don't try to develop a prison ministry if there isn't one. You can team with another church whose passions lie in the justice and prison ministry areas. If you happen to have a solid number of nurses, physicians, and other congregants passionate about the health of the community, focus energies there rather than trying to start a ministry for which there is limited interest or enthusiasm. Of course, you needn't discourage a calling. Rather, as you will see, there will be opportunities to put the passions of even single congregants to work through collaboration with other churches.

Changes in capacity

You should also understand that interests, passions, and capacities will evolve over time. It is natural for congregants to become less passionate or even disinterested in a particular ministry if life calls them elsewhere. For instance, a mother may be deeply interested in working with youth while her children are young, only to move to work on healthcare issues as her kids leave her "nest." A father of three who works with the youth choir may become interested in racial collaboration as he sees his kids struggle with society's racially motivated challenges. Life and people change, and so will their passions and gifts. Let it happen and allow your congregants to grow and move as their passions and gifts pull them.

As these many gifts and passions are discovered, small groups of like-minded Christians will likely form. These small groups will become even more relevant and important as the community of churches begins to unite and knit together the many individuals and small groups into an integrated patchwork of like-minded Christians.

THE CHURCH BODY

In this model, the church, shown at the four o'clock position on the image, is to provide a place for gathering Christians together, as God has commanded us. God knew why this is important and why being part of a church body is critical to our sustenance as believers. Of course, the individual church should provide a place to praise and give thanks to God. It should also be a place of teaching, collective and individual education, mentoring, and deeper knowledge of the word of God.

The individual church should also be a place where congregants can recharge spiritual batteries after what might have been long days of spiritual warfare. Refreshing and cleansing the spirit through interactions with friends, worship and praise, and celebration of God's love does wonders for the beleaguered and weary.

Therefore, each weekly service should not be just a singular event at the end of six days of inactivity. Rather, the typical Sunday morning service should be an opportunity to recharge and revitalize, share great service experiences, exchange ideas for bettering our activities, celebrating successes and building one another up after frustrations and defeats. Each week, successes should be celebrated and challenges discussed. From this, ideation will drive new energies into the week's activities. Even a rote, standardized worship service with a prescribed format and length can be made to incorporate celebrations of activities and acceptance of new challenges.

Thus, the Sabbath Day becomes a time to recharge, re-energize, refresh, ideate, and celebrate. Church, as most Christians think about it, needs to transform from a singular weekly, obligatory hour or morning into the kick-off of a week of passionate utilization of God's gifts and the opportunity to reflect on the previous week's efforts. "Go in peace" needs to transform to "Go and get busy!"

This creates a safe, open, and welcoming environment in which creativity and energy can flow forth into solutions for the community. Without this environment, we can quickly miss opportunities to engage congregants in the application of their God-given gifts and passions. Importantly, it creates an environment in which newcomers are shown what might be a new perspective on Christians and Christianity, one that involves the joy of Christian service, selfless activities, cross-denominational collaboration, and churchwide community engagement rather than stereotypical condemnation of the wicked, guilt, and shame.

THE COMMUNITY OF CHURCHES

As your church moves into the eight o'clock position on the diagram, your church is ready to uprightly communicate and collaborate with other churches, especially those of other races. You'll have your congregation's gifts, talents, and passions aggregated and quantified. Now you can poll other congregations of all types and sizes on their collective gifts and passions, and link together those in your congregation with particular passions and gifts with those in other congregations with similar passions and gifts. Small groups link together to become the large, cross-denominational and cross-racial groups through which action takes place.

This is a critical point in the movement from single church activity to roles within the communal body of Christ, as it is at this point that our doctrinal differences, backgrounds, racial self segregation, socio-economic strata, geographies, pride and arrogance, latent racism, and other encumbrances can erupt to stop or slow progress.

Therefore, the movement from the congregation to the community requires us to first be upright, as described earlier in this book. Uprightness, with all honesty, integrity and objectivity, must be the primary attribute of our thoughts, communications, and interactions with one another and the worldly society surrounding us. This is a critical concept is the work of the church and there are great risks to our success if uprightness is not fully internalized.

Naturally, because we are individuals, there are a great many differences and often great distances between Christians on issues ranging from doctrine to abortion, gay marriage, and politics. For Christian blacks and Christian whites, there may also be underlying animosity, decades-old resentment, bigotry (in the purest definition of the term), mistrust, political ideologies, and the many other walls society has built up between us.

Yet, we must necessarily break down these barriers and heal the age-old wounds if we are to come together for the greater good of our society and the glorification of God. We, as Christians, must be able to sit down together and work through all the facts, opinions, and feelings of a given issue so as to come to upright truths on matters important to the cause, while putting aside the "non-essentials" of doctrine that will only serve to unnecessarily divide us. Focusing on key issues that matter to us all and addressing those issues in a Christ-like, upright manner is the only way for us to get along while fighting for a common cause.

We can therefore continue to disagree about a host of things while still having intellectually honest conversations and developing new ideas to collaborate to solve key issues and problems.

COLLABORATIVE WORK

Moving to the fourth area in the diagram, the eleven o'clock position, each congregation and congregant will then prayerfully take a role in the community's body of Christ, whether as the metaphorical brain, foot, eye, or hand. Depending on the many potential roles each congregation and its members might play in the broader community of churches, our congregants may perform a variety of functions within the body, including all the aforementioned and more. All are equal and thus all have great potential to contribute once the power of God is released within each individual and these larger communal bodies of Christ. Thus, we become unity in action.

As issues are targeted throughout the community, unified actions will bring glory to God, His teachings and our ministries. And as the energy, creativity, and passions flow forth from individual congregations into targeted actions and activities within the community, the community of churches, acting as the unified body of Christ, can become doers within a larger geographic area, creating greater impact.

By becoming doers rather than talking, acting rather than condemning, and working together to make positive changes in the community rather than

140

pointing fingers of blame, we will put the church in a unique and higher place. Our unity of purpose, under the direction of the teachings of Christ, will make us very different from every other charity, social organization and political group. Our unity will show society how much Christ can do. Even as our society becomes more and more divided, we will be different, growing more and more unified, more and more as one body working together.

And through our activities and actions, we will necessarily draw attention. This will bring more people into our actions in support of the joint causes our churches have decided to tackle. Relationships and friendships will be formed. Mutual respect and genuine Christian love will replace the street-corner bullhorn and the public restroom damnation literature. Even without pushing or starting the conversation, our activities will lead people to ask questions, be curious, and be willing to question what they've heard in the media and from society about us and our faith. They can ask questions, debate and challenge, thus coming into a knowledge and appreciation of Christ and His teachings through a newfound lens. And we will be in a much different position to discuss the wondrous love of God with those who will join us or at least pay attention to us. And from this will come the leadings of the Holy Spirit to those who would be saved.

This, of course, starts the cycle over bringing the diagram back to the one o'clock position, as new Christians need mentoring, education, and spiritual growth as they join churches, make friends with congregants and find their own passions for ministry.

The "Congregant to Community" cycle thereby yields a sort of organic growth. Using individual congregations empowered by their churches to act together as a body of Christ to bring change to our communities, new believers will come to realize the power of our faith.

UNITY OR PREFERENCES?

The proliferation of denominations and churches demonstrates that doctrine, preaching style, music, liturgical approach, dress, race, demeanor, existing members, politics, and even service length can all have an impact on the churches individuals choose to join. These preferences have exploded the possibilities for worship, causing some churches to die over time and others to be born and thrive.

Yet, whether we agree on the preferences we choose or even the doctrine we follow, we must never let these issues overshadow the common theme of Christ's message and the simplicity of the Gospel message that will one day bring us all together with our Lord. Whether you dunk or sprinkle should not impact our ability to work together. Likewise, coming to worship dressed in a three-piece suit or barely out of pajamas does not matter when the education of our children is at stake. Unless you are truly and willfully breeding Jezebels within your congregation, we, as Christian brothers and sisters, should be putting aside our preferences and working together.

Most notably, we must not let our political differences divide us. It is no secret that many Christian whites and Christian blacks would vehemently disagree about the last or the next election. These differences are, in many cases, wide at best. Recent political and social events have made these divisions even more profound and troubling, seemingly getting worse each day.

Yet, these too can and should be put aside or, as necessary, discussed uprightly as followers of a single God. This will at least yield a different discussion and likely different outcomes than we commonly see when disagreements happen in society.

SUMMARY

The outside world is perfectly happy to collaborate against God, Christians, and our churches. Society will regularly unite against God's teachings while we are left bickering over music or doctrinal preferences. But as the old saying goes, we must "let go and let God." We must let go of our loyalties to the walls of our silos. Let go of our preferences. Let go of our cynicism, self-righteousness, and pride. Let go of ourselves. And let God direct us, united as upright believers with all our many personal preferences, towards bringing glory to His Kingdom, His name, and His church.

WHAT CHRISTIAN WHITES NEED TO DO

⁵May God, who gives us patience and encouragement,
help you live in complete harmony with each other, as is
fitting for followers of Christ Jesus. ⁶Then all of you can
join together with one voice giving praise and glory to
God, the Father of our Lord Jesus Christ. (Romans 15: 5-6)

INTRODUCTION

If you accept that unifying the Christian community in the United States towards substantive social action is a worthwhile act, and if you agree that our Christian body has been and continues to be divided along stark and bold racial lines, then Christian whites need to know what to do to impact the situation. Action and change are required on both sides of the racial and political aisles. And we, as Christian whites, certainly have an important role to play.

RECAP

Let's be honest. We helped start this. It is partly, if not nearly entirely, the fault of our white protestant forefathers that the American protestant church is divided along such stark racial lines. We can only speculate about how racially split the church might be were racism not part of the Christian American history, and only personal preferences and doctrinal factors influenced our ecumenical choices. But we certainly know that race and racism played a critical role in the early American denominational divisions.

Now, hundreds of years later, we see that the racial silos we initially created have multiplied into the many racially segregated denominations and non-denominational churches that are the Christian black and white churches of today. Individual worship preferences and doctrinal differences have added to the age-old racial divisions to cause both black and white churches to split like amoebas in a petri dish. Thus, the Christian American landscape is peppered with everything from Free Will Baptists to Catholics to Pentecostal to Church of God in Christ and African Methodist Episcopalians.

Ironically, however, this seemingly negative outcome of racism and doctrinal divisiveness may have served God's purposes by allowing a deeper dissemination of Christianity into a broader swath of American society, thereby saving more souls for Christ and growing our numbers while enabling a larger future potential for the impact of a unified church. The American body of Christ is larger, with greater latent strength, than it might otherwise have been. Thus, despite the human failings that created our racial divisions, God has turned our disunity into our current opportunity for greater good and His glory. Note the key word here: *Opportunity!*

As Christian whites, we are now tasked with taking advantage of the opportunities afforded us by the dissemination of Christianity by helping to bring Christians together, unified in action for the glory of God. There has never been a time in our nation's history when dramatic solutions to intractable problems were more needed but yet more elusive. Only God's church can lead the way.

God has given us the people;
history has provided the perfect timing.

Our first steps in this process involves deep introspection, the development of a new way to see ourselves, our churches, and our society, and one very bold act.

GETTING PERSPECTIVE WITHOUT A GUILT TRIP
Through attending many black churches across the country and particularly in the southeast, I came to appreciate the personal preferences and worship style differences that we should all celebrate and enjoy. I have come to enjoy the enthusiasm and energy in worship of some black pastors and their congregants. While I might prefer to remain quiet in my pew rather than verbally engage with the pastor and yell out a hearty "Amen!" I learned to appreciate the variations in styles and approaches.

And through study and mentorship, I came to know and appreciate the role of Christianity, race, and racism in the history of Christian African Americans. Through this, I learned how God has moved in communities very dissimilar from my own and to see the love of God displayed in ways I never considered.

Therefore, learning the history of the black church, black Christianity, and racism throughout our past 200-plus years should not be a self-deprecating exercise for Christian whites. Though many in our society want to see Christian whites relegated to a distant past, isolated from any future influence and burdened with unspeakable guilt, I didn't seek out this information to take a guilt trip or to find way to hate or shame my heritage as a Christian white male, or to find guilt and shame for being a white person. Nor did I go in search of information that would justify or refute any of the various government policies meant to support minorities and the poor, reduce disparities and/or otherwise equalize life's circumstances. Nor did I seek to justify or condemn the divisions that split us even now, or the tools, such as revised definitions and new social constructs, that have been used to create and maintain those divisions.

Rather, I simply wanted to understand the present as it related to the past and the potential for the future. For acknowledgement is not "giving in" or "giving up." Acknowledgement does not mean acquiescing to someone else's political views, or succumbing to unreasonable demands, guilt trips, or abuse. It does not mean that we must put aside moral standards or allow resentment, anger, and hatred against us to thrive. And it certainly does not mean that we put aside expectations of Christian behaviors and attitudes, or be forced into obsequious, ignoble positions or roles. To the contrary, we should be seeking to ensure that all non-Christian attitudes and behaviors are called out and corrected, including any and all of our own. Acknowledgement simply states an understanding and appreciation but needn't carry the harsh punishments that our hateful and vindictive society deems necessary. After all, we are trying to unite with fellow Christians, even if some of us didn't always treat them as such in the past.

Through these perspectives, you will see that we have once-in-a-lifetime opportunities to serve God's kingdom here in America, discover how those opportunities might be manifested, and understand the means by which the glory of God can be displayed. You will come to appreciate the true "power of the blood" and how we can now use that power as a uniting force.

So, if you don't know what a "Green Book" was (at least, before the movie by that name was released), or don't know the prominent and proud role of Christianity in African American history, it's OK. You can learn without taking on a guilt trip or feeling that you should hate your own race for its past.

THE NEED FOR EDUCATION AND ACKNOWLEDGEMENT

As we have seen, society's evolving definitions of racism have labeled Christian whites as racists, in large part due to the religious and social mores

45

and values that we support and teach. Furthermore, according to some of these definitions, all white people, regardless of their conscious thoughts and desires, are guilty of uncontrollable and intrinsic racist thoughts, words, and actions simply by existing as white people in America.

Yet, whether you agree in part or in whole with these harsh monikers and the social philosophies that give them life, Christian whites need to objectively and openly acknowledge the past and current existence of textbook racism. Moreover, if we are to be upright in our dialogue and interactions with our Christian black brothers and sisters, we need to acknowledge that the impacts of the various forms of historical racism still linger even where the ideology itself has died.

Even if traditional racism and its related segregation, violence, and social, economic, and political exclusions had been completely and utterly exterminated in our society, those who once suffered its ill effects must still deal with its impacts. Like a patient whose cure for gangrene resulted in the removal of a limb, the disease may be gone but the bodily damage remains. Indeed, those who cite racism as the exclusive and singular cause for any current plight of blacks in our nation do so in part to highlight the ongoing impacts of the past in order that they not be forgotten.

Furthermore, we cannot develop holistic solutions with our brothers and sisters without appropriately and uprightly accounting for all the many causalities within a given situation, including those related and unrelated to historical and current racism, segregation, and discrimination. Failing to uprightly account for all of the impacts of the past and present can leave us without a complete understanding of the issues we seek to solve. Therefore, this acknowledgement is necessary if we are to develop effective collaborative solutions for the future.

Though this may seem like an intellectual and perhaps unduly painful exercise, some Christian white readers may not have thoroughly considered the full historical context of some of the issues facing our communities today. Let's face it, blacks and whites can see the world through two very different lenses. Without proper consideration of the views of others, it is difficult to fully grasp the perspectives through which they see the world and our society. Thus, it is necessary to delve deeply into the ramifications of history so as to properly understand the present. We can fully and openly acknowledge the past without succumbing to society's demands for vindication and revenge.

To illustrate the need for an acknowledgement of the past as it relates to the present, consider the following perspectives, learned through interactions with Christian black brothers and sisters. As you seek to take the next steps in your communities towards unity in action, consider these examples and how similar circumstances might impact those with whom you seek to align. Uprightly consider the circumstances of the families and communities, their histories, and the limitations society has placed on them. Seek out a deeper understanding of the multiple causalities and nuances that have led to the current situation, and openly seek new perspectives and ideas. You can avoid society's tendency to "dumb down" and cite a single root cause and instead highlight the many influences that are typically involved. As you do so, you will be able to better discern the full, Godly truth in each situation and work effectively with your brothers and sisters in Christ to develop holistic solutions for society's most intractable problems.

THE BARITONE SINGER

On a spring Sunday morning, we sat in one of the many black churches we visited while traveling over the years, surrounded by Christian black congregants. An elderly gentleman, likely in his 70's or even 80's, sat alone on the pew directly behind us. He was tall, well over six feet. He was well-dressed, polite, and friendly. When "meet, greet, and hug" time came, he smiled broadly and welcomed us with a friendly handshake and a warm "God bless you!"

When the hymns began, I couldn't help but notice his strong baritone voice. "He should be in the choir," I thought to myself. But as the words to the hymns flashed on the screens hanging to the left and right of the pulpit, I noticed that he would occasionally go from singing to humming along with the tune. It seemed that it was only when the refrain of the hymn or some familiar passage came up that he would boldly and confidently sing the words. At the time, I thought nothing of it.

It was only when we sat in front of him during another service, and once again heard his strong, though intermittent, baritone voice did I realize that there was an issue. As before, he would sing happily and loudly when certain hymns and passages were played. When other passages played, he would hum or go silent, only to sing again later. At first, I thought perhaps he has a breathing issue, or couldn't sustain his singing for very long due to some ailment or physical restriction, perhaps due to his advanced age. Yet, there was no sign of struggle when he breathed as he sang, nor was there any indication of an issue when we met or when we said our goodbye's after the service.

As this pattern of signing and humming continued, it finally dawned on me. Only when he got to parts of the hymn that he'd memorized, like the refrain of a very familiar hymn or some other familiar passage, would he sing along. For everything else, he would only hum. Even though all the words were there on the two large screens for him to read and sing, he wouldn't. No, he couldn't ... because he was illiterate. This Christian brother, as kind and sweet and passionate about Christ though he was, had never been taught to read.

I don't and will never know his life story, though I later confirmed my suspicions that he had never been formally taught to read. Clearly, he was old enough to have been raised in the depths of the history of repressive segregation. Old enough to have freely been called a nigger; to have walked with the Civil Rights movement and had police dogs turned on him; to have be rejected from educational and job opportunities. And he still lived with the repercussions of it each and every day.

As a white man, I don't think about the impacts of the history of segregation. I am not a racist (though there's little doubt that writing this book will earn me that moniker from someone), so I don't think about or even know how to think about the experiences and impacts of racism that went on decades ago. Yet, those impacts are still around, and continue to limit the men and women who suffered under them.

Think about it. A black man who is now, say, 60 years old was born in the late 1950's. If he was born in the south, he likely grew up in a segregated town that remained segregated throughout at least his high school years. In those days, he was as likely to have been raised in a two-parent, stable family as most white kids. (Up until the 1970's, black men and women were as or more likely to be married than their white counterparts, though the 1960s brought on the beginnings of a steady decline.[xv]) Yet, bright and talented as he might have been, his aptitude would likely never have been used to its fullest potential as segregation might have limited his opportunities to learn and earn.

THE WEALTH OF GENERATIONS

Were this kindly baritone to die today, what familial financial wealth would this aging black man be able to pass along to his kids and grandkids? He could certainly offer that which he has been able to accumulate himself (which is fortunately more than we sometimes think), as well as the incalculable wealth of moral and ethical guidance, the example of a solid marriage and family relationships, his faith in God, hope, optimism, and confidence in his children's future. But would he also be able to pass along any additional financial wealth received as an inheritance from his father? Would there be generational wealth available to enhance the lives and opportunities of his children and grandchildren? Or has the past inhibited the birth and expansion of financial wealth and opportunities that some take for granted?

Consider the limited time in which blacks have been able to gain and grow wealth, educational achievements, and long-term, solid foundations for their families. While wealthy and middle-class white parents are able to pass on the cumulative benefits of generations of education and savings, at best most blacks have had about fifty years. Likely less if they live in the south. That's less than a generation.

It is worth noting that this has become the basis for both what society calls "white privilege," which is largely if not exclusively focused on wealth and finances and demands for reparations. Importantly for the context of this book and our relationships with Christian blacks, this monetary focus diminishes the importance of moral and ethical teachings, work ethic, discipline, the family unit, etc. in the construction of short- and long-term success by taking a myopic view of the root causes of wealth and wealth creation. The financial focus also allows society to paint "rich white people" as wealthy simply due to the status of those who went before them rather than anything done or accomplished. The stereotype of whites, particularly middle-class and wealthy whites, among many minority groups is that they have what they have only because others gave it to them. This simultaneously fosters bitterness, resentment, and covetousness while downplaying the hope, optimism, effort, and attributes, some of which are classic Christian social and ethical mores, that have led to the success of people from all social classes, backgrounds, and ethnicities.

Nonetheless, it is blatantly clear that blacks have a smaller generational wealth pool from which to draw. Take, for example, a black man, 35 years old, with a wife and two kids. He and his wife would have a much easier time generating wealth to pass on, since modern American society now allows for greater educational and earning opportunities for blacks. Still, it is likely that much of the financial wealth passed on to their kids will have been gained though their own efforts rather than from that handed down from past generations. They might obtain property from their parents when they pass, but they might not inherit a large IRA. Hopefully they weren't caught up in the 2008 housing debacle in which many blacks lost homes to Federally induced sub-prime mortgages. (This downturn hurt minorities worse in that more of their personal wealth tends to be tied up in their homes than in cash or investments.)

Moreover, the modern, 35-year old successful black father must face other constraints that even his elders did not. Though his elders suffered from harsh and blatant discrimination, modern culture challenges him, his wife, and his children in ways heretofore unseen. Many schools still don't teach well. Worse, his kids' peers sometimes don't even want to learn or have a bias against learning and achievement. Being studious is still too often considered "being white" and therefore taboo, yielding children who are unnecessarily uneducated even when good schools are available. Worse, some kids are told to avoid education by their parents. His children are therefore mocked by their peers for speaking what he considers proper English, studying, and making good grades.

His kids also face the challenges of an American culture that glorifies violence and hyper-sexuality and promotes incivility, animosity, racial discord, and anti-Christian messaging. Even as he and his wife try to raise their kids in a Christian environment, they are bombarded with the exact opposite in their interactions at school and with peers. While they try to raise their kids to be positive and see the great potential in themselves and others, society teaches that racism may forever inhibit their progress and success and that there is something inherently wrong, or even evil, in being white.

Even some local black civic leaders speak a dire, if subtle, message of near hopelessness in the face of institutional racism that prevents black success and limits black potential. He worries that his kids will hear the wrong messages, become instilled with the wrong ideas and mimic society's angry, non-Christian examples and behaviors.

Furthermore, the households of many of his peers, of all races, are broken apart with divorce or lack of marriage and familial stability for the children. Thus, too many of his kids' peers are from more challenging single-parent homes. And his peers are further challenged with lack of job skills, careers, and long-term wealth accumulation strategies.

Thus, he can still teach his kids the same moral and ethical guidance, faith in God, hope, optimism, and confidence in their future that his father should have passed to him. But the momentum of generational and community wealth, as seen in both its financial and non-financial forms, is just getting started and is still stymied by the "worldly" culture in which he and his children live.

Of course, this is true throughout low-income America. Generational poverty is not just a racial issue, as it crosses racial boundaries and impacts both whites and blacks. Indeed, it is a social issue that impacts all poor people, and is now complicated by everything from less-than-adequate education and healthcare in rural areas to the growth of drug and alcohol dependency, amoral social norms, breakdowns in the family and the rise of single-parent homes, and broken social constructs. But blacks are hurt by both this generational poverty as well the history that put many in that state. Therefore, the modern black family struggles against many externalities, all of which are relevant but also complex in origin.

My point here is that there are distinct differences between current racism, the repercussions of prior racial injustices, and the worldly, cultural challenges black Americans face today that inhibit future generational success and prosperity. All can constrain and limit. Often, the latter two are tightly intertwined for our black brothers and sisters. Sometimes, all three are at play.

As Christian whites, we must endeavor to simultaneously understand the position from which our brethren come while realizing the breadth and depth of the issues that too many Americans, particularly black Americans, face.

THE PERCEIVED RISK OF ACKNOWLEDGEMENT

Yet, too many white people think that the simple recognition of the modern repercussions of our segregated history means that they tacitly or openly support financial reparations, special allowances, or other means by which to compensate or unduly favor blacks for the sins of the past. Or, that recognition gives too much credence to the racial reasons cited for the issues blacks and black communities face, which may only partly strike at the root causes of these modern problems. Or, that this recognition means that whites should inherently limit their achievements and success by standing aside to allow others to move ahead in a newly favored status. Or, that whites should be scorned as "privileged" and (ironically) ashamed of our skin color and the achievements of our ancestors.

Not so!

Rather, the simple recognition of the history of the current state helps us understand the situation our brothers and sisters are in and the challenges they face. It helps us discern how to move forward in a Godly, honest way and on an objective, rational footing. Most importantly, it helps us understand how to best come alongside our Christian black brothers and sisters and offer the right kind of support in a way that isn't demeaning, disrespectful, demoralizing, condescending, or misdirected. It helps us be honest, objective, and completely aware of all the myriad causes and effects of current problems, not just the ones commonly blamed. In short, it simply helps us define, analyze, and develop effective solutions for the problems our entire society and all races and creeds face based on a realistic and holistic understanding of those problems, regardless of their myriad sources.

Time only moves in one direction. We cannot go backward and offer those who would have and could have applied themselves to study and work opportunities a "do-over." Nor can we, in any reasonable way, estimate what might have been and what reality would currently be like had racism not darkened our past. We can no more know the impact of an altered history on our current situation than we can take H.G. Wells' Time Machine into a bygone era to test our hypotheses of a better today.

And though it is a component of many issues, racism is not solely to blame for every social problem faced by our black brothers and sisters. Whites, blacks, and others, both rich and poor, struggle with single-parent homes, the pressures of negative cultural influences, a decline in moral values and the traditional work ethic, the decline in church attendance and Christianity, and increases in sexuality, drugs, and alcohol use among our young people, just to name a few. Causalities are typically quite complex and rarely singular in nature, but they are important to understand fully. If we don't understand the challenges black communities face within the context of the history not of their making, we cannot effectively address them or parse out those issues that are "modern" in nature.

Therefore, the best we can do is uprightly assess the current situation and move forward based on what we have before us, alongside and with the support of our Christian black brothers and sisters. The racism of the past is what it is, ugly as it is. And of course, any and all racism currently still alive, no matter who feels it or towards whom it is directed, needs to be dealt with before more lives are impacted.

This helps change the discussion from the "blame game" of trying to find the same, often errant, culprit for each and every problem to an objective discussion of myriad root causes from which viable and effective solutions can be generated. It offers a means to deal with reality without shame, self-depreciation, or restrictions of future opportunities. It also allows a recognition of blame where it is due and truly present, which can then be combined with a mutual appreciation of both the requirements for change and respect for one another.

Back to the baritone singer. One thing that struck me was his attitude towards me, as a white man. Or perhaps, his attitude towards me as a fellow Christian. He was warm, friendly, and happy. When he could remember the words to a hymn, he would praise His ever-loving God as boldly and cheerfully as he could. There seemed to be no animus in him, at least any that he would let show in church. If there was bitterness in his heart, I wouldn't have known it. He displayed nothing but joy, satisfaction and heart-felt worship to a God who had no doubt seen him through some very rough times.

Indeed, I have met many Christian blacks who are positive, inspired, and passionate about life. They don't look back in bitterness. They look forward with the power of God in them. And that seems to make all the difference.

A FIRST STEP

With that, we should now be willing to openly acknowledge the past without worry of giving up moral and social standards, allowing resentment and hatred to thrive, permitting non-Christian behaviors and attitudes to erupt or continue, or going on a collective guilt trip.

Instead, we can go forward with the confidence of a Godly spirit that can drive us to unify God's churches, and more readily unify with our black Christian brothers and sisters in the uprightness that will make us different from the world. This, in turn, will allow new solutions to age-old challenges, but without the bitter conflicts and harsh divisions of today's society.

Thus, Christian whites can take a bold step towards unity in action, one that will defy the past and tap into the great latent potential of our vast numbers.

Our Nehemiah moment

Imagine living in the days of Nehemiah, in the 5th Century B.C. The city of Jerusalem had been attacked and torn down and its people scattered some 150 years prior (in 586 B.C., described in 2 Kings 24). The remnants of the population finally began to return years later, and had rebuilt the temple (between 535 B.C. and 516 B.C.) And, since the city and its gates were burned many years prior, there was surely also a gradual deterioration of any remaining infrastructure as time, weather, and lack of maintenance took their toll. Thus, over time, there was less and less from which to rebuild. When Nehemiah finally returned, some 150 years after the destruction of the city, he was deeply disturbed to see the condition of the city and its walls and gates.

Immediately, Nehemiah went to Jehovah in prayer. Indeed, the Bible tells us that he "mourned for days, fasting and praying before the God of heaven" (1:5). Yet in the brief recorded summation of his undoubtedly countless prayers, he doesn't start by praying for a miracle, or as a member of the chosen people of God, or for God's wrath upon the enemies of God's people, or as a God-sent messenger with a task to accomplish. Rather, his prayer is mainly one of supplication and admission of sin. Nehemiah 1: 5-7 reads, "⁵O Lord God of heaven, the great and awesome God who keeps covenant and steadfast love with those who love Him and keep His commandments; ⁶let your ear be attentive and your eyes open to hear the prayer of your servant that I now pray before you day and night for your servants the people of Israel, confessing the sins of the people of Israel, which we have sinned against you. Both I and my family have sinned. [7]We have offended you deeply, failing to keep the commandments, the statutes, and the ordinances that you commanded your servant Moses."

Despite being sent on a proverbial "mission from God," he stops and clearly states his own sin. Furthermore, and importantly for this discussion, he confesses the sins of his people AND the sins of his father's family. Only at the end of this prayer, and only after these admissions of generational wrongs, does Nehemiah ask for God's assistance and blessing on the task at hand. Only after these prayers does he ask in Nehemiah 1:11, "Give your servant success today by granting him favor in the presence of this man." Nehemiah's prayer is a simple confession of generational sin from which the state of the city had come, followed only at the end by a request for success in the task to which he was assigned.

This admission of guilt and the guilt of past generations as a focal point of prayer continues in Chapter 9, after the walls are rebuilt (in a stunning 52 days, by the way) and there is much to celebrate. In Nehemiah 9:2, all the Jews came together in worship and, wearing sackcloth and with dust on their heads, professed their sins and the sins of their ancestors. Nehemiah 9:16 tells of the Levite priests speaking of their ancestors' sins, describing them as "arrogant and stiff-necked."

Even after perhaps hundreds of years and a successful reconstruction of the temple, the city and its protective walls, there is an ongoing admission that the sins of past generations had led to the miserable state of affairs from which they had been finally delivered, including the exile of the Jews and the destruction of Jerusalem.

Furthermore, there was the admission that the current sins of the Jews were not to be forgotten, as if the past sins were a warning to the current and future generations. Thus, one lesson for us in our modern times might be that although the current generation has learned from the sins of the past, we can nonetheless still remember as a means to help prevent future wrong. Lessons learned from past sins should not be readily forgotten, even as God's blessings pour forth in the present.

"We didn't do it!"

Perhaps there were those among the Jewish people who felt that it was the sins of their fathers which had led to the destruction of the city, and not theirs. Perhaps they felt that they were "better people" and not deserving of such ongoing self-flagellation. There might have been the thought that, "We're better than they, more educated, refined, and sophisticated. We have learned from the errors of the ways of our fathers' families, and don't act like that now." Or, perhaps there was simply a general "Can't we all just move on?" mentality. "Why revisit the painful past? We know the sins of our fathers, and how they disobeyed God and the commandments of Moses. Why do we need to ask for forgiveness yet again? Haven't we already covered this?"

Perhaps there were also those who knew their familial histories and knew that their fathers and father's fathers were true men of God and did indeed follow His commandments. While there may have been some or even a majority of Jews who failed to live the lives they were called to live, there were surely some who were obedient to God and His laws. And the lineage of those latter families may have taken offense to the notion that they needed to pray for forgiveness of sins that neither they nor their forefathers committed.

This rings of what I hear from many of my white friends who are, perhaps rightly so, tired of being mischaracterized and judged as modern-day racists when they are decidedly not. "I didn't do it! I don't think that way, even if my father and his father and his father did!" Good Christian whites, striving to be as accommodating and understanding as possible, may admit to a current state that is built on a history of segregation and racism. Yet, they will also state emphatically that those conditions have long since passed away, even if their remnants are still with us and fringe elements of our citizenry still think in bizarre ways.

Alternatively, sometimes whites will take on the "modern racist" yoke by guiltily claiming "white privilege" in martyrdom fashion, often without full recognition of what it means or what to do with it.

But this is not about shaming our beliefs, history, or skin color. Yes, we recognize the sins of the past and the continuing evil where it exists. But we can do that from the same position of wisdom as the Jews did as they prayed. When the Jews went to God, they did not anticipate His ongoing wrath, nor did they expect Him to continually shame them. Likewise, when we go to God for forgiveness, we do not expect that He will continue to pour out shame on us. If we are sincere, and if ours is true repentance, He forgives. Period.

Collective prayers for forgiveness

Therefore, in Nehemiah's time, there was no reticence to delve deep into the past and bring it to the present in the form of prayers and supplication. Chapter 9 tells us that all the people came together to simultaneously praise God and ask for the forgiveness of the sins of generations, even while they were celebrating the tremendous achievements and blessings of opportunities that God had allowed for them. The rebuilding of the city walls meant that the city and its people could now prosper as before, in security from external enemies, and in peace through strength. And God was clearly with the Jewish people when they rebuilt the walls. God was in their mission. So the continued prayers over sins committed long ago served, in part, as a reminder of the wages of sin to the current generation, an admission of God's supreme reign, as well as a respectful and humble thanks for the forgiveness ultimately granted.

As part of our own unification process, and because we seek a different way to unify Christian Americans, perhaps it is time for a collective prayer from Christian whites to recognize the sins of our fathers, specifically vis a vis the American church. A prayer to recognize that Christian whites are responsible for the damage done to God's church in our nation. A prayer to acknowledge that even though many Christian whites were on the front lines in the fight against slavery and segregation and for the Civil Rights Act and the freedom and equality of all men and women, there were those among us who were not. There were those who claimed Christianity and thought of themselves as living Godly lifestyles who also harbored known or unknown racial animosity or prejudice, who had succumbed to the worldly thoughts and ways of an errant society, who failed to recognize their black brethren as equals, or who just didn't stand up to take the Christ-like side.

Thus, even those Christian whites whose heritage and personal feelings have always led them to think of their black brothers and sisters as equals need to recognize that there were plenty of Christian whites who did not feel, think and act this way. There were those who simply did not feel, think and act as Christ would have. Were this not the case, we would not have the Christian black denominations and the racial divisions in God's church that we have today.

To my knowledge, Christian whites have never come together in a way that recognizes the sins of our past and present while simultaneously calling for unity around specific social actions that would impact our society, our children and our faith and bring glory to God. If so, I don't recall the event or see its impact. And even if we have tried it in the past, let's do it again. Why not? Obviously, it didn't work the first time! We shouldn't give up on the power of prayers of millions of unified Christians. In the Bible, many of the great heroes prayed multiple times over various situations. Think of Elijah, Abraham and the instructions to Naaman. If we have prayed collectively, we certainly haven't done it seven times!

Silliness? Overkill? Impossible? Only if we perceive it as such! But Nehemiah has shown us the example of what can happen when a people, unified towards action and accomplishing something great, come together and pray for the sins of past generations as well as their own.

Making it public

And let's be clear. We need to make a very big deal out of this. Nehemiah didn't ask the Jews to all go home and pray silently in their bedrooms or keep it silently in mind as they went about daily life. Instead, he brought them all together, out in the open, in the bright light of day. And in a very public, unabashed and upright way, he and the Jewish elders prayed for forgiveness for everyone to see.

Similarly, we cannot expect to have an impact on the relationships with our Christian black brothers and sisters, past, present, and future, by praying in our silos among a few of us. Rather we must unite as many as is logistically possible and make a public display of our prayers. Using technology, special dates on the calendar, coliseums and stadiums, and whatever means that God presents to us, we must make our prayers as public as humanly possible, as if we are trying to get the attention of the angels in Heaven. If done correctly, with the right approach, this will lead not to shaming and degradation, but rather it will serve to create new opportunities for collaboration and cooperation among Christians who heretofore have remained siloed.

This is no small feat. It is a God-sized task, to be sure! But it may be of critical importance for unification in your community. Failure to make this happen may cause us to miss a unique, historically significant opportunity to create a dialogue that has never been seen before. Without these public prayers, even if only within small communities and groups of white churches throughout the nation, we may not be able to jump-start the conversations that will lead to the collaborations our nation so desperately needs.

Bad examples

A few attempts at something similar have been made, albeit on a small scale and with the wrong intentions. The few examples I have seen thus far are more about blame, shame, guilt, and punishment of whites than starting afresh and forgiveness after prior sins are admitted. Society's way is not to forgive ... that's Christ's way. Rather, society's way is to continue to see the errors of our history, even long after an offense is committed. This is particularly true if one is part of a group that society has decided to scorn, such as is the case with Christianity. Thus, when society tries something like this, the effort generally yields something other than forgiveness and unity. Commonly, the results are little more than further shame and degradation.

One event, in particular, asked young white people to "lay hands" on young black people, recite statements about the depravity of their race and the evils that their race had committed, and ask forgiveness. Yet, after this guilt-ridden verbal self-flagellation, there was nothing. No forgiveness. No solidarity. No forward progress. In short, nothing positive was accomplished other than shaming those who sought forgiveness.

Indeed, the simple recognition of wrongdoing does little more than beg further restitution, since there is no forgiveness or settlement. The crime is merely highlighted and continues to demand its justice. Furthermore, the failure to grant forgiveness does little or nothing for the relationship between the parties, and indeed may harm it. It certainly doesn't bring people together. Therefore, the striking attribute in this ceremonial guilt-trip was not so much the request for forgiveness but rather the lack of forgiveness and the lack of closure. The wound, however deep, remained open.

Such events do as much damage as good, if they do any good at all, since unless we can all come away with a better, more unified and co-equal society, little will have actually been achieved.

Of course, Christians know forgiveness well, since we have been forgiven by the pure grace of our Lord and Savior. Therefore, Christians can and should be the ones who show the way to a better place in our society through these and similar events. Ours is the way of forgiveness of our brothers, not merely the highlighting of one another's sins.

IMAGINE

Imagine a group of churches of different denominations, socio-economic geographies, and both races coming together to try to address local social issues, particularly justice and health. After many inter-church discussions, phone calls, meetings, and a few gallons of coffee, they have formed a group to start a cross-cultural collaboration. The formation of the group has taken great time, energy, and hours and hours of prayer by passionate, committed prayer warriors.

Not all churches in the city wanted to participate. Some of the white churches declined to participate, primarily because they were not convinced that such an effort would fly, given the split in the culture and the history of racial divisions among the area churches. There were also those who expressed that the effort was a diversion and not a role that a church should play, as it did not involve saving souls for Christ. If saving souls was not part of the purpose, they said, it was not God's will and thus not something in which they would involve themselves.

Furthermore, some cited the work they were already doing in local charities and expressed a reticence to take resources away from these existing efforts. Some smaller congregations worried about whether they would stretch their thin resources too far. Others worried about funding, what social issues would be chosen and the ultimate benefit for their individual churches.

Likewise, many black churches declined to participate, cool to the idea of integrated collaboration. "We are already doing that," some politely said, implying that no changes or assistance were needed. "We've been doing that stuff for years. Now, if you want to support us, you are free to join in. But we already have a program set up and it's working just fine."

Some black churches were simply not interested. Ironically, they gave some of the same reasons [excuses?] as the white churches for passing on participation. Current ministries were working fine for their targeted areas, and there was no need to pull resources or divert attention from their current ministries to their people. Furthermore, they were concerned that it was just another passing fancy to make the white congregations feel good about themselves by helping the "poor, pathetic, and incapable black folk."

Thus, there was growing frustration. If there wasn't enough enthusiasm to carry the day, the risk of failure was high. The white churches worried that without more black church support, the effort could become "too white" and thus not optimal for success. Sure, they could press forward as a group of predominantly white churches, but they really wanted to this to be an act of the entire body of Christ, not just a few pieces.

So, with the support of the group's black congregations, the white churches decided to make a very public statement. Using the local high school gym on a Sunday morning during the traditional worship hour, they would bring their congregations together for a public prayer meeting. They would close their own doors on that Sunday morning, cancel Sunday School, and make their way to the gym instead. They would, of course, invite the black churches that had chosen to participate to come and join as well. They would also invite all the other churches in the community, of all races and denominations, to come and witness what would be a very unusual prayer service, the likes of which had never been seen in this community before.

There, they would hold a multi-congregational prayer service. They would celebrate the bringing together of the small group of churches for collaboration on the key issues facing their communities. They would pray for guidance and providence from the Holy Spirit on the actions they would take, the challenges they would face and the results they would see. They would pray for the leadership of each church and the members of the various congregations who would spearhead the collaborative efforts.

Then, the white churches would pray a special prayer, a prayer of repentance for themselves and past generations. They would pray for forgiveness from God for foolish ways, the use of stereotypes, the condescending attitudes, and any racial animus that had ever dwelt in their hearts or the hearts of their forefathers. They would pray for forgiveness for the segregation in their community that had led to so much pain, so much hate and so many lost opportunities. They would pray and remember those times that to them seemed an eternity ago, the results of which still lived on in too many ways. And they would pray a vow to stop the madness and work together with any and all Christian blacks, their brothers and sisters in Christ, to bring change to their community, to be upright, to become the Race Police for the community (more on this later), and to show their community Christ's message through their thoughts, words and deeds.

This would not be a prayer designed to continue or exacerbate blame, nor create shame or guilt for being white. Rather, these prayers would be meant to recognize the sin that existed and any that continues to exist and call it out.

However, just as any Christian does when they pray to a benevolent, loving God, they would pray knowing that repentance is not about shame or self-hate. The prayers of the Jews in Nehemiah were not about degrading the Jewish people, shaming their heritage, or denying their value in the eyes of God. Repentance is about moving forward in a renewed relationship with, in this case, both God and fellow Christians.

So, as the next part of their prayers to God, they would ask all those present to pray, unified in a commitment to come together to bring glory to God through unity in action. They would vow to leave the past behind and look into the future, to commit time, resources, money, and whatever their congregations had to offer to help the collective group move in their neighborhoods, their schools, their courts, their hospitals, and their churches for the betterment of all and the glory of God. Through this, repentance turns to unity, and unity into power.

HERE?!

If this were your community, could this happen? Would you even be able to start something with your fellow Christian whites? Would you get enthusiastic participation, cautious consideration, or push-back? Would you get participation from any of the black churches, or would you have to prove your goodwill first? What would that day in the gym look like? Would anyone close their church doors on a Sunday morning and show up for the sake of the community? Would there be an excited and packed gym, or would the day be an embarrassment for the organizing churches, displayed in the local media as a silly Christian stunt? Would the local blogosphere mock your effort as racist, condescending and trite? Or would your turnout blow away every optimistic expectation, with churches from across your city showing up in great numbers? Would the crowd spill into the halls of the high school, even forcing you to move to the football stadium? Would there be such enthusiasm that the entire Christian community, optimists and skeptics alike, from all denominations and doctrines, would suddenly be thrust into action?

If you cannot imagine the success of a similar event in your community, how can you expect to break down the silos of your congregations and optimize the effectiveness of your efforts? How can you expect to tap all the latent capacity within your many churches to reverse the societal downward spiral that will consume our children and many of our churches?

If you cannot imagine this, then what is your dream for the future of Christianity in your community?

Is it one full of Christian unity or the same struggles for membership and financial sustainability, communal relevance, and effective evangelism?

This one bold act will open up a wealth of opportunities for collaboration and cooperation and may even serve to pressure our various church communities to "put up or shut up" on solving our nation's largest social ills. Either the united church can do it, or something else will take our place.

A SECOND STEP: COLLABORATION

However, this is just one step, albeit a huge one, in the process of creating unity through action and bringing glory to God through our collaboration. This one step will serve as a catalyst for the difficult activities of unification and bringing change to our broken society.

And even while this is being done, there is much more that Christian whites can do towards unification, collaboration, and cooperation. Some involves reaching out and learning how to collaborate and cooperate with a community from whom we have been separated for decades and even centuries. Some involves direct action in conjunction with our Christian black brothers and

161

sisters. And some involves deep introspection and developing new perspectives on our relationships with and attitudes towards all God's people.

Getting started

Breaking down the barriers that divide our churches will require some significant work within both the Christian black and Christian white communities, since there is often such a gap between us. Of course, the Nehemiah moment will set a tone for your community and shine a harsh, bright light on any separations that exist. Racially segregated churches are often within blocks or miles of each other. Politics bleeds over into Sunday morning and further divides us. Therefore, healing these gaps will require outreach from both white and black churches to mend old fences, create new dialogues, and develop new strategic visions for all communities.

When trying to start a working relationship with your Christian black brothers and sisters, there are a few, commonsense but often missed considerations. These will be important as we look to bring together large swaths of the Christian American population to shine God's glory on our society through our actions, words, votes and voices.

And as you begin this long process, keep in mind what this is not. This is *not* about swapping pastors once a month, having the black folks come sing at your service once in a while, or sharing a meal on a Sunday after church. This is *not* about the occasional gathering of local pastors, or revivals, or meetings to talk. *Nor* is this about a large white church "adopting" a small black church (or vice versa).[lxvi] *Nor* is this about Thanksgiving turkeys or Christmas presents for poor families. Rather, this about ongoing, collaborative action, change, and doing.

Of course, some of these initial forays will be easy, some will be harder, some will seem impossible. Some churches will readily want to integrate efforts to impact our society, welcoming and sharing as much help as possible. These churches, large and small, from a variety of denominations and socio-economic environments, will readily step forward to join in the efforts, providing whatever assistance they can muster.

Others will seem hesitant, perhaps having been burned by a previous outreach or collaborative effort that didn't end well or resulted in little more than empty promises, frustrations, and broken relationships. These will need nurturing and encouragement until they see the uprightness with which you come forth. Often, they might take a "show me" position, wanting to see demonstrations of your commitment to the cause, only joining after you have proven your good intentions and willingness to stick it out for the long

162

haul. Only then will they open up and begin to participate and support the efforts.

And still others will seem impossible to penetrate, as age-old divisions, racial boundaries, and contentment with self-sufficiency add up to a silo wall that is thick, tall and fortified. I can certainly see some of the churches I have visited falling into this heavily isolated category. These churches will never be satisfied with your "proof of commitment" or your loyalty to the cause. They will see each and every foray as a sign of your racism and arrogance, every attempt at dialogue as an attempt to control and manipulate, and every outreach as an affront and a slap in the face. Hopefully, these will be few. And though they may come around and eventually join in, you should expect to work around these intransigent churches to make progress with the others in your community.

Thus, you can expect every kind of response, from a warm and loving welcoming to a door shut in your face. Still, God commands us to persevere and bring together the entire body of Christ, not just a few parts. Thus, your persistence and patience are required.

Intra-race collaboration

If we cannot get churches within the respective communities to collaborate, we certainly won't get black and white churches to collaborate. Indeed, getting the predominantly white churches from a given community or town to come together to collaborate on anything except disaster relief might be more challenging than we think, particularly if the end goal is an even broader community-wide collaboration with even more churches. Ditto for the black churches. There may be competition, denominational and doctrinal divisions, etc., that would serve to keep us in silos and comfortable. There are myriad reasons why churches don't collaborate now, which have been discussed elsewhere in this book.

But clearly this is a critical first step. If, for instance, Christian whites seek to make the initial foray, they'll likely want more than just one church to step forward. Likewise, for the black churches wishing to take the first step. Thus, before you start down the path toward leaping over racial boundaries like Superman, you may need to first cross some other boundaries that keep your black and white churches from an integrated approach to community-wide problems.

And as you begin to come together as intra-racial churches you can muster the impressive force of will that would help initiate the inter-racial collaboration that will begin to break down the age-old silos.

163

Communication

This is perhaps the most obvious, but just start communicating. Patience is not a virtue that we should possess here. Once things start and get moving, great patience will no doubt be required. But to start the process, none should be expected or needed. Someone simply must start the conversations. (And it doesn't even need to be said at this point that these conversations must all be approached uprightly). To start things off, you may need to begin with the basics of the relationship. Much like going on a first date, you'll need to discover more about each other and your respective passions, feelings, perspectives, backgrounds, and philosophies before proceeding with the furthering of the relationship. For some, this will be an exciting venture into new Godly interactions and Holy Conversations. For others, it will seem painful, disquieting or uncomfortable, at least at first.

Clearly, race still plays a role in our society, whether we want it to or not. It is hard to believe that a very small but extremely toxic and divisive segment of our white population still thinks themselves racially superior to others. More subtly, there is still racial discord in the form of prejudice and stereotypes that keep our people divided.

Likewise, there is plenty of racial hate on both sides of the racial divide, some stemming from old habitual thoughts, some from decades of mutual intolerance, and some from more recent events that have ripped the slowly healing scabs from centuries' old wounds to unleash a new kind of hatred, racial animus, and discord.

Therefore, you will quickly need assistance from your Christian black brothers and sisters to help you understand the implications of the many definitions of racism and what is meant by the various terms now so freely used in secular society. Fortunately, anyone can start this conversation, and it will likely need to precede any others. Even if it seems too sensitive a topic to start off with, or just too difficult to deal with, this must be discussed at some point. ALL parties need to know the definitions of the terms you will be using, else there will never be clear dialogue.

Christian whites will need to understand the perspectives of their Christian black colleagues in order to understand how they view the world, whites, and society. And Christian blacks will need to understand the attitudes and perspectives of their Christian white counterparts on race, race relations, history, the current status of society, and the roles of race in society, the economy and our institutions. Therefore, a solid understanding of perspectives and deep discussions of the racial terminology of the day will greatly help you as you move forward.

Once this footing of the foundation is laid, you may be ready to move to a relatively narrow topic set, such as one or more of the four areas mentioned in this book (justice, race, healthcare, and education). You might start by asking "What keeps you up at night?" "What is this community most concerned about?" "What angers you the most about this topic?" Or, start with these questions in a more open-ended discussion, thus allowing you to locate your targets based more specifically on the needs of the community.

Then, of course, let the other folks know your concerns about the various topics. If this is collaboration, both sides should be fully expected to contribute to the solutions in all communities. This is not meant to be a one-way conversation, "complaint session," or one-sided action, with one side swooping in to save the day for the other. Both should be expected to join in fully and participate.

From these discussions will come targets for intervention and change. And these initial discussions should generate other discussions, perhaps with larger groups, and more in-depth and perhaps even more heated exchanges. And note that, if you aren't rubbing on some sore spots, either your Christian community is lot more closely aligned and integrated than many, or you aren't pushing hard enough on the difficult topics at hand.

But once or as you begin, consider the following additional, concrete steps to make your case before those whose minds we need to change. These steps will go a long way towards helping you move toward unity.

Support versus overtaking

From the perspectives of some if not many of our black brothers and sisters, the charitable efforts of Christian whites are viewed with at least some degree of skepticism and mistrust. This tendency evolved from many years of well-meaning but sometimes overpowering or misunderstood efforts to help predominantly African American communities.

While God calls us to help the poor, clothe the naked, and offer shelter to the homeless, the Bible doesn't offer direct guidance on the how. Thus, Christians, whether they be missionaries, volunteers in foreign countries or in local communities, have a tendency to come in, take over, and try to run things in their desire to do God's work and show mercy and compassion. The explanation for this is typically quite benign. Some seek to follow their God-given calling to share and give. But there is a right way and a wrong way to do that. And Christian whites have sometimes done it the wrong way.

This has resulted in the following statements, all of which came from Christian black brothers or sisters. "When we see white people coming, we go the other way." The black pastor added and clarified, "When we see [otherwise well-meaning] Christian white folks coming to "save our day," we know they just want to swoop in, pretend they have a solution, and feel good about themselves." Similarly, another black pastor put it this way, "White folks want to come downtown to do their good stuff, then go back [to the suburbs] and leave us with all the hard work to do."

Yet another black pastor offered this, "White folks tend to come in and take over and leave us and our ideas out." Citing specific examples, he expressed his frustration with the "just stand aside and let us handle this" approach to charity work. In the past, Christian whites had given his black community the sense that they were not good enough, smart enough, or gifted enough to do anything for themselves. White folks were therefore seen as thinking that they had the best ideas, since they weren't living in poor neighborhoods with lousy schools, crime, and drugs.

Furthermore, some in this community were left with the impression that Christian whites felt that only black and poor communities have problems and issues. Even though history shows that we help folks of all races, creeds, and socioeconomic situations, including those in our stereotypical white communities, underlying sensitivities to whites helping black communities had erupted. This, needless to say, led to cynicism and a deepening of the divisions between Christians. Finally, and more importantly, the solutions the pastor described to the problems being addressed were, in his words, "too simple and too easy to do any good at all."

Likewise, a sister shared this, "These are our problems, we don't need [rich] white folks telling us how to fix them. They don't know anything about us!" This was in reference to some commissions that local white politicians [which presumably included some Christian whites] had started to address inner-city crime and drugs. As her comment demonstrates, there was a sense of a lack of understanding of the communities being helped, thus a frustration that the usual crime prevention solutions would be put forth. It was felt that pre-conceived notions and a lack of objectivity and depth of understanding would be combined with a "get out of the way" approach, yielding few, if any, tangible and truly valuable outcomes.

The result is an all-too common sense that Christian whites may want to do good works but may not fully understand the communities and peoples they seek to help. Likewise, there is a sense, right or wrong, that Christian whites commit to causes only or mainly to feel good about themselves rather than to do actual humble service. Whether legitimate or not, in part or in whole, some Christian blacks are simply not as welcoming of collaboration as Christian whites might hope or expect.

This, of course, mimics the "Toxic Charity" concept mentioned elsewhere in this book. That is, charity can do more harm than good through a "we'll do it for you" approach. By leaving the accepting community perhaps helped but without the skills, knowledge, and direction to take the ball and run, the community is left dependent rather than independent, subservient rather than self-sufficient. In this case, the toxicity is complicated by the insult of resentment and a sense of condescension felt by the accepting communities.

Obviously, the simple solution is to come alongside, support rather than overtake and collaborate rather than do.

Don't assume you can't learn

All are equal in God's eyes. All are gifted. So, let us remember that we are all brothers and sisters in Christ. There are latent talents throughout all our congregations, with passions that run deep on a great many issues. Tapping these passions and abilities and uniting them with like-minded Christians in other congregations and communities is the key to broadening our influence and impact.

Remember, too, that though all races suffer from the impacts of poverty and abuse, the black community has faced issues that most white communities have not. Thus, there may be solutions that they have found from which we could readily learn, particularly in times of trouble. Certainly, they have faced troubles that we as whites can neither imagine nor fully understand. Moreover, the breadth and depth of ministries in the black church, the close-knit church communities, and the deep, abiding faith of the oppressed should be part of all communities.

And as God has gifted us all with specific talents, abilities, and strengths, we should always be ready to call on all parts of the broader Christian community for resources rather than simply relying on those within our own church communities or denominations. A white church is no more able to solve the larger societal problems on its own than a black church and vice versa. But the broader the community of churches united in action, the larger the pool of resources from which to draw. As we unite the Christian church around specific actions and goals for our communities, we'll need all the resources that our united church community can bring to bear.

Thus, we must remember that all are able. These God-given talents, passions, and abilities will shine through and be used more effectively as we align the strengths, passions, and aggregated capacities of our many congregations.

BECOMING THE RACE POLICE

Obviously, racism continues to exist in many forms. The extent to which historical and/or current racism still impacts our communities and those whom it harms deserves our immediate and ongoing attention. Whether it is "the" or only "a" root cause of a particular issue or social ill is for upright Christian blacks and whites to determine on a case-by-case basis, using all the tools and approaches described herein and more. As part of this effort, there is a special role for Christian whites.

As we see throughout the nation, race and racism continue to divide our communities and churches and taint our attitudes and perspectives. The terms are pervasive in today's political and social discussions, sometimes used carelessly and without regard for meaning or context. As discussed in detail earlier in this book, the ever-fluid definitions have poisoned the waters of dialogue and collaboration, yielding divisions that could be with us for another generation or longer. As the need for unity grows, society continues to seek ways to divide us further and keep race as an impenetrable barrier. Yet, there is no upright arbiter of the instances when current events, sociology's latest theories, or accusations erupt. Since racial dialogue is so inherently toxic, and since even the hint of racism or an accusation thereof immediately yields animosity and resentment, rational discussions are made impossible. We are thereby left without the means to repair the scars that our own actions and words continue to reopen. And thus, our children, steeped throughout their lives in the negativity and hopelessness of society's new definitions and the growing hatred and bitterness of our society, will have little chance of seeing a different world in their lifetimes if we do not act.

It is into this fray that Christian whites must go. Assuming we accomplish the first tasks of presenting ourselves as seekers of upright thinking, speaking, and action, we can work directly with our Christian black brothers and sisters to make Christianity the best arbiter of these discussions and issues.

Specifically, once we establish ourselves as being upright in the eyes of our Christian black brothers and sisters and of those around us, Christian whites can take on the role of objectively and honestly assessing each institution, each social, business, educational, and judicial model, and each social and political situation that arises to determine whether it or any element within it is truly racist, as defined by a mutually derived and defined standard.

To do so, Christian whites must be very clear about the definitions we will use, open about the criteria by which we judge, and transparent about our findings and analysis. Let the proverbial chips fall where they may. Upon deep, objective analysis, we may uncover age-old patterns of behavior that haven't been modernized. We may discover thinking that is mired in previous centuries and stereotypes that perversely influence behaviors, interactions, and decisions. We may find relics of a segregated society that live on in the systems of government, education, and the economy despite the advent and promotion of modern moral and ethical standards. We will sometimes find the hatred of previous generations, and sometimes exaggerations, urban legends, deceptions, and false accusations. Very likely, we will unearth Jacks crying wolf, pure hatred and 1850's thinking, and everything in between.

And we must always be ready and quick to remove our own preconceived notions, examine each situation with fresh, completely objective eyes, and see the perspectives of others, especially those claiming to be unjustly treated because of their race. We must be ready to critically examine the systems our forefathers built and all facets of the institutions that we might assume to be just and righteous.

We must furthermore be Spock-like in our willingness to avoid conclusion-jumping and too quickly taking one side or the other. Indeed, there may often be no side to take, since many of the issues our society faces are multi-faceted with myriad causalities and deep roots that grew and spread throughout our nation's history. Thus, our role will be to point out both when racism is at play, where it is only partly at play, and when it is not an actual factor.

We must work to show that our assessments are indeed wholly upright, such that God Himself would be pleased with our approach and our conclusions. We must communicate with our Christian black brothers and sisters, helping them understand the conclusions we have drawn as we seek their support. We must all come together to decide on an appropriate upright answer, a path forward and the changes that are required, regardless of whose ox is gored or which veil is removed.

Of course, as we detect racism or even old or new stereotypes that need to be erased by whatever means, on either side of the racial aisle, it is our duty to our Christian brothers and sisters, our society and our God to call them out and aggressively seek to eradicate them. If, and only if, we are pure and holistic in our assessments, and if, and only if, we are willing to "call them as God sees them" (rather than "call them as we see them"), will we establish the Christian white community as worthy of the collaboration of Christian blacks and the respect of the rest of society.

Thus, Christian whites need to become a sort of race police, chasing down racism when and where it exists, calling it out as we find it, and explaining the breadth and depth of the real issues when we do not. We must be willing to take hits for our objectivity, knowing that any side of a given situation has vested interests in the sides taken. We must remain true to our uprightness, seek out the whole truth, and be prepared to stand before our God and our society on our determinations.

Furthermore, and importantly, we must work closely with our Christian black brothers and sisters to ensure that racism doesn't further spread in either community. Hate is hate, and can never be justified, even if against those who have repeatedly mistreated us. Hatred should not be allowed to fester within the black community even as we eradicate it in the white community. To prevent this, we must collaborate and communicate openly and with all uprightness with our brothers and sisters, such that we are constantly seeking Christ's perspectives rather than our own or society's.

Our politicians, government institutions and "intelligentsia" won't do this, as many seem to thrive and prosper from division. Likewise, the various associations, organizations, political parties, and interest groups all have earthly agendas, clouded views, and spoken and unspoken biases. Thus, as Christian whites, we must take up the role of Race Police. Only then can we come together with our fellow believers to properly identify, isolate, and eradicate racism's remaining vestiges and prevent its resurrection.

SUMMARY

There is a definitive lack of trust among our Christian black brethren, created by a long history of division that abides within our church community today. Yet, this offers us great opportunities. The racial divisions of the church likely allowed a spread of Christianity where it might not have otherwise penetrated. With this comes greater numbers of Christians who could come together to combat an increasingly secular and lost American society. All we need do is break down the silos that keep us isolated from one another, whether by race, denomination, or geography, and unite in action to impact our society.

Therefore, this is about "doing different" rather than "doing better." We've tried doing better, and it has only gotten us so far. We're tried sharing a few meals together, adopting churches, and giving away Thanksgiving turkeys and

Christmas hams. But this is about changing society through Christ's love and our actions, not feeling good about our charitable tendencies.

Doing different sometimes has to start with something bold, something unique, and something eye-opening. Big changes happen because big catalysts arise. Sometimes, something has to snap. And in the case of Christian racial unity, something very big must become a catalyst. Bringing together southern white Baptists and C.M.E.'s, white Presbyterians, and the Church of God in Christ, A.M.E.'s, and Catholics won't be easy. And it won't happen if we try the same things we've tried in the past.

Therefore, Christian whites must do things and think in ways that run deeply counter to the ways of this world, and indeed the ways of our past. We, as Christian whites, must put aside our pride and create those Nehemiah moments that will clearly display our intentions and willingness to go well beyond what has been done in the past. Christian whites can publicly address the sins of our past without yoking ourselves with the misguided labels and distorted accusations of the present.

By doing so, we reach out to our Christian black brothers and sisters and come alongside them, as partners, to fix the ills in all our communities, in all socio-economic classes, throughout our nation. Then, united Christians can become the arbiters of truth, integrity, honesty, and objectivity in our racial conversations, taking Jesus Himself as an example and showing the way for a divided society.

Will we stumble along the way? Of course! This is a rough path we take, and our alliances will mostly be new. This will not be like love at first sight. Rather, there will be errors, mishaps, and our worldly mistakes all along this path to collaboration.

And of course, our society, such that they notice, will notice these stumbles. They will mock and do their best to divide whatever unity we can muster. Ours will be a constant struggle to stand together, firm against the howling of a society determined to see us fail.

Yet, stumble we will! And we must take each stumble as an opportunity, each error as a learning experience, and each failure as another step down this long path to which we have committed. Better to stumble and bumble our way down this road than to stand at the starting line and argue.

And only then will we lift God's church to be what it should be, a shining example of what God's love looks like here on earth.

WHAT CHRISTIAN BLACKS NEED TO DO

*¹How very good and pleasant it is when
kindred live together in unity! (Psalms 133)*

*¹²Just as a body, though one, has many parts, but all its
many parts form one body, so it is with Christ. ¹³For we
were all baptized by one Spirit so as to form one body—
whether Jews or Gentiles, slave or free—and we were all
given the one Spirit to drink. ¹⁴Even so the body is not
made up of one part but of many. (1 Corinthians 12: 3 – 6)*

*³Make every effort to keep the unity of the Spirit through
the bond of peace. ⁴There is one body and one Spirit, just
as you were called to one hope when you were called;
⁵one Lord, one faith, one baptism; ⁶one God and Father of
all, who is over all and through all and in all.
(Ephesians 4: 4 – 5)*

*¹³But now in Christ Jesus, you who were far away from
God are brought near through the blood of Christ's death.
¹⁴Christ himself is our peace. He made both Jewish people
and those who are not Jews one people. They were
separated as if there were a wall between them, but
Christ broke down that wall of hate by giving his own
body. ¹⁵The Jewish law had many commands and rules,
but Christ ended that law. His purpose was to make the
two groups of people become one new people in him and
in this way make peace. ¹⁶It was also Christ's purpose to
end the hatred between the two groups, to make them*

into one body, and to bring them back to God. Christ did
all this with his death on the cross. [17]Christ came and
preached peace to you who were far away from God, and
to those who were near to God. [18]Yes, it is through Christ
we all have the right to come to the Father in one Spirit.
(Ephesians 2:12 – 18)

PERSPECTIVE

I used to regularly have lunch with a white pastor friend who led an all-white congregation. About once a month, we'd meet for fried chicken at local, rather famous roadside eatery (which is a nice way to say a chicken shack). After all, good friends and good fried chicken on a picnic table, what could be better? Since I'd I moved away from his city, we only get together on a rare occasion. While I was on a business trip back to his area, he agreed to meet once again at the same eatery.

I'd already asked him to review and critique this book, so he had an electronic draft version. As we ate, he went down the list of things he would change, add and delete. He liked certain chapters, made some verbiage recommendations, and had many thoughts on the style. Then he came to his short but important list of concerns.

He looked me in the eye, and said, "I get that you needed to write a chapter on what white Christians need to do. That was good. You're right. We need to do more … a lot more!"

He then paused and said, "But you also wrote a chapter on what black Christians need to do." "Yes. Yes, I did." He stared at me for a long moment. Then he glanced quickly over his shoulder, as if out of a habit when talking about a sensitive subject in a public place. He looked me in the eye, learned towards me and lowered his voice nearly to a whisper to say, "But you're a white guy."

Had he not been deathly serious, I might have chuckled. "Yeah, I know," I said, trying to avoid trivializing his comment. "I figured that out a long time ago."

He stared at me for another moment, as if he didn't think I'd understood the gravity of his comment. Then he said, again quietly, "But you're a white guy. How can you even do that?!"

These comments seemed to be a profession of our current social inability to discuss serious racial issues without great consternation and fear of harsh backlash, particularly among white folks. As a pastor, he seemed particularly disturbed and cautious about creating negativity or anger.

To me, his message was a significant signal that society has been successful in keeping upright conversations from taking place, even between Christian brothers and sisters who should otherwise have no issues with coming together as followers of the same God. His concern was both profound, meaningful, and well-taken, particularly given the context of this book.

But in the end, obviously, this chapter remains in the book as what I feel is a necessary component of the grander scheme of things. I pray it will have its intended effects to help bring Christians together across hundreds of years of divisions within our faith.

INTRODUCTION

This chapter was one of the hardest to write. Hard because I am writing from a white male perspective, having had no experience living in the skin of a black person. Hard because I must try to walk a fine line between the sensitivities within the current state of race relations, the obvious need for immediate and dramatic changes in the dialogue among Christians, and the desperate need for large-scale social action. Hard because society has made these toxic subjects, full of verbal entrapments, incorrect interpretations, and harsh, quick judgments, and assumptions. Hard because so many lie in wait, hoping to misinterpret even the kindest of words into anger-filled messages of hate and division.

Yet, this is a chapter that must be written in order that we might at least lay the foundations of the concepts for future collaboration and unity in action. Society seems to have found many ways to keep Christians divided into camps. Our own church-based divisions are harsh enough, given the silos created by our denominations, style and personality preferences, and church identities and loyalties. And even now, our churches continue to split over music, gay marriage, doctrine, and myriad other reasons.

We might be able to justify two churches having different worship and music styles, since they can still readily collaborate to create change within a community. After all, we all worship the same God despite our preferences and doctrinal opinions.

But, as already discussed, it is the racial and related political divisions within God's church that are the most damaging and damning. Getting a Christian Methodist Episcopal church and an all-white southern Baptist church to collaborate on a specific social cause might be a little difficult. Or a lot difficult! After all, Christians have lived in these divisions for almost 200 years since racism helped found the first all-black denominations. So, here we remain, as divided as society itself, often more so.

Moreover, today's racial politics serve to drive more wedges between our churches as Christian blacks rail against what they view as blatant racism in politics and social institutions while Christian whites rail against being dubbed racists for following and espousing Christ's teachings in the public realm. Americans have a long way to go to heal their racial divisions, but there are few, if any, significant signs that the God's American church, as a whole or in part, is taking the lead towards unification.

Thus, not only are we failing to heal our own Christian divisions, God's church isn't taking its rightful and proper role to lead the nation out of its bitterness, resentment, vengefulness, and hatred toward a Godly perspective. God's church, if it participates at all, is an "also-ran."

Now that we have examined what the Christian white community must do, and a white Christian male's perspective on race and racism, it is time to address what the Christian black community needs to do to help raise God's church to a new level of prominence and influence in American society.

Unfortunately, however, what is being asked of Christian blacks herein are the harder of the many tasks, far more difficult than anything asked of the Christian white community. Not that Christian whites have it easy, mind you. Clearly, they do not. Rather, the requests of the Christian black community simply may require far more patience, strength, and faith.

Here is a short list of just a few of things being suggested for Christian blacks to do if unity in action has any hope of becoming a reality. Christian blacks will need to:

- Put aside the deep-seated feelings that have come from generations of abuse by fellow Christians.
- Replace resentment, anger, frustration, and generations of rightly-held mistrust with respect, love, and full cooperation.
- Walk shoulder to shoulder with those who have repeatedly mistreated you.
- Look to the future and see the great potential that lies ahead in Godly unity rather than to the oppression and hatred of the past.
- Constantly seek objectivity and reject stereotypes by seeing each situation anew, in its fullest context and with the freshest of eyes.
- Accept help from a former enemy when it is offered.

- Humbly and freely ask for help from that same enemy without concern for pride or rejection.
- Split with a society that may seem to support your racial cause while simultaneously opposing many of the standards, social mores, and policies that all Christians should oppose.
- Seek the whole truth by amending, as necessary, seemingly logical and justifiable explanations for current issues and problems within our communities with a deeper analysis, introspection, and the asking of politically and socially unpopular questions.

In sum, Christian blacks must take a long, hard, steep, uphill road instead of the well-worn and easy path.

Of course, none of this is the way society has suggested you handle these ongoing issues. Indeed, modern society and the rage of our youth recommends that blacks embrace their resentment, heighten their anger, focus on the abuses of the past, refuse to forgive, direct their frustrations, and target their enemies with rage, bitterness, self-justified retribution, and hatred.

Yet, as Christians, we know that this is not the way Christ taught to act, nor is it the way we will ever reach viable solutions for our communities.

As Christians, we are called to "do different."

RE- RE- RE-DEFINING OUR TERMINOLOGY

As explained several times already, the definition of racism has been rewritten over the years. Given the changes to the definition and the broadening of the term's application, when you call a white person a racist, he may not even know what you mean. But, it is almost guaranteed that he won't like it. Ditto for using similar and increasingly common accusations such as privilege, fragility, and the concept of innate, inbred, and uncontrollable racism. Let's face it, we cannot start conversations with insults or terms that are interpreted to be insults. One can no more start a conversation with a white man by calling him a racist[lxvii] than one can start a conversation with a black man by addressing him as "Boy" or "Nigger." It's simply a non-starter which leads to nothing but more division, anger, and resentment.

Furthermore, if the definitions are used to falsely classify whites, even only slightly, then the misuse of the term does not correspond with walking uprightly and will surely lead to ongoing divisions. Just as false stereotypes of African Americans hurt and cause resentment and division, so too do the false stereotypes of whites and Christian whites. When we mischaracterize anyone, for whatever reason, we are not speaking as Jesus spoke and commanded us to speak. We thereby fail to set a proper example for society, our children, and our fellow Christians.

And we therefore will not set ourselves apart from a society that is bent on the maintenance and deepening of racial and political divisions for its illegitimate purposes.

Defining racism

In asking several friends, both whites and blacks, to define racism, only one took the textbook definition, while others tossed in interpretations that had little to do with the word itself. This speaks to the variation that has come into our discussions, which has obviously led to some of the confusion and bitterness around the use of the term and its modern derivations.

Thus, before we begin using terms like racism, there must be a mutually understood, precise definition amongst Christian blacks and whites. That definition, by whatever means it is derived, must be precise, clear, concise, conclusive, and exclusive. That is, it must be used precisely and not loosely, include the necessary elements that give the word its power and exclude any elements that confuse and obfuscate its applicability.

Take these examples of the definition of racism. From the Merriam-Webster dictionary: "A belief that race is the primary determinant of human traits and capacities and that racial differences produce an inherent superiority of a particular race."[lxviii] A more "modern" definition states: "Racism is a system that encompasses economic, political, social, and cultural structures, actions, and beliefs that institutionalize and perpetuate an unequal distribution of privileges, resources and power between White people and people of Color."[lxix] Each is different, the latter describing a social construct or system while the former describes a belief or opinion. Both might be correct. Either can be damaging if used inappropriately or if used without the understanding of all parties.

Indeed, because of the expansion of the definitions of racism away from its more simple, straightforward origins, racism is now said to mean a great many things, many if not most of which no longer refer to hatred or individual beliefs. Rather, racism is now defined as a component and cause of system behavior, the outcomes of system performance, or the system from which outcomes emanate.

Moreover, the adjectives added to racism (e.g. institutional, systemic) create new forms of racism that seek to describe certain outcomes and disparities seen within the various elements of society. Thus, racism's definitions are not only more numerous but also fluid, inconsistent, and evolving.

However, like an arrow fired at a proper target, this and other terms can be used to do justifiable damage. But when fired at the wrong target, in the wrong way, or even accidentally, bad things immediately happen. Words have meanings. But their power is only well-utilized and maximized for good when properly directed.

Moreover, the definitions of the terms we use should further our discussions, not hamper them. As we collectively agree on definitions and uses of these terms, they will better aid us in furthering our conversations by reserving the rhetorical acidity only for its intended purposes and targets. Accurate definitions and utilization yield more effective results. If the weapon of the word is fired at an appropriate target, the goal of its use is achieved. Assuming the goal is righteous (unlike many of society's hidden goals) then the result will be advancement of God's cause.

As discussed, racism now has a broad variety of meanings, all extremely negative, loosely applied as the user desires. Instead, to carry its true and legitimate power, the target/recipient must fully understand the definition of the term used by the accuser, else the accusation can have unintended and/or negative consequences and impacts on both parties. Most important, misuse and abuse of terminology can result in diminishing the user's ethical and moral position with the accused, thus nullifying any efforts to communicate. Therefore, the definition must be historically accurate, since the importance and relevance of the term spans generations. The definition in a Webster's dictionary published in 1970 must still be applicable today if we are to speak across generational boundaries. A racist of 1970 cannot be different from a racist of today, else we will become mired in the historical contextualization of various interpretations of the word. This, of course, is exactly what has happened today.

Definitions must also be precise, free of the adjectives that create its mutations and variations. When we add our spin and our own interpretations to our terminology, using additives and derivations the original term was never meant to carry, we muddle our efforts to communicate. Of course, the term racism can and should continue to be used, as there are still far too many racists in our society for the term to be retired. But with precise definitions and appropriate utilization, it will carry real meaning and the power of uprightness when it is used. Christian whites will know how and when to use it, as well as precisely what it means when it is used by Christian blacks. This can do nothing but help our dialogue and show society what it means to live and think uprightly as Christians.

Other racially charged terminology

Since some of the modern social theories have at least some degree of credibility, we as Christians must address the historical and current social environs in which the races interact by properly addressing the terminology we use to describe our institutions, systems, and social structures. These terms include but certainly are not limited to bigot/bigotry, Nazism, nationalism, fascism, homophobia, xenophobia, islamophobia, personal responsibility, hard work, and other terms used in the modern culture to degrade, insult, harm, and divide. Whether to describe long-standing stereotypes, media presentations of racial attributes, modern cultural aberrations and norms, or aging attitudes now considered ignorant, all must be accurately portrayed in order to avoid the blanket use of insulting and demeaning terms that only serve to stop dialogue and inject vitriol. In order to uprightly discuss these issues, our terminology must be defined and used properly.

Of course, we need to address the modern variations of racial terminology such as modern, institutional, and systemic racism as well as white privilege and other forms of racist characteristics said to be nearly encoded within the DNA of Christian whites and white people. Because these are terms generated by modern society, their use is often solely intended to divide, demean, and harm rather than generate dialogue and develop solutions to real-world problems. Therefore, these, like racist, carry their own power and thus must be used properly, if they are used at all.

And because these can seem more nefarious and even more negative than the term racist, society's modern definitions can generate even more resentment and anger when used. Without properly defining these terms and using them within their proper context, their use can result in even worse outcomes.

Moreover, and importantly for the future of our faith, we can no longer make broad accusations about the "other side" without sweeping Christian brothers and sisters into the mix. Christian blacks must carefully use terms that do not unintentionally create injustice rather than stop it or paint Christian whites with an undue brush. And, of course, Christian whites must think uprightly as we discuss the contexts and nuances of societal realities so as fully understand the perspectives of our Christian black brothers and sisters.

In the end, whether a term is used to explain the distribution of wealth, injustice in the criminal justice system, poverty, crime, health status, educational disparities, or any of the myriad other issues our society faces, we must use our terminology from a point of mutual understanding of the context of its use, the precise definitions, and the harm or good that can come from the use of the terms we create.

Therefore, in order to fully understand where we are as a society and the ways in which groups of united churches can move God and Christianity to a more prominent and honorable role, it is imperative that we have deep and upright conversations about the various modern terms used by and in society.

Leading the way

However, it is critical to note that is it up to Christian blacks to lead the way here. No one else, no other group or organization can or will do this. Certainly, Christian whites cannot define and redefine these terms on our own, since we will be accused of simply deflecting accusations by wordsmithing or making rhetorical excuses for our true inner feelings and hidden racist attitudes. After all, we are the common targets of these accusations and insults. So, any efforts to define, redefine, or reign in the use of modern racist accusations and terminology will be seen as mere self-serving deflections of the ugly truth and would therefore be readily discounted.

Rather, led by Christian blacks, Christians of both races must come together to derive proper definitions for the harshest terms in our society and come to an appropriate understanding of the historical contexts and challenges of moving our nation forward. Just as Christians united across racial lines and join hands to eliminate slavery and lead the Civil Rights movement, Christians must unite and show our nation what civic and racial unity looks like. It is our calling to be upright and different, love our brothers and sisters, and seek restoration in broken relationships.

And for God's glory to be shown, Christians cannot take a back seat to the solutions society might derive. If we merely follow society's lead and direction, or, worse still, if we are part of the ongoing divisiveness that cripples social progress, God will be seen as an "also ran" in cultural restoration. Our churches and our God will be seen as no less political and every bit as worldly as the society we claim to be broken and in need of the God to whom we all allegedly belong.

If however, Christian blacks choose to avoid taking the lead role in these discussions, or refuse to support their brothers and sisters, the effort will be immediately shut down. Intransigence will be seen as tacit support for society's definitions by which all Christians, particularly Christian whites, and all whites are condemned. And thus, Christianity will remain tainted with hypocrisy and as racially divided as our society.

TRUSTING CHRISTIAN WHITES ON RACISM

Just those five words alone may make many Christian blacks pause and ask, "Are you crazy?? How can you know racism, stereotypes, prejudice, and hate if you've never felt it? How can you know what it's like to be looked at in a certain way or spoken to in a certain tone that exposes the speakers' negative, preconceived attitudes towards you? You've never had to have "The Talk" with your sons and daughters. You couldn't possibly detect what is directed at us any more than you can see radio waves!"

Well, truth is, we may not be able to without help. And we certainly won't have credibility on the issue without that help, given the vitriol coming from a society that directly accuses Christian whites of being the very racists blacks resent most. As discussed, the revised definitions of racism place an accusation squarely at the feet of Christian whites and, more generally but less specifically, all white people. Without an alliance that joins us firmly and permanently in brotherly Christian love, and without the alignment and agreement on the proper definitions of key terms, Christian whites will be left shouting our defenses to the winds of a society that hates what we all believe.

Thus, both groups, as Christians, will suffer as we are shunned as hypocrites, idiots, and liars. There are no good outcomes for Christian blacks from the stereotypes society has placed on Christian whites, whether historically justified or not. Christianity, the body of Christ, and the effectiveness of the church in society will be inherently diminished by the injuries inflicted on one part of the body of Christ. Just as in football, a great offense is of little good when the entire defensive squad is on the sidelines with injuries. There are only so many points the offense can score without help to prevent progress by the other team.

Of course, Christian whites must uprightly evaluate racism and its many roots and tendrils in our modern society. Christian whites then need to become society's "race police." Just as Christian blacks must be at the forefront of defining terminology, Christian whites must take our place as the only voice that can call racism as it is seen without being discounted as Jacks crying wolf or improperly using harmful terminology. Our voices will ring true, even as we confirm or deny racism's existence. Through upright dialogue, education, and historical perspectives, Christian blacks will be able to support their white brothers and sisters in our efforts to reclaim the moral high ground from those who have unjustly taken it and who fail to use it as Christ would.

Yes, there are now several nationally known groups who claim to speak for all blacks, such as Black Lives Matter. But too few are based on or espouse Christian principles. And few, if any, would support the notion of the unification of Christianity across racial boundaries. Therefore, you will need to come alongside Christian whites as they come alongside you. Stand shoulder to shoulder, have our backs just as we will have yours, and support our efforts as we take on new roles and new challenges within society.

Thus, all Christians of all races and creeds need to put aside politics, preconceived notions, and stereotypes, think deeply and discuss uprightly our past, present, and future. Both sides must evaluate old loyalties, whether political, social, or economic, if they conflict with our mission of unity in action and the will of God for our faith and our nation.

Of course, this will be more difficult than it sounds. But doing so will place Christians in a position of strength we have never seen before. Not since the first arrival of Christians to our shores hundreds of years ago have Christians possessed such unified strength through which they might challenge Satan's influence. Our unification has always been hindered, through both society's influence and our own sinfulness. Therefore, American Christianity has always been tainted with divisions. But now, using power of our unified numbers and the legitimizing impact of walking uprightly, we have a unique opportunity to put God in His rightful place and bring necessary change for our society.

FORGIVING

I was having lunch with a middle-aged, black pastor friend one weekday afternoon. Though I didn't attend his church, we came to know each other through charity work. As we munched on barbequed pork, we chatted about his congregation, his vision for the community around his church, and the fate of the city in which we both lived. Occasionally, perhaps not often enough, our conversations would shift to local and national racial politics and issues. Sometimes our opinions differed, often not.

As I told him about the idea for this book, he was curious about its purpose and target audience. As we discussed options, I asked him a simple question. "Before we go any further, I guess I need to ask a basic, fundamental question. Without knowing the answer to this question, there's not much point in writing one book or twenty. Can black folks and white folks ever live in harmony in this county?"

Almost without blinking, and unfortunately without any sarcasm or jest, he answered, "You mean the white folks who raped our daughters, lynched our

182

boys, and kept us in chains for two hundred years!? You mean THOSE white folks?!?"

Ouch, but yes, those white folks!

In many cases, of course, forgiveness has already happened. We see reconciliation at the workplace, in schools, and within and between some churches. Certainly, we see it in individual relationships among neighbors, friends, couples, colleagues, etc. In many ways, racial divisions have been significantly narrowed throughout our society.

Yet, we also continue to see evidence of how deeply divided we remain as a society and how scars can be so readily reopened. Think Ferguson, Baltimore, and Charlottesville, and the pending 2020 Presidential election. There is clear anger, frustration, and resentment in the black community which seems perfectly justifiable to many. Indeed, there are elements in our political and social systems that would prefer to see this resentment live on and the divisions continue and exacerbate. Instead of forgiveness, our society seems to prefer rage, vindication, harsh and sometimes false accusations, shaming, silencing, and even violence. When it comes to matters of racism, many in our nation are far more ready to accuse than to objectively investigate, much less forgive. And when a wrong has been done or an accusation made, the quick response is to score a permanent mark on the perpetrator and all those like him or her. By society's standard, no forgiveness is allowed. Thus, communications fail, our nation remains split, our children are raised in unnecessarily divisive environments, and our future as a nation looks less promising.

Moreover, there is a growing chorus of Christian authors, pundits, pastors, and professors who are using the tainted history of the American white Christian church to demonize both previous generations and modern-day Christian whites. Their messages often include calls for not only the acknowledgement of the sins of the past but acknowledgement of rampant current racism within the Christian white community as well as monetary, social, and emotional compensation from white churches. Recommendations include the payment of reparations by whites churches, funding of black church plants, etc. Yet, even if these demands seem reasonable and fair, there are no concurrent calls for forgiveness, unity, and collaboration to show society a more Christ-like way to love, interact, and find solutions to problems. Thus, though their intentions may be pure, their approaches seem to mimic society's rather than those that would strengthen our faith and encourage our potential to reach an increasingly lost society.

This is where the Christian black church must again step up and into the fray. In the chapter to Christian whites, it was recommended that they do as was done in the story of Nehemiah and pray for the forgiveness of their own sins as well as the "sins of [their] Fathers." You probably already know the passage well, but here's a quick recap (in case you didn't read the chapter meant specifically for Christian whites, as this story was directed toward them).

The city of Jerusalem had been attacked and torn down, its gates burned, and its people scattered some 150 years prior to the arrival of Nehemiah and Ezra (in 586 B.C., described in 2 Kings 24). The remnants of the population finally began to return years later and had rebuilt the temple (between 535 B.C. and 516 B.C.) However, the city and its people were still at risk of attack and persecution because the walls of the city had not been reconstructed. When Nehemiah finally returned, some 150 years after the previous destruction of the city, he was deeply disturbed to see the condition of the city and its walls and gates.

Immediately, Nehemiah went to Jehovah in prayer. The Bible tells us that he "mourned for days, fasting and praying before the God of heaven" (Nehemiah 1:4). Yet, in the brief recorded summation of his undoubtedly countless prayers, he doesn't start by praying for a miracle, or as a member of the chosen people of God, or for God's wrath upon the enemies of God's people, or as a God-sent messenger with a task to accomplish. Rather, his prayer is mainly one of supplication and admission of sin. From Nehemiah 1:5-7:

> *"⁵O Lord God of heaven, the great and awesome God*
> *who keeps His covenant and steadfast love with*
> *those who love Him and keep His commandments;*
> *⁶let your ear be attentive and your eyes open to hear*
> *the prayer of your servant that I now pray before you*
> *day and night for your servants the people of Israel,*
> *confessing the sins of the people of Israel, which we*
> *have sinned against you. Both I and my family have*
> *sinned. ⁷We have offended you deeply, failing to keep*
> *the commandments, the statutes, and the ordinances*
> *that you commanded your servant Moses."*

Despite being sent on a proverbial "mission from God" to rebuild the city's walls, he starts off with and clearly states his own sin. Furthermore, and importantly for this discussion, he confesses the sins of his people and the sins of his father's family.

Only at the end of this prayer, after these admissions of generational wrongs, does Nehemiah ask for God's assistance and blessing on the task at hand. Verse 1:11 reads: "Give your servant success today by granting him favor in the presence of this man." Nehemiah's prayer is a simple confession of generational sin from which the state of the city had come, followed only at the end by a request for success in the task to which he had been assigned.

This admission of guilt and the guilt of past generations as a focal point of prayer continues in Chapter 9, even after the walls are rebuilt and there is much to celebrate. In Nehemiah 9:2, all the Jews came together in worship and, wearing sackcloth and with dust on their heads, professed their sins and the sins of their ancestors. Nehemiah 9:16 tells of the Levite priests speaking of their ancestors' sins, describing them as "arrogant and stiff-necked."

Thus, even after perhaps hundreds of years and a successful reconstruction of the temple, the city and its protective walls, there is an ongoing admission that the sins of past generations had led to the miserable state of affairs from which they had been finally delivered, including the exile of the Jews and the destruction of Jerusalem. Furthermore, there was the admission that the current sins of the Jews were not to be excused, as if the past sins were a warning to the current and future generations.

I have therefore strongly recommended that Christian whites step forward and ask for the collective forgiveness of past sins of our predecessors. To my knowledge, Christian whites have never come together in a way that recognizes the sins of our past and present while calling for unity around specific actions that could impact our society, our children, and our faith.

But likewise, Christian blacks need to pray for whatever is necessary so that you can forgive your Christian brethren. Whites know the sins of the hearts of past generations of our people, including Christian whites. But only Christian blacks can speak to any such sins in their own hearts, whether past or present, that may prevent forgiveness and the ultimate unity of Christians across racial boundaries.

And, as a result, you may need to examine your own hearts and seek out those thoughts, resentments, hostilities, and feelings that you harbor towards whites and, whether directly or indirectly, Christian whites. These feelings may be perfectly justifiable in the eyes of men. But just as Christian whites may need deep introspection, cleansing, and healing, so too may some Christian blacks.

And in some communities, where deep separation exists, forgiveness may need to come even before repentance from Christian whites. Even if only to draw attention to the need for Christian unity, the Christian black church

185

needn't always wait for Christian whites to act. Christian blacks still need to pray for healing for our nation and thereby help their Christian white brethren move down the unification path. So, whether in response to repentance or initiating action through the forgiveness of the sins of past the current generations, the Christian black church will need to take bold and meaningful steps if unity is to have any impact on our nation. Repent as you need and forgive as God leads you to do.

Yet, even with unity among Christians, no one is under the illusion that hate and racism will suddenly cease to exist. Even if all Christians come together united in action against them, hate and racism may never be completely extinguished, any more than any other sin of the minds of men. Though our united efforts will surely help promote its demise, no one should be surprised if evil continues until Christ comes again.

But as we all know, hate does not justify more hate, certainly not from Christ's perspective. You already know the great quotes of Dr. Martin Luther King, Jr. on this matter. Were hate justifiable, Christians of the early church would have been angry warriors and murderers rather than martyrs and missionaries, given the crimes committed against them. And just because racism continues to exist does not mean that we must succumb to its pull and divide our churches along the same lines as society. Instead, all Christians should set the example for the rest of society by rejecting the very hatred, resentment and divisiveness that racism has and continues to spawn.

This is not an easy request. Indeed, this is not forgiving "seventy times seven," but seventy million times seven or more! For many, it is a nearly impossible feat given that these sins and the results of previous sins continue into our current age, and the sheer number of people impacted over hundreds of years. Certainly, given the current political environment, forgiveness is being made even harder.

But by not being at the forefront of this issue, the American Christian church, both black and white, has failed to take a proper role in social transformation, evolution, and healing. Thus, we are missing great opportunities to show Christ to our very broken world.

Therefore, this step is necessary as both a means of healing for the Christian community and a means to open up collaborative opportunities with the Christian white community. We, as Christians, cannot stand shoulder to shoulder if we have not come to terms on the very issues that have and continue to divide us.

Make it public

Nehemiah didn't ask the Jews to go home and pray for forgiveness in the privacy of their bedrooms. He brought them all together, in the bright light of day, to pray in front of everyone. Nehemiah knew the power of collective prayer and the power of groups of people under the same accord to create change and maintain momentum. He asked the people to make their feelings public.

Furthermore, we are told that we are to come together, as Christians, to commune with one another. This brings energy, support, love, and a sense of belonging to our day to day lives. Such gatherings are particularly important when specific issues are to be addressed, just as in the times of Nehemiah. Our efforts to unite as a Christian body of Christ must therefore be made publicly, unabashedly, and confidently. Whether gathering to create mutually agreed definitions of racism, dialogue on social issues, rhetoric towards each other, the collective repentance of the Christian white church, or the actions we choose to take in our communities, ours must be a public display of God's love for His people and all those in society. Our actions, done with Christ-like uprightness, will shine our light to a dark, lost, and ever-seeking world. But to do so, we must make our efforts public.

Think of a meeting of Christians in the town square. Think of keeping your church doors closed on a Sunday morning and instead meeting fellow brothers and sisters in a parade of faith through the middle of town. Think of communing in your local high school football stadium. Or better yet, imagine filling a professional sports stadium with Christians united to ask and receive forgiveness and unify in action.

Imagine what might happen if we all could come together in such a fashion! Just imagine!

OUTREACH

It is preposterous to say that outreach can only go in one direction and a fool's stereotype to assume that white folk always need to start the conversation with their black brethren. Why do some of us assume that black folk should not lead the way on outreach and collaboration on society's issues, particularly those so important to our churches and our children? Nonsense! Everyone has God-given gifts, talents and abilities and we should take advantage of every passion for God's callings.

My point here is simple. Nothing says that Christian blacks shouldn't be the ones to initiate the outreach to their white brethren. Maybe this happens far more often than many know, but one could see how this might be constrained

187

given the history of whites' efforts towards collaboration. If the Christian white churches would learn from the thinking in this book, they should be ready to humbly and graciously collaborate if the community writ large will be helped.

This kind of collaboration will be particularly important given the issues that God's American church must tackle. Justice, race, education, and health are not issues that one church or even one race can solve on its own. These are complex issues requiring the uprightness of Christians and their passion for both Christ and those around them.

Yet, according to my black pastor friends, this is a particularly difficult challenge. Asking black churches to offer aid or leadership to white churches seems almost nonsensical, given the previous relationships. But our tainted history should not stop Christian blacks from taking the initiative and leading all Christians towards our brighter future. By taking the initiative, starting the conversations, and leading the way, Christian blacks can show the way of the future, teaching both society and many Christian whites that forgiveness, collaboration, and harnessing the miracles of the power of God are as possible as a handshake.

Note that this does not mean simply taking initiative within your own communities. Clearly, that already happens! Instead, this means reaching out to Christian whites with whom you may never have collaborated before, or with whom previous collaborative efforts yielded poor results. This means "going big" and moving outside our church and community silos to break down the walls of the silos that surround white congregations to align interests, develop working relationships, and tap the latent power of our unity in action. Never forget that we have a very big God who can do some very big things!

It is therefore vital that Christian blacks take initiative not just in their own communities but reach out to engender solidarity with their white brethren.

Outreach to break down our many silos should not be difficult or strange. It should become the norm on both sides of the racial aisle.

ACCEPTING PARTNERSHIPS

Based on my conversations with fellow brothers and sisters, it seems that black folks have had issues with white folks trying to swoop in to do good things. While their hearts may be in the right place, it seems that white folks tend to want to come in and take over. This, naturally, leads to issues of dignity and resentment that comes from a seeming condescension towards "black communities in need."

One example that comes quickly to mind is a large, suburban, all-white church that tried to "adopt" a small, downtown all-black church. Through funding and other generous means, the whites supported the "adopted" black church for several years before the relationship fell apart. Small wonder that the effort ultimately failed, since the very concept of "adoption" implies a superior entity taking on the custody and care of a lesser entity. We adopt babies and helpless children, not able, capable adults! So, not surprisingly, the term "adopt" is itself was likely considered condescending.

This can also lead to what some have called toxic charity.[lxx] Toxic charity and similar concepts have demonstrated the unintended consequences of the well-intentioned, help in recipient communities. Those consequences include unemployment, financial dependency, and a dearth of entrepreneurship, ideation, and creativity in problem-solving. Essentially, if charitable organizations swoop in and do the necessary work, it leaves communities without the skills, resources, and problem-solving capabilities to fix their own current and future problems. Proponents of the toxic charity concept[lxxi] state that charity can ultimately do more harm than good. In the context of Christian collaboration, the toxicity comes in part because the supposed benefactors of the assistance come to resent the givers for their superior attitudes, lack of cultural awareness, and real or implied condescension. Thus, the "swoop in and take over" resentment in black communities has caused unintended, but legitimate, resentment and resistance.

So, as you develop partnerships and align to address key social problems, you need to work with your white brothers and sisters to ensure that the roles they play will be appropriate for needs required and are sensitive to the history of similar efforts. The roles of white churches may be little more than getting white folks to show up in greater numbers at School Board meetings in support of initiatives that will help kids in predominantly black communities and schools.

Or, it may be little more than standing up against urban renewal programs that displace black communities and businesses in favor of strip malls and boutique coffee shops.

Or, it could mean working in inner-city homeless shelters alongside Christian black churches, rather than parallel to them, to stop the incarceration of the mentally ill.

Regardless, the approach needs to be different than it has been in the past.

Yet, it is important for the Christian black community to remember that it is not productive to shut out partnership offers just because the offers come from Christian whites. I have seen this happen in my own efforts to volunteer in black communities, so I know just how real this attitude can be. While perhaps caused by bad history, shutting yourselves off and fortifying your own silo walls will not get the job done. It will only make the desired results more difficult to obtain.

And of course, there will be issues that communities can manage without the assistance of other churches, whether of the same or a different race. The bigger issues, however, will need all the power that unity in action can muster.

Therefore, both communities must be open to communicating their needs such that confusion does not arise. This is where upright dialogue leads to important discussions on the importance of unification, alignment, and the power of the use of all the elements of the body of Christ. Each brings their own skills, capabilities, and God-given talents to the efforts. And each should be allowed to use those for the greater cause without concern for their race, which church or side of town they come from, or who their pastor is, or who is running things.

The issues that we need to address (education, racism, justice, and health) are huge and complex, with God-size solutions. Petty squabbles about who is doing what should not impede our efforts. Rather, if we see ourselves as individual components in a larger body that is trying to attack a much larger problem, we will find that our race doesn't matter as much as our willingness to serve someone other than ourselves and our personal interests, motivations, and egos.

We must be loyal to the cause, not loyal to our pastors, congregations, and churches.

DO WE HAVE AN OPTION?

And really, do we, as Christians, have a choice but to unite? As we see society erode, honesty and integrity become contextualized, and truth become evasive, there is a void in our society's heart into which something will flow. Who else has the power and the calling to show society how to live uprightly? Who else is called to come together in such vast numbers, 200 million and more strong, to address important social issues? What other group, political party, or entity has the singular light towards which we walk, and which guides our lives, thoughts, and activities? And what other mass of people has more motivation to address a decaying society that threatens the futures of our precious children?

Christians must necessarily become THE voice of objectivity, honesty, and integrity in all manner of these issues. Through our uprightness and collaboration, we will all constantly strive towards our goals of dramatically impacting our society for the glory of God.

BUMPS IN THE ROAD

Will we stumble along the way? Of course! This is a rough road we take, and our alliances will mostly be new. This will not be like love at first sight. Rather, there will be errors, mishaps, and our worldly mistakes all along this path to collaboration.

And, of course, our society, such that they notice, will take note of these stumbles even as it challenges any progress we might make. They will mock and do their best to divide whatever unity we can muster. Ours will be a constant struggle to stand together, firm against the howling winds of a society determined to see us fail.

Yet, stumble we will! And we must take each stumble as an opportunity, each error as a learning experience, and each failure as another step down this long path to which we have committed. Better to stumble and bumble our way down this road than to stand at the starting line and argue.

We must be doers. We must "do different." And we must "do" together.

SUMMARY

None of this would even be remotely possible were it not for our God from whom we draw our strength, our power, and our passions. Only through Christ, and living uprightly as He showed us to live, can these things be achieved. Only through Christ can society be turned for the better. And only through our unity in Him can God be glorified.

Forgiveness for decades of previous and ongoing injustices, accepting assistance from those who used to look down on you, trusting Christian whites to work with you to objectively seek out and destroy current racial injustice, and conducting outreach to those who once rejected you is difficult to say the least. But certainly not impossible.

For God's church to take its rightful place in society and thereby bring glory to God, new hope to the lost and new believers to our faith, we must cross seemingly impenetrable boundaries and break down silos hardened by mistreatment, frustrations, and society's influences. We must come together as a body of Christ rather than small pieces of the whole, united in action, to impact our society with a strength in numbers not seen before in our nation's history.

Only through this will we see God glorified and in His rightful place in our society.

CONSIDERATIONS FOR UNITY

¹Therefore if you have any encouragement from being united with Christ, if any comfort from his love, if any common sharing in the Spirit, if any tenderness and compassion, ²then make my joy complete by being like-minded, having the same love, being one in spirit and of one mind. ³Do nothing out of selfish ambition or vain conceit. Rather, in humility value others above yourselves, ⁴not looking to your own interests but each of you to the interests of the others. ⁵In your relationships with one another have the same mindset as Christ Jesus. (Philippians 2: 1-5)

CONSIDERATIONS FOR UNITED CHRISTIANS

Now that we have covered some considerations for both Christian blacks and whites as you move towards uniting in action for the glory of God and the betterment of our society, we need to cover some mutual considerations. Christians can do great things when they bring forth their hearts and minds in the spirit of God. Through unified focus, we can amplify our current and latent resources for the issues at hand, showing our hate-filled, anti-Christian society what Christian uprightness looks like while bringing glory to God through unity action. With our passion and our convictions, we must bring a restorative dignity to those we serve through which they will come to know that they, too, are precious and valued in the eyes of almighty God.

DOING GOOD AND NOT SO GOOD

Working in other communities with which we are unfamiliar can be fraught with unforeseen issues, especially when the local churches and entities are not fully engaged. While we want to do good works as we are led to do by the Holy Spirit and the blessings of our salvation, this is not as easy as showing up with a smile, a Bible and some work clothes.

In order to be as effective and efficient as possible, it is important to engage with those local to the problem we seek to address. This might seem a no-brainer, but it is not uncommon to see churches diving into communities without working with Christians already in that community.

And the more difficult the issue, the more we need to engage with local entities. Certainly, when trying to address justice, healthcare, or race, our efforts are far less likely to succeed without the full and passionate engagement of all the resources in the targeted community.

Therefore, with our compassion and desires to help we must also bring the dignity and respect that will allow those in need to help themselves and someday help others. All are precious in the eyes of God. And we must bring this attitude with us in every endeavor we undertake.

In the end, if we think about it, many of those we try to serve generally don't need us. They need God and His restorative power. Our role is simply to be tools that God can use to help those in need. Thus, we can be hammers, screwdrivers, shovels, and saws. But we should take no claim in the finished work, since our role is that of a tool in the hands of the Master Craftsman.

Furthermore, pretending that we, as Christians, can somehow ride in to save the day for the needy, like the Allies into WWII Germany, is foolishness. We must recognize that all our efforts are for naught if God isn't first and foremost in our hearts and minds, and if local Christian leaders are not leading the way in their own communities. Yes, we can come alongside. Yes, we can provide support, power to the unpowered, boots for kicking down barriers, and logistical and other support. We can unite in common causes for the glory of God and the betterment of our society. Indeed, we are explicitly called to do this in God's Holy word.

But it is God's work, not ours. And it is through doing the will of God in united action that will bring the dignity that is so vital here.

THE POWER OF DIGNITY

Dignity is not mentioned often in our Bible, but it is an important concept both biblically and in our society. When it is referenced, dignity is twice being taken away. In the Book that bears his name Job's dignity was "driven away as by the wind" as people ridiculed his terrible situation and the circumstances into which Satan had cast him. He was friendless, having lost everything from his livelihood to his family. Even his wife mocked his continued faith. His dignity, as a man, a citizen, and businessman, had been swept away.

In Proverbs 5:9, young men are warned away from the lustful attractions of adulteresses "lest you lose … your dignity to one who is cruel." Thus, dignity is lost when sin enters, and Satan overtakes.

In Exodus 28, the Lord commanded that Aaron and his sons be made priests and adorned with robes of the finest materials "to give them dignity and honor." Thus, honor and dignity can go together, speaking to the sense of self-worth and uprightness that dignity affords.

And think also of the attempt to rob Jesus of his dignity throughout the day of His crucifixion. He was stripped of His clothes, paraded through town and a gauntlet of mockers, made to wear a crown of thorns, spat upon, and hung on a cross. There was no human dignity offered in His death.

Today, throughout our society, there is a dearth of dignity, particularly amongst the poor and minority communities. This helps explain at least some, if not much, of the behaviors and social trends we see in modern society. Hyper-sexuality, gang membership, violence, disrespect for women, rebelliousness, and general anti-social behavior can be traced back, at least in part, to the need for and the lack of provision of some form of dignity.

For instance, in working with at-risk teenagers, volunteer leaders will profess that dignity is an important element in relationship building, trust, and good behavior. Teens who've lacked dignity in their lives crave it and are highly sensitive to any affronts to the dignity they have and seek.

Similarly, those who deal with the working poor will consistently profess that their clients routinely quit solid, well-paying jobs because a manager or boss disrespects them. Some may think it foolish, but the denial of dignity cuts people deeply thereby causing them to act in ways that might seem self-defeating. If dignity is damaged, threatened or taken away, a visceral, negative reaction results which can limit their future interactions with the rest of the culture. By contrast, a man, woman or child who has dignity can rise above the fray.

Dignity comes not from taking a handout or having someone else do the work for you, but rather from the work of change itself. Charity does not typically offer dignity, hence the term "toxic charity".[lxxii] Dignity comes when the hand that helps lets go, allowing the recipients to do for themselves. There is even great value in failure, for from failure comes learning. And that learning, and the successes that rise from prior failures, yields the dignity necessary to move forward.

Thus, it is important to keep in mind that we must offer the same "dignity and honor" to all with whom we work. As Christians, this should not be hard given what we know of the pure equality of God's grace. Yet, it is an easy concept to forget, particularly when we are dealing with people in far different socioeconomic conditions. It is perhaps easier to feel pity than to offer dignity. But we can only walk beside or behind those with whom we share dignity.

Therefore, if Christians are constantly solving for issues in poor communities, whether mixed, black, or white, without the leadership and intense and full cooperation of the members of those communities, more than dignity can be lost. Trust, leadership, self-satisfaction, and relationships are also at risk. If we are to team with our brothers and sisters to work in all our communities to fix the major problems of the day that plague our entire society, then we must be equal partners.

Moreover, we must step aside and offer assistance without insisting on commanding leadership. And this requires us to stand together, shoulder to shoulder, side by side. In many cases, Christians will need to simply support the existing efforts within these communities rather than bring our own.

Regardless, always keep in mind that the role of the Christian church may not be to lead when working outside its community. We will likely need to follow and do what we can to aid the efforts of others.

STEPPING OUT

Solving for society's intractable issues, whether the four mentioned throughout this book or others, requires all Christians to step outside of their churches and go out into the communities of others. Of course, we do this through myriad local ministries, every week of every year. Rare is the church that doesn't do something for those in its community, whether providing food, shelter, clothing, resources, education, etc. But we typically do these things from within our silos, meaning that these activities may be less effective than they could be. To change this, you must unify with like-minded Christians in churches throughout your community and in the communities you seek to serve.

So, if yours is a predominantly white church in the heart of a large city, you will need to move outside your walls into other communities where unity with the power of other churches can enhance what you are already doing or would like to do.

Likewise, if you are in a small town or rural community, where segregation in the church long ago ended by melding people of all races and creeds together, you need to move outside of your church's walls to align with other, like-minded congregations and find targets for actions for the good of your entire community.

And if you happen to live in a segregated community, where whites and blacks have long been divided into racial enclaves, you'll need to work hard to find ways to build bridges into and throughout those divided communities, using activity as a link to engage fellow Christians throughout local congregations. Or, if yours is a suburban church, one of several in your area, you'll need to determine how best to combine the strength of your current and latent resources to bring the power of unity to the efforts of all the surrounding churches.

Of course, that does not mean that Christians should abandon the work in their own communities and congregations in favor of other communities, or discontinue the missions, charity, and other works for which the church, generally, is well known. To the contrary, these efforts should be continued and may even be enhanced by the alignment of goals and the efficiencies gained through unity.

Moreover, it is foolishness, though perhaps errantly stereotypical, to think that white communities face no troubles or issues, or that only minority communities have issues or need help. Whites, including Christian whites, do not live trouble-free lives in isolated bubbles of happiness and joy. As a recent example, the epidemic of opioids and heroine has hit whites harder than minorities. Teenage suicide, divorce, drugs and alcohol, poor education, injustices, poverty, and myriad other issues find their way into every corner of our society. Everyone struggles with something, and all communities need help in some way.

In order to address the root causes of key social issues in all communities, Christians need unity in action to bring their power to the problems. This means both working in your own communities as well as other communities wherein help is needed, regardless of ethnicity. And this is why both power and focus are so important.

Bringing your power to the problem

It is said that there are two kinds of organized power. Organized money and organized people. The first and most commonly cited is the power of organized money. As seen in politics, for instance, organized money buys access and desired outcomes, pushing causes and opportunities that will generate more money, influence, and power. Whether on the left or the right, political power is constantly wielded through the influence of money.

Likewise, consider the power of organized money in marketing and messaging, where money buys access to an audience through which influence, preferences, and thought patterns can be created or molded. Or the organized money in crime and evil whereby, for instance, drug traffickers and other criminals use their deep pockets to buy the weapons of violence, overtake neighborhoods, and buy the subservience of corrupt police and politicians in other countries.

Then there is the power of organized people. Collectively, people can bring power in democratic societies, even if they don't bring pockets full of cash. The power of people is in their collective voices, united around specific issues, causes, and messages. Throughout history, the power of the people has been shown to be irresistible.

Of course, this people power can be used for either good or evil, depending on the group or those directing the group. History is replete with examples of both the power of the people to do both evil and good. Think of the power of people to do good as reflected in the American Civil Rights movement versus the power of the people to do evil in communist and socialist revolutions, riots and mob violence, or the scourge of radical Islam. All were led by impassioned leaders, and all harnessed the power of mass groups, yet the purposes and outcomes were very different. Some movements led to social progress, others led to destruction, death, torture, slavery, and subservience. Millions have been freed, and millions have suffered and died, through the use of the power of people.

But when put to God's use, the power of organized Christians can do great things. Across the country and throughout our history, churches have organized their power to address issues. Think of the Great Awakenings through which millions were brought to the word of God. More recently, organized churches have fought for or against various issues and policies of our society, from civil justice to charter schools. Often, these were localized efforts, focused on specific issues of the day, rather than prolonged and sustained efforts. But regardless of the example, we see that there is power in organized people.

And we all know that God speaks of our spiritual gifts, notably in 1 Corinthians 12. God calls us to use the gifts, talents and all available means to serve the body of Christ. And in this context, we will all need to assess and inventory our gifts, talents, and resources so that we can better gauge the aggregate capacity we have to address the problems we face. We can do this on an individual basis as well as a congregational basis. This will help the community of churches understand their aggregate capacity to impact local community interests, select targets for interventions, and avoid over-committing valuable volunteer resources.

Some will use their talents, others will contribute their time, some will use their political and social influence, and still others will use their God-given wealth. For example, a pastor of a white church in a relatively affluent area of a southern town once told me, "We don't have huge numbers, but we have power." That is, his congregation included lawyers, doctors, judges, and prominent businesspeople in his city. "We can bring that to the fight," he proclaimed.

So, even though our churches don't have the billion-dollar revenues of publicly traded companies, or the money of billionaires to buy access to the circles of the rich and powerful where deals are made and influence peddled, we have roughly 54 million Americans regularly in our congregations with another roughly 150 – 200 million claiming Christ as Savior.

As we have seen, however, we are locked in our 350,000 silos, making our work less effective than it should be. Thus, in order to better tap into this enormous power source, we must break down historical racial, doctrinal, and denominational barriers in order to bring Christians together once again such that we can exert the power of our people in the doing of the will of God. The key is to direct those people, en masse and in localized groups, to become power by focusing on a few, important issues and problems of our society.

If we, as Christian black and white churches, are united towards common goals in our communities and guided by our uprightness and the spirit of God, then we will know how best to allocate resources, utilize our power, and attack the enemies in the culture.

Unified, our collective role may be simply kicking down the barriers that stand in the way of justice, or education of our children, or the development of effective healthcare solutions. We can use the influence of both black and white communities and churches and the power of people to make a way for those who need their paths cleared, while allowing them to walk that path with or ahead of us, not behind us.

This is why unity is so important. Through the aggregation of our capacities to serve, we will find more resources with more talents, passions, ideas, and creative solutions than we will as individual small groups or congregations. A united group of churches, all moving towards the same goals, is simply more powerful and accomplishes much more, more quickly than single churches and siloed efforts.

Focus and alignment

By focusing on a few key issues and their root causes, we can use our numbers to create great movements of change. We should seek to focus on issues that a) we, as united Christians, can impact, b) we can impact without large financial investments, c) will impact our society and thus bring glory to God, d) will impact multiple communities, not just our own, and e) will draw non-Christians into the effort.

Of the myriad issues we might be facing, those discussed herein (race, education, healthcare, and justice) are consistently present in communities throughout the nation. These are issues of interest not just to Christians but to all people of all creeds and backgrounds. Importantly, they commonly need only the power of people to help direct the solutions rather than millions or billions of dollars of investments.

Focusing will also help us align more quickly and consistently. Focus will help us create internal and external momentum as people see our unity in action. Our momentum will create new energies and bring in new volunteers and alignments with other like-minded individuals and groups. We will thereby be stronger, able to stand up to the forces that will no doubt be arrayed against us.

Thus, focus brings alignment. Alignment brings attention, as we show ourselves as a broader and deeper force. Attention brings even more people to join in our efforts. And as we grow, our organized people bring more and more power.

PUSHBACK

But as we succeed in uniting Christians across racial lines, some members of our worldly society simply will not like it. Normally, unity and common cause between blacks and whites for nearly any reason would be a great thing. But many will push back not because we are blacks and whites working together, since that happens every day throughout our society, workplaces, neighborhoods, and community organizations. Instead, they will react negatively because we are *Christian* blacks and *Christian* whites coming together.

Though they shouldn't, there are many groups and individuals who will fear what our unity will do, what our numbers will achieve, and the glory we will bring to the God we worship. Even as we target important community issues such as justice and education, they will worry that our future targets will include something precious to them, whether a social or political cause, their power and prestige, or long-held beliefs. Or, they may simply fear Christianity's influence. Think unfettered access to abortion, gay marriage, or transgender acceptance.

And thus, we must be ready to defend against an inevitable onslaught of derision, harsh reactions, horrible accusations, and every kind of barrier. For this, the Bible offers another valuable analogy for us as we try to predict and prepare for the reactions of those whose positions and power we will threaten.

The lessons again come from Nehemiah and the unusual way in which the people were forced to work as they rebuilt the walls of the city and replaced its mighty gates.

As the story is told, the Jews were gathered and focused on a singular task: the rebuilding of the walls of the city. Like our soon-to-be-unified body of Christ, their Jewish body was made up of groups of Jews, organized as families, each assigned to its role in rebuilding the various important wall sections and gates.

Throughout the story of the rebuilding of the walls of the city, Nehemiah describes the anger and resistance of local tribes and people. The Bible tells us that as the word of the initial rebuilding effort spread, so did the resistance from the local tribal leaders. They feared a strong city wherein the Jews could live, defend themselves, and expand their population and influence. This resistance grew quickly into plotting for attacks against the Jews rebuilding the walls.

Nehemiah 4:8 reads, "They [Sanballat, Tobiah, the Arabs, the Ammonites and the people of Ashdod] all plotted together to come and fight against Jerusalem and stir up trouble against it." In verse 11, Nehemiah tells us, "Also our enemies said, 'Before they know it or see us, we will be right there among them and will kill them and put an end to the work.'" Thus, the Jews faced significant external threats from the tribes and peoples who did not want to see them succeed in their plans.

Furthermore, Nehemiah 4:19 reads "The work is extensive and spread out, and we are widely separated from each other along the wall." Imagine small groups of Jews working on specific areas of the wall, spread all around the circumference of a city the size of old Jerusalem. By necessity and the requirements of the project, they could not be united in one large group, which would be harder and more costly to attack. Rather, they were spread out along the walls in small family clusters, making them more vulnerable to attacks which could severely hamper or stop the entire effort.

To combat these threats, the Jews needed to protect both their work and themselves. In Nehemiah 4:16 - 18 Nehemiah writes "¹⁶From that day on, half of my men did the work, while the other half were equipped with spears, shields, bows and armor. The officers posted themselves behind all the people of Judah [17]who were building the wall. Those who carried materials did their work with one hand and held a weapon in the other, [18]and each of the builders wore his sword at his side as he worked."

And to deal with the distance between families and the spread of groups around the city, the text also tells us that the workers needed a plan in case of an attack against one area or family. Nehemiah 4:20 reads "Wherever you [the Jewish people] hear the sound of the trumpet, join us there. Our God will fight for us!"

Thus, the Jewish people, united to rebuild their city and its walls, were forced by threats of external attacks to remain armed and vigilant against those who would attack them. The work would go on, but with the added effort, cost, and stress of ever-present physical threats. This was no small feat, and required significant collaboration, cooperation, planning, and foresight.

Do you already see the analogies? We, as Christians, are rebuilding a city ... a society ... a nation. And like the Jews of this Biblical story, we have sinned in our past by what we have done and what we have failed to do. Our fathers sinned against their brothers and sisters, and we against ours.

Just as the small Jewish clans and families were spread out along the great circumference of the city, we are some 350,000 individual congregations spread throughout the country, in disparate communities in disparate denominations.

And like these Jews, we will be up against powerful forces which will seek to stop us. Therefore, we need to be just as prepared to face what might be a scaled and united onslaught should we unite for the singular task of rebuilding our Jerusalem. If we are ill-prepared, we will surely be defeated.

Sources of attack

Notice in verse 4:7, the clans that quickly aligned against the Jews. Horonites, Ammonites, Arabs, and Ashdodites. While these might have been otherwise peaceful but disparate neighbors living separate lives in separate societies, they quickly came together against the Jews. Similarly, groups and organizations once independent and unrelated will quickly join forces against the work we choose to do.

Attacks will most certainly come from moneyed interests whose power, influence, and funding our proposals and ideas might expose or threaten. All you need to do is look at efforts to create institutional change in the education, justice, and healthcare systems to see how quickly those entrenched interests come together, circle their wagons and launch coordinated defensive counterattacks. And the politicians who are supported by these moneyed interests and loyal voting blocs will use their legal and political power to throw roadblocks in our paths.

Just as we try to array our people power for good, so too will our opposition array its power towards us.

Maintaining the racial status quo

Many alliances between Christians are looked upon with some scorn and caution, as shown when any of us rise to challenge modern social injustice, moral corruption, deviance, and sinfulness. But an alliance between Christian blacks and Christian whites may draw special ire from many who are bent on maintaining the racial status quo, miring us down in our imperfect, racially divided history, and, consciously or not, keeping Christians siloed and far less impactful.

There are those in both the black and white communities who are quite content with racial divisions, regardless of the impact on society and our children. They may want to keep racial separation and animosity in place because, for various reasons, it benefits them politically, financially, and/or socially.

Whether political pundits, popular political groups, social justice organizations, old-school ignorant racists, or those professionally and personally committed to certain political and social beliefs, there are plenty of people who benefit from the disunity of the races. For them, racial unity would mean a loss of influence, power, and prestige, and the end of their notoriety and popularity.

Similarly, some within all these groups will oppose what they see as the deceptive salve of an elusive equality and harmony between the races. Resentment causes some to feel that whites must take a secondary position due to the history of subjugation of minorities, as a sort of payback for the sins of the past and present. For them, whites deserve to be made under-privileged so as to allow others to prosper in the absence of white oppression.

For some of these people, benignly seeing skin color is not only an unachievable dream but one that is now wrong-headed. Rather, they believe that external cultural and ethnic differences must always define who we are and our value relative to others. Without these traits as primary factors, the reasons for varying social, political, and economic outcomes have no legitimate, singular, and acceptable cause.

Of course, God's vision of oneness and sameness is antithetical to this viewpoint. The very notion of a society in which one's character defines who we are is no longer acceptable or even a goal. Instead, the goal has become differentiation such that many groups and sub-groups can constantly be pitted against each other, with characteristics rather than character becoming the single root cause of all negative outcomes.

This, in turn, helps justify everything from sexual choices to hatred of others and helps insulate personal decisions from scrutiny. This also allows history rather than the future to define us. Recall from previous pages that society does not allow for forgiveness. Rather than seek reconciliation and improvement, society continues to seek to punish for mistakes that may have happened decades ago.

Similarly, society asks us to focus on historical racism rather than any racial progress made. This, too, keeps God's notion of oneness and unification at bay, since keeping the past the focus of the present keeps prior sins alive, inhibiting us from becoming what God would have us be.

Ironically, many of these people will speak of racial harmony while promulgating the very lies, misconceptions and stereotypes that society uses to keep the races apart. Using misconceptions of whites and Christianity, they continue to demonize traditional social norms as oppressive and support the notion that all whites are racists. Moreover, rather than admit that change can happen and that their way of thinking must eventually pass away along with racism itself, they continue to highlight any and all gaps that remain while discounting and minimizing any progress made.

Many of these impassioned people have the best of intentions in continuing to highlight what they consider to be ongoing racial injustices. Yet their efforts to spotlight racism inadvertently helps society discount any improvements and deny any non-racial root causes for current social, economic, and political circumstances. This encourages the blaming of only one villain. Society will therefore typically point to our racist history rather than our potential future, past sins rather than future collaboration, and highlight any incident involving race as testament to a complete and total lack of societal progress. In the end, this breeds suspicion rather than promoting trust.

Anti-Christians

Of course, attacks will come from those who were and are anti-Christian, or at least anti-Christian-white-male. They will see our unity as a threat to their way of life, their freedom to make personal, sexual, and communal choices, and their social influence. Their allegiance to non-Christian values, social mores, and personal choices and the stereotypes of Christian white men will result in many choosing the wrong side, even if society might benefit from the work Christians will do.

The disdain for Christians and Christianity may be so strong that it will even cause them to oppose the very unity that they may have worked for in the past. Even if we do not seek to change or influence the issues and causes they hold to so dearly, such as abortion or transgender recognition, they will see any foothold that Christians might gain as an eventual threat to their personal, social, or sexual interests.

Thus, even if we do not challenge their interests directly, as if almost by habit and without consideration of our actual goals and objectives, they will nonetheless join in opposition to our efforts.

Furthermore, as some lifestyle and sexual choice advocacy groups have co-opted the Civil Rights mantra, it is critical to their success that blacks and whites remain separated and in conflict. If blacks and whites come together, by whatever means and to whatever extent possible, these groups lose many of their fellow culture warriors, leaving them to fight for their causes with far fewer allies and far less political power. If they lose the original Civil Rights fighters, particularly those whose influence in the Movement was so strong, they become isolated minorities fighting for their personal sexual and moral choices rather than fighting for what they would like us to see as their God-given rights.

Attacks from within our races

And from within the ranks of the two races, there will no doubt also be negativity towards our unity in action. Remember that even the great Dr. Martin Luther King's approach was not universally loved within the black community of the Civil Rights era. Some, impatient for changes that were long overdue, favored violent protests against their centuries-long oppressors. Followers of Malcomb X, both Muslims and non-Muslims alike, favored more radical protests, total separation from "white devils," and hatred rather than love.

Similarly, there are now voices within our communities that continue to push for more separation, re-segregation based on race, retributions for prior and current sins and injustices, and mistrust, disdain, and even hatred of whites.

Thus, collaborative Christian blacks may be quickly labeled as patsies, turncoats, Uncle Toms and subservient fools. They will be depicted as abandoning the cause of their people in favor of an alternative, if subtle, form of slavery via their alleged subservience to Christian whites and ongoing white supremacy.

And within the white community, there may be pushback from some whites who do not want to be honest and objective about the aftermath of centuries of their mistreatment of others. They might be overly sensitive to a holistic perspective on race relations and the role of the white church in the racial divisions of God's church today. Therefore, they may refuse to acknowledge the ongoing influence of past sins or take ownership of the need for unified repentance and new social action.

Some whites will be quick to say, "Can't we just move on!" rather than asking forgiveness for the sins of their fathers and patiently working together. And sadly, there will also be those who, for purely racist and hateful reasons, do not want to see blacks and whites unified for any reason, even if the society and all our children benefit.

Thus, the attempts of Christian whites to align with Christian blacks might be portrayed by our opposition as described below. Just to predict a few examples of things you might hear:

- Whites are trying to co-op blacks into the white church (for nefarious reasons).
- Whites are silencing black frustration and racial pride and uniqueness by taking over black churches.
- Whites are taking over what the Christian blacks are doing in their communities.
- Whites are trying to coopt blacks into working for their interests and/or in white communities to solve white-centric problems.
- Whites are trying to cover up modern racism by making Christian blacks believe that whites are on their side, when in fact they are just showing their true, unconscious, racist beliefs in their own racial superiority.
- Whites are trying to put Christian blacks back in chains through their attempts to take control of black communities via black churches.
- Whites are placating blacks by taking their attention away from Institutional racism and the oppression that is inherent in the system.
- Whites are showing their racism by trying to pretend that equality can ever exist in a nation like America, born as it was through oppression and genocide.

These attacks and the portrayals of Christian whites may make our work more difficult, but it certainly will not be impossible, for God will be on the side of the upright.

Yet, we must nonetheless be aware of the potential impacts of these many attacks from their many sources in order to best combat and nullify them.

Ramifications of the attacks

Importantly for our efforts to bring dramatic change to our broken society, even though most anti-Christian attacks are directed at Christian white men, society ultimately draws no distinction between white Christianity and black Christianity. All are injured even if only some of us are directly attacked. And as Christianity is weakened in society via its ongoing assaults on Christian whites, our faith is damaged within the black community, as well. Even if only by virtue of the association with Christianity in general, which society views as racist, homophobic, and generally anti-everything, it is harder for black churches to promote Christianity to their youth, promote Christian values in the culture, and generally impact society. Certainly, it is far more difficult for Christian blacks to unite with Christian whites to impact our society. Society thereby makes it easier to keep black churches and their congregations isolated and siloed, perhaps impacting their own congregants but with little chance of broad and deep social impact.

Our society has a thereby created a way to reduce the influence of both groups while only needing to openly attack one. Through targeted attacks, our opposition can malign many Christian moral and behavioral standards and reduce the influence and strength of Christianity within both society and the African American community, particularly among the youth who see Christianity through the lens of society's portrayals of Christian white men.

And so, from these groups and others with similar feelings will come a rise in attacks. Disparate groups will unite against us, analogous to those who joined to plot to attack the Jews rebuilding the walls. Just as clans aligned against the Jews in Nehemiah's time, so too will opposition forces align as we unite to do God's work in our society. And just as in Nehemiah's time, we must be ready to defend ourselves.

SUMMARY

Matthew 25:40 calls many of us to action and to be led by the Holy Spirit to do for others, particularly those in the greatest need. The Bible also clearly explains the need for the church to come together as one and for Christians to be bound together by their love of Christ.

Yet, our churches largely remain tucked in their silos, perhaps doing good works in the community, but rarely, if ever, collaborating with other churches just around the corner, down the street or across town. Indeed, churches may be doing the same work in the same communities on different days and yet be completely unaware of the overlapping resources and efforts.

Through our unity in action, we can become more effective and efficient, use our precious Christian resources more wisely while bringing more power to the problems we seek to solve. Through our unity, we can do more with less, make greater impact, and simultaneously demonstrate to a divided and hate-filled world what following Christ is all about.

But, just as Nehemiah and the many Jewish families faced oppositions and threats of violence from local tribes, so too will we face opposition if we are noticed. And if we are not noticed, we're doing something very wrong!

As we try to unite, the Sanballat we face will be our politics and our loyalties to political parties, politicians, and single-sided views of the world. Our Tobiah will be our loyalty to our individual congregations and the siloed work they do. Our Ammonites will be the comfort of the words of racially divisive leaders who focus on our differences rather than our unity, our past rather than our future, our hate and mistrust rather than our love and mutual interests. And our Ashdodites will be those anti-Christians who believe their personal choices and anti-Christian goals will be threatened by the strength of upright Christians displaying the power of God through unity in action.

This will only intensify as we delve deeper and become even more prevalent in our communities through our united and focused actions. The more active we become, the more impact we will collectively have, and the more opposing forces and powerful interests will feel threatened.

Only Godly uprightness will take us, as Christians, to a different place and through this mire of worldly thinking to effective solutions for our communities. We simply won't get through these obstacles and constraints to unity in action without the uprightness that God calls us to exhibit towards and with one another and our world.

Uprightness will allow us to work together, within and through difficult questions, complex issues and painful, self-exposing revelations of causality. And without this, we may never break down the barriers that keep God's churches in siloes. Certainly, we will never have the impact on our society that God has called us to have.

But, please do not be fooled. Attacks will come. Some will be subtle, some will be overt, some gentle, some cautioning, some viscous. We may even get back to the days of seeing our churches burning! Indeed, Christianity in America has been under some degree of subtle and not-so-subtle assault for many, many decades. Some of this we have brought upon ourselves, some has been brought upon us by external forces seeking our demise as an influence in society.

Thus, just as Nehemiah instructed the Jews as they rebuilt the walls of Jerusalem, we must work with one hand and be ready to fight back with the other.

INTRODUCTION TO
THE FOCUS AREAS

After all the build up from these many pages, you might expect a lengthy treatise on the areas in which the Christian American church should focus as a collective body of Christ. Of course, a quick glance forward will tell you that this book is nearly complete. It took this much to explain the history, the "why" and a bit of the "how" before getting to the actual "what." Perhaps surprisingly, the "what" is rather simple.

Part of the reason this section is relatively short is that each local community will have its own specific circumstances, demographics, constraints, history, politics and policies, and people. Thus, while these general themes of this book can remain intact and widely applied, the specific and pressing issues a given community needs to address may vary.

For instance, in one community, the Justice theme might be focused on the incarceration of the mentally ill and the lack of adequate communal resources to better care for these patients. In another, racial discord is the issue that keeps its people from moving forward to a better place. In another, the most pressing issue might be a lack of a drug court through which non-violent offenders and the addicted might go. In yet another, the issue may be more effective justice as a countermeasure to school expulsion.

Likewise, under the Healthcare theme, one community's most urgent problem may be childhood obesity. In another, it might be a lack of ownership of health status that drives destructive behaviors. Or it might be opioid abuse, high rates of alcohol dependency, or common industry/work-related diseases. Or all the above.

Furthermore, your church and community may have very specific reasons for rejecting the proposed focal areas and developing your own. You might choose an entirely different topic area based on your local community's needs, such as post-industrial nature conservation.

The next several chapters outline the "what and why" of the four recommended focus areas. It will be up to your community to prayerfully consider the specifics that will bring your community of churches together for the glorification of God through unity in action.

THOUGHTS ON SYSTEMS THINKING

As you read through the next chapters, you may come to think about the sheer complexity and enormity of the issues facing your community. Race, justice, healthcare, and education are huge, complex, interconnected issues without quick, easy solutions. Each may have tendrils that reach further than you currently know or understand. Each of the four may intertwine with the others. And each is therefore harder to solve than even those involved are often willing to admit. This might make envisioning a different reality daunting.

Creating and implementing solutions to complex problems requires a very different way of thinking, a way that most of us are not schooled or trained to do. It requires not just "thinking outside the box" but simultaneously thinking about multiple boxes and everything both within and outside them. It requires us to think of the seen and unseen consequences of our ideas, actions, and changes; to consider the motivations and agendas of people who think very differently than we think; and to consider how multiple people, each with a different relationship to the problem, might react to the solution(s). Thus, creating solutions to complex problems requires a very different mindset, approach, and toolbox.

Unfortunately, detailing the many approaches to change management would require a separate book. So, you will not receive all the answers in this chapter. But, below are some helpful hints to get you started and keep you on your path to success. Please consider the following as you are joining with others on your journeys to bringing glory to God through your unity in action.

Remember that God is involved. None of this is about us. Rather, it is all about Him and bringing Him glory through our unity in action. Importantly, none of these issues are impossible to solve if we keep God in the forefront. ALL things are possible!

Maintain uprightness. You must, at all times, strive to be upright in your thoughts, words, and deeds. Never lose it! Never allow bias, personal interests, stereotypes, etc., to enter your work. Doing so will ensure that relationships will falter, groups will break up, direction will be scattered, enemies will find ammunition, and your efforts will suffer. By maintaining vigilance in your uprightness, you will instead ensure that the right problems are addressed the right way, in the right time, with the right approach, based on proper guidance from God.

Remember, uprightness is what makes us different from the world, and what will make our solutions inherently more effective. Moreover, showing our uprightness is an important element in showing the world a different way to act, interact, and love one another. So critical is uprightness to success that I would recommend you start every group meeting with prayers for uprightness in everything you think, say, and do.

Maintain humility. Remember, this is not about you, your pastor, or your church. It is about God, His glory, and helping others to see Him in a new light. This can be extremely difficult as you start planning the details, roles, and responsibilities, since the solutions you develop may or may not involve you or your church.

Furthermore, not everyone can be the heart or brain of a community's body of Christ. It may be appropriate for others to take the ball and run. If necessary, you must be willing to step aside and let God work through others, even if you only get the satisfaction of having helped them get started. As long as the causalities you seek to impact are legitimate and solutions you develop are valid, let God's work be done through whomever He chooses.

Set priorities. You cannot do everything at once. Nor can you attain all your goals through one single act. In order to keep from trying to do everything at once or trying to do too much and thus failing to do anything, set priorities.

This should include determining the one or perhaps two things that will give you the biggest possible impact for your time, money, and effort. Then, do that above all else. Set everything else aside, avoid distractions, and focus on the one or two things until they are achieved.

Setting priorities can also help you manage multi-faceted, long-term strategies and avoid moving too quickly or neglecting critical elements that should be addressed before others. Without prioritization, you will find that your efforts become scattered and your timelines are unduly and dramatically extended.

Set goals. This may sound trite. But I have seen far too many bold ideas die for lack of clear, well-defined, quantified, and timed goals. Whether you use the SMART approach (**S**pecific, **M**easurable, **A**ttainable, **R**elevant, **T**ime-constrained) or something similar, your group should always set forth goals to be achieved.

Generally speaking, and no matter which approach you use, there are three very important elements in any goal. First, describing them in detail generates enthusiasm and promotes visioning of the "future state" of the problem. Without specifically defined goals, it will be more difficult for you to gain additional support and grow your numbers. Be sure to specifically define the what, how, and when.

Second, making them quantifiable gets you away from "doing better" and into the realm of determining how much impact you can or need to make. Churches are good at generalized goals, such as "reaching out to the community through the love of Jesus Christ." But only when it comes to determining budgets do many get specific about numbers. Be sure to quantify your expected impact, as it will help you create realistic visions for the future.

And third, putting a due date on each goal and sub-goal gets you away from "someday" and "eventually" into specific deadlines on the calendar for which you and others can be held accountable. Giving your group deadlines by which to achieve certain goals will prevent delays and excuses and allow better planning and execution.

So, rather than say "We'll improve reading scores for our kids," you might say "We'll improve third-grade scores on annual reading competency exams from 25% to 75% by December 31, 2021." Set your goals such that anyone can readily grasp them.

Think short- and long-term. Remember that these are likely issues that require a long-term approach. Yet, the solutions to each problem have short-term changes that will create a path to a long-term success. For instance, you may not be able to solve for all the community's healthcare issues within one year, but you can influence specific patient populations, such as diabetics, within that time span. Impacting diabetes will then allow you to impact other healthcare and non-healthcare issues, such as obesity and joblessness. As you look towards and plan strategies for your long-term goals, think of the short-term changes that will move you forward towards the ultimate objectives.

Consider the interdependencies. This is perhaps one of the most difficult, since there are so many facets to the four issues discussed in this book. Take education as an example. If education were as simple as hiring new teachers, we'd have done that already (indeed, many have tried this approach to no avail). Instead, in addition to staff quantity and quality, issues in education and school performance are related to housing availability, community and ethnic culture, family relationships, crime and safety, familial stability and history, and geography, just to name a few. You will need to capture these interdependencies in some form of interdependency diagram or map (just search the internet for the phrase "interdependency diagram" or "interdependency map" to see myriad examples). This will help you catalogue and assess the potential relative importance and impact of each. Those with high relative Impact (such as the impact of home environment on educational success) may require you to develop solutions that do not seem directly related to education, such as parenting classes for parents with kids under three or specific after-school interventions for troubled middle-schoolers.

Look upstream and downstream. Part of the interdependency analysis should include a look "upstream," to the sources of the problem, and "downstream" to the outcomes of the solution or change.

Looking upstream can give you hints as to how to prevent the situation from occurring in the first place. For instance, trying to improve high-school graduation rates may require you to address high-school discipline and expulsion policies as well as address reading skills as early as kindergarten, since the latter may eventually impact the former. Both, in the long-run, impact graduation rates.

Looking downstream helps you examine the intended and unintended consequences of your actions. As an example, consider the story of a veterinarian who went on a crusade to prevent the euthanizing of stray cats. Her goal was to save (literally!) one million cats. The approach was relatively simple: get animal shelters to avoid killing (a.k.a. euthanizing) stray cats and instead spaying or neutering them and returning them to the outdoors (a policy generally called TNR: Trap, Neuter, Return). The thought was to eliminate the moral and ethical issues of killing captured cats and instead allowing them to live without further reproduction. Eventually, it is thought, the number of stray cats should go down as reproduction rates decrease.

But while a great idea if you are a shelter owner or cat-lover, the ecological impact makes it a very questionable solution. According to Federal Wildlife agencies, feral cats are known to be responsible for killing billions of birds, including the extinction of thirty-three species, as well as countless beneficial snakes, lizards, rodents (yes, there are some!), and even crustaceans. Cats are considered an invasive species where they roam, having an often-disastrous impact on the ecology of the area. And because cats will kill even when they are well fed, normally docile housecats that spend time outdoors are known to instinctively become "natural born killers." By allowing captured strays to return to their previous outdoor habitats, even if spayed/neutered, they will continue to kill, unconstrained, until they die.

Thus, what appears to be a good idea in one respect might have disastrous consequences that we do not foresee. It is therefore critical to consider all the upstream and downstream interdependencies of the actions we might take.

Understanding the interdependencies, whether upstream, downstream, or right in front of you, is perhaps the hardest part of complex problem solving. Whether hidden or obvious, unexpected outcomes plague our solutions, nullifying results or even creating more problems than our solutions fix. Documenting the interdependencies, then determining their relative importance, are critical steps in ensuring that you target the correct problems and develop effective solutions.

Untie the web. As you create your interdependency diagrams, think of "untying the web of causality." This means understanding the difference between causality, correlation, and the presence of a specific condition or outcome. This is important, as properly ascribing the right causes to a problem will allow you to effectively solve it. Alternatively, failure to find the real, true causes will often result in playing the "blame game," chasing the wrong solutions and wasting time, energy, and money, or becoming frustrated.

Take, for example, incarceration rates among black men. Some would say the issue is, at its heart, caused by systemic and institutional racism and nothing else. But might there be other causal factors that influence the outcome? The tendrils of this issue may be many in your community, and might include everything from sentencing guidelines related to the "war on drugs" to lack of effective mentors in middle- and high-school; an American culture that glorifies violence and the mistreatment of women; income and housing instability for inner-city families; and lack of reliable transportation to job opportunities, just to name a few. Pinning the problem on a single cause often leaves us struggling to fix the problem, as its causality is commonly more complex.

Get and use data. Data can be critical to any intervention. However, too many times, we try to use emotion rather than data-based facts to drive our efforts. This can work for those who are on your side but demonstrably fails if your target audience is opposed or skeptical. If your audience doesn't feel the same drive or emotional tug, data can help you create in their minds the need and the necessary sense of urgency. Without data, you may find yourself having to be the loudest squeaky wheel in the room, yelling rather than discussing, and turning away those who you need as advocates and supporters. Indeed, society seems to say that if facts don't support your position, you just need to yell louder and be more adamant. That is not a good path to success, however.

To properly and effectively use data, keep a few things in mind. First, data can be wrong, manipulated, and misrepresented. As the old saying goes, "There are lies, damned lies, and statistics." We all know and have seen how data can be used incorrectly to make a point that its upright use would not support.

Whether to support a political position, an environmental theory, a problem's causality, or a government policy, data can and has been manipulated to produce intentionally erroneous outputs. This intentional or unintentional misuse leads to errant conclusions about causality, oversimplification of complex interdependencies, waste of precious resources, and failure to fix the problems at hand. Thus, of course, your data must be free of bias, deceitful manipulation, or even the sense of impropriety if you are to effectively and humbly represent the body of Christ.

In other words, your data must be at least as upright as you are.

Secondly, remember that data can come in many forms, both quantitative and qualitative. The latter can include feedback from the community in which you are working, interviews and interactions with those impacted by the issues you seek to address, and other "soft" data. All qualitative data can and should be turned into something that can be quantitatively analyzed, else you run the risk of generalizing and misrepresenting your sources. Keep in mind, too, that interviews and surveys, while "directionally informative," are easily manipulated and can thereby be misleading or misinterpreted.

For instance, you might get general feedback from a community about the constraints in public transportation. But stating broadly that "this neighborhood demands more and better bus routes" would misrepresent the feedback received. A more accurate representation would state that "73% of respondents who were aged 19 to 65 stated a general need for better transportation to high-employment areas."

Likewise, the statement "people love to have access to open spaces and parks" could be better represented using a specific volume or percentage of local residents who regularly use local green spaces during specific hours or days of week.

The more specificity you can add and the more accurately you can turn your qualitative data into quantitative data, the better off you'll be.

Third, you should also know that data in and of itself can be as lifeless as the paper or computers on which it resides. Once you have error-, bias-, and manipulation-free data, it needs to be transformed in order to be useful for your efforts. Data must be turned into information.

This may be as simple as taking "raw" data in the form of a bunch of numbers in a spreadsheet and turning it into compelling charts, graphs, and other visual representations. People respond to a colorful chart much quicker than they will a spreadsheet of even the most relevant numbers. (For an excellent reference on this, look to Edward Tufte's famous books on the "Visual

Display of Quantitative Information."[lxxiii] His work will inspire you to create something far more compelling than a PowerPoint chart).

Next, that information must be transformed into strategy. Information is just pretty charts and graphs if nothing is done to turn it into strategies, plans, and decisions. Turning information into strategies can again require the use of visualization but may also require good storytelling and a vivid description of the future state you wish to see. This may be the most difficult part of the data transformation process, yet the planning and strategy will mean the difference between endless discussions and action, stasis, and success.

Lastly and importantly, we must always uprightly interpret what we have. Too often, we want our analysis to prove our point, support an existing assumption, or back up our long-held opinions. But this is how the outcomes of medical or environmental research swings in favor of those funding the research effort. It is how those who have strong and vested opinions seem to find data that supports their cause, while never finding any data in opposition. Just as data is open to abuse, so too are our interpretations of data.

However, as upright people of God, we must be prepared for our opinions and desires to be denied if our upright data sources tell us otherwise. Our personal interests may be subjected to harsh revisions if objective analysis reveals that our explanations of reality are incorrect. This can be particularly true when we point to a single cause for a community's circumstance when in fact multiple causalities are at play.

Yet, using the truth is never a bad thing. If our data and analysis lead us to change our strategies, we can rest assured that we are moving forward as God would have us do, uprightly pursuing goals that are honestly derived and supported by our integrity. Moreover, uprightly developing strategies will lead to better results, as we will address the right causes at the right time in the right way for the right reasons. This will allow us to show society that uprightness is indeed a better way to live, act, and love, and that God can do wonders when we walk His path.

Data and how you use it, then, is critical to your efforts to bring large-scale change to your communities.

Avoid distractions. As you've likely seen in movies or in real life, a common tactic of those wishing to remain undetected is to create a distraction. Think of the fire started down the street from the bank that distracts police while robbers do their dirty work. Or, the spy who draws guards away from their posts in order to gain access to the safe where top-secret plans are kept. Create a distraction, and you can go about your business undetected.

216

Similarly, it is common for those protecting their status, position, or power to distract us as we try to bring forth social change. Think of the politician who blames the other side of the political aisle, the police chief who blames state government, or the Governor who points a blaming finger at Washington, D.C. Think of the school superintendent who denies accountability for poor student performance even though some of the causality may lie with some of his teachers or a lack of effective and fair discipline policies. These are all distractions designed to take us away from our hunt for the true causalities and send us chasing unicorns rather than solutions.

So, if someone in a position of power or who has a vested interest in the status quo tells you to look right, look left. Or they tell you to look up, look down. Too often, those whose sacred cows you seek to gore will try to distract you from the root causes and best solutions for your issues.

Be willing to make mistakes. You will, and so will all those who participate in your efforts. Society isn't very forgiving. Nor are those who oppose change. But we must be willing to admit when we get it wrong. That is part of being upright, and thus a necessary part of our efforts. So, be sure that all participants in your group are OK with being wrong, messing up, going backwards, and starting over if necessary. Some of the best lessons are learned from mistakes.

Don't require perfection, but don't be too casual with planning. Both are equally damaging. Once you have a reasonable plan in place, more forward. You might not make it all the way in one try, but you'll accomplish nothing by continuing the planning process forever.

However, don't be so quick that you use the mantra, "Fire, ready, aim." Move too quickly, without properly researching the problem and its many interdependencies, and you're sure to fail. Instead, find as many of the interdependencies and causalities as is reasonably possible, use as much data as is reasonable, then move forward knowing that you'll likely find more along the way.

Use non-experts. It is usually best to include those who are NOT deep deeply entrenched in the environment or system you want to change in your solutions development efforts. Using only industry experts can easily result in becoming mired in "we've already tried that," "we can't do that because …," and other constraints to free thinking, ideation, and creative solutions. Allowing fresh ideas from uninvolved parties prevents the "same old, same old" solutions from being the only ones proposed and allows new ideas to flow more freely.

For instance, if your efforts are in education, you likely do NOT want current and former teachers and school administrators leading your group. Keep them involved and engaged, of course, as their expertise can prove valuable. But don't rely on them for all the ideas and solutions. Too many are too close to their fields to be able to step back and see the world with fresh eyes. Too many have been in their fields long enough to have deeply seeded opinions and entrenched ideas at the ready, whether right, wrong, fresh, or severely aged. The result is that, too often, other participants will defer to their field expertise and avoid putting forth ideas and solutions that may work. Without "outside eyes," you may find that your ideas are inherently limited to the limited vision of those who live in the system.

Read up on the "systems thinking" concept. I highly recommend you read Peter Senge's seminal work, <u>The Fifth Discipline: The Art and Practice of the Learning Organization.</u>[lxxiv] Senge is considered the grandfather of Systems Thinking, and his work is an insightful read. These and similar works will help you understand both the necessity and value of looking at your problem in a systemic way, considering the many variables that drive its existence.

These are but a few of the many hints and ideas that might help propel your efforts to a faster and more thorough success. Use these and others as you dive into the following Areas of Focus or other areas your community of churches deems valuable.

AREAS OF FOCUS: HEALTHCARE

As Christians, it has long been part of our heritage and calling to serve God through the provision of healthcare. Almost since Luke, a physician by trade, wrote his gospel, Christians have been involved in healthcare. History shows that from the fourth century through to the present age, Christians have been prominent in the building and running of hospitals, hospice centers, and charities to promote health and wellness, particularly to the poor and needy. In your city or nearby, there is likely a Baptist, Lutheran, Catholic, or other Christian supported hospital. Indeed, Catholicism currently supports some of the largest health systems in the United States, including Catholic Health Initiative and Sisters of St. Mary.

But you needn't own a hospital chain or work in a clinic to have an impact on the health and wellness of your community. Throughout the American church landscape, there are myriad church-based, health- and wellness-related programs. There are healthcare ministries, disease-specific support groups, regular wellness check-ups, blood drives, disease screenings, health cost-sharing programs, exercise classes, health education, and even gyms and sports facilities.

Yet, despite it all, the health of our congregants and our communities remains less than optimal, often quite poor. This is due to myriad reasons, not the least of which are:

- Profit and financial motivations that run counter to the best interest of communities and patients.
- Lack of collaboration between healthcare providers and their communities.
- Lack of sharing of insurance company data that could impact wellness.
- Failure to fully integrate communal resources, including families, friends and fellow congregants, into the care of patients.
- Poor chronic disease management options.
- Perhaps most importantly, a general lack of "Health Ownership."

Furthermore, the late 2000's brought tremendous change to the healthcare system, both positive and negative. The greatly praised requirement to cover "pre-existing" conditions came along with legislated increases in required coverage for all health plans, rapid and huge increases in premiums and deductibles, and restrictions to access for those with even the best employer-provided plans. Cost-shifting to the insured and away from the insurer has become more and more prominent and problematic. And as these and other dynamics impact both the insured and uninsured, many insurance products are simply out of reach for many Americans. Even when insurance is affordable, more and more Americans are under-insured due to reduced benefits, much higher deductibles and co-pays, and restriction to clinical access, expensive drugs, and specialty care.

This creates both challenges and opportunities for Christians to use their influence among their congregants and their communities to impact health, healthcare, and wellness.

This chapter will suggest some ways in which you can take action in your community to help solve for some of the most pressing and dire issues your churches face: healthcare and healthcare costs.

DOING THE RIGHT THING

There is an old saying that we all know, "No money, no mission." Applied to many areas, it essentially means that without funds, there is nothing to pay for the work that needs to be done. Whether tithing to fund church operations and pastoral salaries or donating time and money to charitable ventures, without some source of money and resources there can be no mission. Thus, healthcare providers, both for-profit and not-for-profit, must balance their desire to do the right thing (which is nearly universal) against the cost, revenue, and reimbursement challenges they face every day. These latter challenges grow every year, as government policy and insurance company reimbursement practices make the provision of care an increasingly financially challenging venture.

Still, hospitals typically provide millions upon millions of dollars in unreimbursed care. This is commonly both part of the hospital's commitment to its community and a requirement of Federal, state and local statutes and the tax code. Thus, hospitals provide care for which they know they can only get a write-off and do so willingly as part of their mission to serve their communities. This is a prevalent attitude in many inner-city hospitals in low-income areas that serve as true safety nets for their communities.

More recently, hospitals have merged to create larger, more monopolistic entities within large regions. Legislative approvals for these mergers are often contingent on the development of specific "population health" plans that include the development of programs to keep communities healthier, often with little or no financial benefit to the hospitals. Similarly, many physicians, nurses, and other healthcare workers routinely give their time and knowledge to charity work with no financial benefits. This can come in the form of local charitable work and free care to indigent populations, national and international disaster relief, and international Christian healthcare missions. Organizations such as Doctors Without Borders and Remote Area Medical are just two of many provider-volunteer driven charity groups. And Christians with valuable healthcare skills and knowledge readily give of their God-given gifts and talents when the need arises. Thus, given the right situation, charitable cause and maybe even a few disincentives, healthcare providers will readily collaborate on "no money" missions. This means that hospitals and care providers are now more open than ever to collaboration with local community organizations which share a vision for a healthier population.

COLLABORATION

One of the themes of this book is obviously collaboration among and between churches and congregations, particularly across racial boundaries. Nowhere is this more of a pressing need than in healthcare. As churches try to impact health and wellness, cost and Health Ownership, there are myriad ways to intervene. And of course, interventions are more impactful when churches collaborate and work together for the greater good and the glory of God.

CONGREGATION HEALTH NETWORKS

A terrific example of a great start to collaboration with hospitals comes from one of the most innovative cities in America, Memphis, TN. Years ago, the CEO of Methodist Hospital initiated a program to engage local churches in the care of patients as they were discharged from that hospital. Later called the Congregation Health Network, this model has been replicated and deployed across the nation to better care for patients outside the hospital once they have been discharged.

Though the model continues to undergo improvements and changes as implementations drive further innovations, the essential elements of the concept are valuable as examples of collaborative care models. As a patient checks into the hospital and is registered, they are asked if they belong to a church and, if so, which church. If the patient belongs to one of the collaborating congregations, the congregation's representative is notified of the hospital admission (with the patient's permission, of course).

From there, a congregational representative works with a special hospital team focused on Congregation Health to better care for the patient, tend to the patient's home needs while they are in the hospital, and help prepare for the patient's post-discharge care. Tasks that need to be performed, from caring for the patient's cat to mowing the grass to watching over an empty home to bringing food to a lonely spouse, can be part of the support provided by congregants.

In addition, important in-hospital tasks might include "navigation assistance," through which the patient's care is monitored by a volunteer nurse or physician congregant to ensure high quality care and the best possible outcomes. Furthermore, post-discharge care can be aided and amended by members of the congregation's care teams to include small, but important tasks, such as transportation, grocery shopping, diet monitoring and management, minor clinical monitoring (e.g. temperature, blood pressure, heart rate, weight), and other in-home tasks that can help keep the patient from clinical deterioration and unnecessary readmission.

To further help communities help care for themselves, Methodist Hospital and the Congregation Health Network also set up multi-week training sessions on the "How To" of care for patients with specific diseases. By training friends, family members, and other volunteers in the care of patients with diabetes, COPD, and other diseases, the community could better care for itself, improving outcomes and helping to establish a better awareness of diseases and their causes. These training sessions are wildly popular and well attended.

At last count, there were over five hundred churches signed up in the Memphis Congregation Health Network and hundreds of volunteers trained. Significantly, the hospital was beginning to tally the financial savings from the program, which showed great promise for further deployment of the model. The Memphis Model, as it is often known, is but one example of the kind of impact churches can have on the health and wellness of their congregations beyond the traditional offerings of potato salad and deviled eggs. While delicious and certainly made with love, food is only part of our health needs when illness strikes or surgery is required.

Ironically, even within the many great faith-based healthcare ministries and programs, it is unclear whether churches are collaborating between and among themselves as part of this and similar programs. We tend to care for our own.

But what might happen if we were to collaborate across churches and between congregations? How might we improve the capacity to care for those with chronic diseases, the indigent, the homebound, and the recently discharged? How might collaboration and cooperation among and between churches of various socio-economic areas aid in the management of everything from diet and exercise to prevention of disease, the improvement of outcomes, and the overall reduction of care costs? Taken to the next level, the Memphis Model could be readily expanded to do just that.

Care Circle Networks

I first began writing about this concept over eight years ago, before the current spate of healthcare/insurance reform started, and it became the topic of my second book.[lxxv] The Care Circle Network (CCN) expands on the more common community care models by providing more care through currently disparate but widely available communal resources. By linking together congregations, pharmacies, civic clubs, volunteers, schools, and other communal resources, Care Circles are built around individual patients under the guidance of the patient's physician. This augments the care provided by physicians, clinics, and hospitals by bringing familiar, friendly, and personally vested care resources to the patient without the cost of traditional clinical resources.

These patient-centric Care Circles complete both non-clinical and clinical tasks to help patients better manage their own health and wellness without the excessive cost and hassles of traditional care models, unnecessary trips to EDs and clinics, and unnecessary deterioration of health status.

Care Circles thereby augment the capacity of the healthcare system, reduce the pressure on clinical resources, redistribute non-clinical workload and help establish a culture of Health Ownership in the local population (more on this later). Importantly, it allows congregations to work directly towards the health and wellness of their fellow congregants by weaving otherwise disconnected resources directly into their care.

Thus, physicians' efforts to care for patients in their homes and communities is augmented, essentially extending the reach of physicians while not increasing the cost of care. Furthermore, congregants can more readily become engaged in the healthcare system.

For young people, this may be the start of a new and promising career. For the retiree, it may be an easy way to give back. For the healthcare worker, it is a great way to extend the blessings of their training and education to their Christian community. And for the generally service minded, it is a means by which to serve their fellow man in a meaningful, lasting, and community-altering way.

Importantly, Care Circles Networks can be expanded to link multiple congregations together to address specific diseases impacting specific congregations or geographic areas, such as diabetes, obesity, and childhood asthma. By pulling clinical expertise and volunteers from multiple congregations, the capacity of service and availability of resources are greatly expanded.

Furthermore, those in clinical roles who might otherwise be unable to contribute due to work schedules (e.g. physicians and nurses) can now have a way to aid in meaningful local ministries. Just helping a poor elderly widow navigate the health system, understand the care being provided, and discern her healthcare bills would be a huge blessing!

By collaborating, multiple churches can also gain the strength of numbers to ask local hospitals, clinics and other providers for cooperation and support (including financial support) for these programs. Indeed, it isn't hard to see how even ten small churches with one hundred congregants each could push for support, since one thousand local people is a lot for any provider to disregard.

Chronic disease management

It is a commonly known fact that a small percentage of the population uses a vast majority of healthcare spending. Depending on whose numbers you use, chronic diseases, such as COPD, diabetes, and others generate close to one half or more of the total cost of the U.S. healthcare system. While "end-of-life" care and the care of the elderly are commonly cited as the largest expenses, aggregate data analysis[lxxvi] shows that this is not the most expensive group of patients. Rather, all patients (not just the elderly) with chronic diseases would be a better place to target care interventions to reduce cost, improve quality of life, and change long-term clinical and community outcomes.

Thus, in a similar vein to the aforementioned Memphis Model and Care Circles, cross-congregational collaboration can target specific chronic diseases and patient populations with or at risk of chronic diseases. Through these initiatives, personalized care from Christian volunteers can be offered with the aid and oversight of patients' physicians so as to:

- Help improve clinical and wellness outcomes
- Break down barriers that keep patients from better self-management

- Improve patient compliance through peer support and compliance accountability
- Provide Christian prayer and moral support
- Bring necessary clinical education to our communities
- Engage our youth, families, and communities in the awareness of the need for Health Ownership

The collaboration of Christian congregations, particularly across racial boundaries, can bring needed resources to bear where there are currently limited and siloed efforts. And, of course, as we do this, God will receive glory as we impact our communities in profound and meaningful ways.

CREATING HEALTH OWNERSHIP

This term has been used several times already without actually being defined. The term Health Ownership simply means that we own our bodies and take care of them as our most prized possession. Instead, most of us take far better care of our cell phones than we do our bodies. Think about the obviously unhealthy guy who fusses over the tiniest detail of his prized car or boat, while drinking beer and eating pizza and hotdogs. Or the overweight teenager who will go out of her way to protect a laptop but won't hesitate to eat fried chicken and a Coke for lunch with a Snickers for dessert. So, suffice it to say that most of us treat our bodies more like tents than temples despite the scriptural directives on the care of the body.

Health Ownership is simply the recognition of and respect for what God has given us in our bodies. We should own our bodies like we do any other prized possession, no matter what society says about it or its condition. Just as we must appreciate all the gifts God provides, no matter how different from those provided to others, so we must appreciate what God has given us and treat it as just that … a gift from God.

A lack of Health Ownership is the actual root cause of some if not much the excessive cost in the American healthcare system. Despite diet fads, exercise crazes, and the impact of what is considered beautiful in our society, far too many of us have either given up or never actually started taking care of God's most precious gift, our bodies. Instead, we fail to do even the basics of bodily maintenance, even when prescribed by physicians and common sense.

As an important part of this discussion and our unity in action, this is an area wherein Christians can demonstrate the wise and profound, yet simple, principles that make the Bible such a relevant document for everyday living. Whether from the examples of the diet in Daniel's fast to references to the human body as more than a garbage dump, Christianity has much to say about how we care for our God-given gifts. Even those in poor health or those with disabilities can find comfort in the scriptures and through the generosity and love of the Christian body of Christ. United in action, we can demonstrate these important principles as we help our communities develop better health practices and habits through Health Ownership.

Moreover, we will demonstrate that we are a caring, loving people who are focused on far more than the damnation of sinners. We will prove that ours is holistic, loving God who cares deeply for all His children and all peoples. Through our unity in action, we will bring healing, health, and wellness to an increasingly sick nation, providing assistance, relief, and support to those for whom the healthcare system often does not work well.

IMPACTS AND THE GLORIFICATION OF GOD

This effort will put God's church directly in the midst of one of our nation's biggest issues, helping to fix the nation's healthcare system without driving up costs or demanding that patients make do with less care, increased out-of-pocket expenses, and mediocre service. God's church will do what governments, hospitals, and health insurers cannot — make the system work without more money and additional paid resources. Naturally, we are merely the conduits for this activity, driven as it is by the messages and teachings of our Savior. Thus, to God goes the glory for all we do throughout all these areas of focus.

And as we shine through the misperceptions of society, the lies told about us and Jesus Christ, and the hatred arrayed against us, we will show ourselves to be upright people whose God deserves the respect and admiration we give Him each day. Through this, those non-Christians who work with us will become curious and seek to understand what drives the joy in our giving hearts. From there, the Holy Spirit can show them the truth about God, His love for all mankind, and why our way is the best and only way to live.

AREAS OF FOCUS: EDUCATION

CURRENT STATE

O f all the focus areas in this book, education is perhaps the one wherein churches already work in the most. There are likely few churches that are not in some way working towards better education for our children and adults. Some churches are working only with their congregants' children, and some only on Christian education. Many have pre-school programs, youth after-school programs, back-to-school backpack giveaways, adult and child literacy programs, English language learning, daycare, and many other similar efforts directed at kids and parents of both congregants and non-congregants. A few run full Christian schools and academies, of course. And many young parents choose a church based on its youth programs and the ability of the church to serve the needs of both parents and kids.

For many churches, the effort is focused on preventing the loss of a child to a bad educational start. It is said that kids who cannot read by third grade are doomed to a life of struggle, and far more likely to end up incarcerated. And far too many of our nation's children and young people perform well below what is considered even passable math and reading skills.

It should not be surprising, then, that many churches focus on young readers to ensure a good start to a better path. Still others collaborate directly with school or school districts to help kids and teachers through volunteerism and support, both human and financial. Thus, of the four focus areas, this is the area where churches have and continue to do a great job of bringing resources to the needs of our society.

NEEDS REMAIN

Despite all that churches are doing in education, this is another area wherein collaboration could create better outcomes, more capacity to serve, and greater efficiencies. Through collaboration with one another, united churches could add to the power they could bring to the problems.

By working closely and strategically together, churches could target specific schools or specific geographies for specific interventions. Churches with greater financial and legal resources might team with other churches to bring needed policy, program, and funding changes to impoverished areas through interventions and pressures targeting School Boards and policy makers at both the state and local levels. Volunteers from multiple churches could more easily and completely fill gaps in services, aid more kids in targeted schools, bring perspectives from one community to another, and generally do more, with greater efficiently. And the collaboration of committed volunteers from multiple churches of multiple socio-economic cohorts can use their resources, time, and even monies far more effectively than they could either as silos or through complete reliance on school administrators and state and federal education systems.

Importantly, through collaboration between Christian blacks and Christian whites, more could be done to set examples for our children that would help negate the negative, racially charged, and depressing messages they receive from society, the internet, television, and even from teachers. Demonstrating how Christian blacks and Christian whites learned to collaborate and love one another, the value of giving and volunteerism, showing hope in the face of troubled times, and the love and care that Christ exhibits through Christians will be powerful, if subtle, messages that our kids can take to heart.

Christians united in action could show how racism is overcome, love conquers hate and resentment, and that God's love knows no limits. Just being there, caring and supporting can have an incredible impact on the lives, attitudes, character, and future of our children. But being there across racial and socio-economic barriers can take your church from a single, siloed, and often unheralded intervention to a community-wide strategy, all while demonstrating how uprightness is lived out through Christians.

HOLISTIC STRATEGIES

We all know that poor performance in school is not always the result of bad teachers, poor facilities, or a child's innate lack of abilities and potential. What happens to kids before and after they leave school is as or perhaps even more important than what happens to them during classes. A fourteen-year-old who is raising her siblings because her parents are largely absent will likely struggle to do well in class, even with the best of teachers. The teenage girl who might have to sleep in several relatives' homes on any given week may experience greater scholastic struggles than her peers, if only for the difficulty in concentrating on homework assignments.

Likewise, children from broken families, those bused to distant facilities, and parents working multiple jobs all make parent-child-teacher interactions and support more difficult. Some parents are unable to support their kids due to work schedules. Some are unable to effectively raise their kids due to the influence of drugs, alcohol, environment, poor life choices, disease and health issues, divorce, lack of familial or community support, and myriad other issues and constraints. Filling these gaps can mean the difference between a child whose future is full of hope and promise and one full of challenges and troubles.

However, since many of these issues are very often interrelated, addressing one without addressing the others may inherently limit the desired impacts. For instance, failing to address community health issues can leave kids unnecessarily vulnerable to disease and illness which could in turn hamper current and future educational and job performance. Similarly, failing to address transportation, housing, and other social justice issues can negatively impact both short- and long-term success in education and life, as both kids and parents are unduly burdened. And long-standing racial animosities can tear communities apart and leave our kids unprepared to live in a multi-racial society if left unaddressed.

Fortunately, collaborative churches are in a great position to untie the web of causality and help deal with these the issues that drive some of the poor performance we see, particularly among the poor. United church volunteers from multiple committed congregations can strategically target justice, race, health, and education legislation and programs in a multi-pronged effort to impact the entire community. As myriad services are provided, churches can build strong relationships with parents, kids, and adult students that will help them win both the battles against poverty, crime, poor health, and the ever-present worldly influences that lead to poor life choices and outcomes.

Moreover, united Christians could do further work to counter the cultural rot that our children are being exposed to and the lies and deceptions they are being taught in society. Whether demonstrating to misdirected kids that learning and education should not be shunned, teaching both white and black kids proper definitions and perspectives on race and racism, or working to instill dignity, respect, self-respect, and a work ethic in the kids who need it most, united Christians can bring better education to our kids while showing a new way to live and interact. These and other efforts will show Christ for who He truly is and do wonders for the next generation.

This, in turn, means that collaborative churches should work to develop holistic strategies that account for at least the issues listed herein, and perhaps other key social issues. This holistic approach will help you envision how to use your church's resources (including human, administrative, financial, technical,

229

and space) to best help you help your community, your fellow churches and other Christian organizations.

Remember that by assessing your congregation's gifts, talents and availability, you will know the resources you have to deploy to any given issue or ministry. By combining the gifts, passions, and availability of your congregation with those of others, you will amass teams of Christians that the communal body of Christ will be able to deploy.

Moreover, as you collaborate with other churches to develop your holistic approaches, you can bring more power and attention to specific goals and objectives for the community. Just as Nehemiah brought together Jews against the "nobles and officials" of his day,[lxxvii] we can bring together congregations to make greater change happen faster via the power of our people coupled with the vision of God's hand in our society.

Never forget that we are at least tens of millions strong, with dozens of churches in even the smallest communities. Those numbers are hard for anyone to ignore! Harnessed with passion and the uprightness of Godly Christians, those numbers can make great change happen.

NCAASI

One great example of a church-school collaboration program is the National Church Adopt-A-School Initiative (NCAASI), born from a church organization in Dallas, TX called The Urban Alternative. For nearly twenty years, The Urban Alternative, under the visionary leadership of Pastor Tony Evans, has worked with schools and churches across the Dallas, TX metro area. Now a nationwide program, NCAASI trains church leaders on the "how to" of engaging with schools and lending a helping hand. Under these programs, church volunteers do literally anything that the schools need.

Christian men and women might simply serve as mentors or might work as crossing guards at intersections. They might work to help kids with math and reading, or simply be a resource for troubled teens and their parents. NCAASI purports that ministry starts with service, which is shown first through example and deed. Thus, many schools and school boards welcome the help of local churches, despite the vocal concerns of some who fear the "subtle indoctrination" that could come from the mingling of kids and Christians. The key is to stress partnerships rather than evangelism.

NCAASI has trained hundreds of churches across the country and continues to expand its reach. Thousands of children and parents have been touched. If your church is considering starting or expanding your work with education and schools, NCAASI is a terrific re source. (www. http://churchadoptaschool.org).

230

SUMMARY

Education is one area in which there is already plenty of work being done. However, even though you are likely engaged in some form of education ministry, please consider collaborating with other churches to bring strategic alignment to your efforts. By breaking through the siloes that keep you apart, you will find there is greater capacity to act and better opportunity to impact your communities.

AREAS OF FOCUS: JUSTICE

JUSTICE AS A BIBLICAL CONCEPT

Justice is mentioned numerous times in the Bible. Depending on the translation, the word and its derivations are used somewhere between 30 and 180 times. Perhaps most famously, Micah 6:8 simply reads, "What does the Lord require of you, but to do justice, love mercy and walk humbly before your God." This command is quite clear and should remind us of the simplicity of both the gospel message and the roles Christians are to play in our society.

And it is also clear that, given the number and context of the passages, justice is an integral part of God's character and His expectations of us. Psalms 33:5 reads, "[God] loves righteousness and justice; the earth is full of the steadfast love of the Lord."

Psalms 37:28, "For the Lord loves justice..."

Psalms 99:4 refers to God as "Mighty King, lover of justice."

Clearly, God sees justice as highly important, as Proverbs 21:3 explains "To do righteousness and justice is more acceptable to the Lord than sacrifice."

Other Biblical passages link justice to the uprightness, integrity, honesty, and objectivity we've already covered in this book. It is made clear that these critical elements must be present in our thoughts, words, and deeds and thus our interactions if God's required justice is to be done.

For example, Deuteronomy 16:19 reads, "You must not distort justice; you must not show partiality."

Leviticus 19:15 states clearly and strongly the need for objectivity, "You shall not render an unjust judgment; you shall not be partial to the poor or defer to the great..."

Psalms 37:30 explains the relationships between justice and Godly wisdom, stating "The mouths of the righteous utter wisdom, and their tongues speak justice."

And Psalms 106:3 tells us "Happy are those who observe justice, who do righteousness at all times."

But it is also clear that "doing justice" (or even as other versions translate it, "act justly," "do justly," etc.) is not a passive action. "Do justice" is an outward action.

This contextual reading seems to beg for action beyond the walls of our churches and homes. Of course, we are to "do justice" there, too. But it strikes me that there is far more to these verses than acting within our personal sphere. After all, few of us preside over courtrooms wherein justice should be fairly administered, or work in banks where the poor might be given fair and just loan consideration. If we are to do justice, it must be practiced both throughout our lives and our society.

Yet, when most people think of justice, they think criminal justice and the righting of wrongs and the punishment of wrongdoing via the court systems. Biblically, however, justice is a broad and sweeping term with implications that go well beyond the courthouse walls to include all human interactions. Indeed, since injustice can occur anywhere there are interactions between people, whether financial, personal, or social, so too can justice. And since the definition of justice is so broad, the activities associated with doing justice are equally broad. Therefore, the doing of justice is meant to be an active, outward, and broadly engaged function for Christians.

Furthermore, this call is meant to be proactive rather than reactive. Rather than reacting to injustice, the Bible constantly refers to acting in the name of justice because simply reacting to wrong doesn't necessarily advance the cause of doing right. By doing justice only after injustices have been done, we merely sweep against the tide. Instead, the proactive advancement of justice not only addresses injustices as they happen but also works to solve the root causes of the issues from which the injustices arise to prevent their occurrence in the future.

Moreover, justice is, in many ways, a core component of the other areas of focus highlighted in this book. For example, justice in the education system speaks to the need for fair, equitable, and reasonable punishment for wrongdoing, fair and equal access to funding, educational opportunities, good teachers and able administrators, quality educational materials, as well as expectations for personal behavior and effort.

Likewise, justice in the healthcare system speaks to fairness in accessibility to care, the fair treatment of the ill regardless of socio-economic condition, as well as personal responsibility for the management of one's health.

And doing justice in race relations can be as simple as taking a Godly view of all mankind regardless of race, or as complex as detecting age-old biases within the systems of society.

Thus, doing justice requires us to actively engage, seeking out injustices in a variety of circumstances and venues, and applying the principles of Biblical justice not just to widows, orphans and the poor, but throughout our society.

IGNORING JUSTICE

It is relatively easy to ignore the need for justice when justice is an unseen but assumed part of your life. We don't think about justice when we are regularly being treated with due justice, or when we have the resources to fight for justice when we feel wronged. Similarly, what we might consider injustices are quite different based on our socio-economic condition, the environments and communities in which we live, the power we can wield, and the way we are able to deal with issues as they arise.

Some have the power, money, and relationships to fight against injustice, while others have little or nothing with which to engage. The former might view the latter's justice issues as self-inflicted or overstated. The latter may feel that the former has an unfair advantage in dealing with life's injustices.

Perhaps this is why the Bible repeatedly calls for justice for the poor and widows by those who hold power over them, and the conscious effort to do justice for those who could readily be abused and who otherwise might not have the position to demand it or the resources to fight for it. God's Word suggests that we must always be mindful of those who need assistance, to include assistance with the attainment and maintenance of justice in these considerations.

Therefore, we should always seek to empathize with those who seek justice and seek to support their causes even and especially when others do not.

INJUSTICE AND UPRIGHTNESS

Justice inherently requires us to think, speak, and act uprightly. If Godly justice is to be achieved, it cannot include bias, hidden agendas, or animosity. Justice demands uprightness, and uprightness requires guidance from and attention to God and His teachings. It should therefore come as no surprise that a significant reason for the lack or distortion of justice is the lack of Godly uprightness in our society. Without God, uprightness is difficult if not impossible. And without uprightness, justice suffers.

Think of circumstances in which injustices have been done. Were the perpetrators of the injustices thinking and acting uprightly? Did they exhibit an open and clear sense of honesty, the purest of integrity, and absolute objectivity? Did they evaluate the situation or circumstance with clear eyes, or did they violate the Old Testament entreaty, "You must not show partiality …?" Were their motivations impure? Perhaps they were simply misguided by preconceived notions, biases, or personal or business interests. Perhaps they were motivated by opportunities for personal enrichment, personal power, or the advancement of a cause near and dear to them, even if doing so required them to act unjustly. Perhaps they convinced themselves that they were acting justly, when an objective evaluation of the situation would have told them otherwise.

At the core of many, if not most, of society's injustices is a lack of Godly uprightness. Of course, what else should we expect from a society that has been gradually distancing itself from God for decades?

Similarly, the demand for justice requires its own uprightness. It is quite possible and often quite easy to treat injustice with more injustice, to punish the doers of injustice with unjust treatment, and to display an unforgiving and unfair heart in the undoing of injustices. It is also often easy to allow those who need help to act inappropriately and unjustly because of their position and the injustices being done to them. Indeed, as we look across world history, millions upon millions have died from what was little more than hate and revenge when justice was put aside, and violence took its place.

Therefore, as we seek to obtain or do justice and correct injustice, we must never use revenge, paybacks, or undue retribution, as these are not the way of Christ. Wickedness cannot be solved through more wickedness, no matter the justification. As Dr. Martin Luther King, Jr. famously stated, "Hate cannot drive out hate; only love can do that." Thus, as we seek to correct wrongs and fight for justice we must be prepared to do the justice that God requires of us, allowing Him to be the ultimate judge of those who have wronged us and others.

It is also important to keep in mind that one individual's injustice may be another's justice. There are often two or more sides to a justice case, leading to two if not more versions of what is and is not justice. Rare is the accused who takes his punishment well, since valid or invalid justifications can be created for just about any thought, word or deed. All we have to do is look to how the Bible was misused to justify slavery and the ill treatment of our fellow man through the ages to see how human minds can twist the truth.

And so, it is very clear that the most difficult of tasks in our pursuit of justice will be the attainment and maintenance of uprightness. This is also why

Christians are well-positioned to take on the doing of justice. Society, by its very nature, does not abide by the standards that Christians should and could apply. Society has little motivation to walk uprightly before God, and thus can readily fall prey to the motivations and causalities that lead to injustice. Christians, on the other hand, should be able to represent uprightness in everything we think, speak, and do.

Justice, Race Police, and collaboration

Nowhere are upright Christians more needed than in the issue of race and racial justice. Society has simultaneously made a hash of the messages of Christianity while it promotes animosity, resentment, misunderstandings, revenge, and hatred between the races.

To combat this, as mentioned in previous chapters, Christian whites must become the "Race Police" with the support of upright Christian blacks. In these roles, Christian whites must seek out instances wherein injustices might be happening, especially when those injustices are based, partly or wholly, on racism.

Likewise, Christian blacks must be upright when evaluating the circumstances of injustice to determine whether the injustice is being caused in part or in whole by racism, or due in part or in whole to other factors such as poverty, misuse of political and economic power, negative cultural pressures and standards, old habits, manipulation of charity, outdated biases, prejudicial judgments, evil intentions, and other root causes. Only through this open and upright collaboration will Christian blacks support the words and deeds of Christian whites. And only with this support will Christian whites be able to take the role of objectively calling out racism and its related diseases as they are detected.

This upright collaboration will be especially important in our criminal and civil justice system, wherein our nation wrestles with high incarceration rates for black men, issues with the management of non-violent drug offenses, the incarceration of the mentally ill, the use of for-profit prison management systems, and rise of new illicit drugs and addiction epidemics, just to name a few. Our justice system should serve our citizens by protecting them from criminals but do so in a way that would be pleasing to a truly objective overseer. As upright Christians, black and white, we can be that overseer and help our nation heal its many wounds and move towards the attainment of justice for all.

SUMMARY

Of course, any time we do God's will through our thoughts, words, and deeds we bring Him glory and please Him. Clearly, the Bible tells us that He loves justice and the doing of justice pleases Him. It is an expectation of our behavior, our thinking, and our interactions with each other.

Yet, our society has not been particularly good at the dissemination of justice. Fortunately, our nation was founded in such a way as to allow for the continuing pursuit of that which is more perfect. Our Constitution was written to be solid enough to stand withstand the pressures of both autocrats and the violent mob while being flexible enough to change in support of the pursuit of freedom and justice.

In some sense, our Founding Fathers in part wrote an aspirational document which would help guide the nation to a better place. But we haven't yet fully arrived. There are injustices all around us, from minor to atrocious. They touch every aspect of life, particularly for some. Indeed, justice is an issue in many of the other problems of our day, from drugs to crime to mental illness, including the other three areas of focus recommended in this book, healthcare, education, and race.

But as Christians, we are in a unique position to bring a very different perspective to the issues of justice throughout our society if we take the opportunity to do so. By joining Christian blacks and Christian whites together and uprightly collaborating on the key justice issues in our communities, we can quickly show ourselves to be quite different from the world via the means through which we deal with justice. We can point to justice issues as they show themselves in myriad situations and show how upright people, even those of disparate backgrounds and socio-economic conditions, can come together in the pursuit of objective, pure truth and justice.

This will show Christianity as something far better than society shows it to be. Our unity in action will thereby help open the previously closed eyes, hearts, and minds of new generations of Americans. From there, we will collaborate together, work together, and begin friendships and lasting relationships with one another. God will lead those who do not yet know Him to a relationship with Christ.

Our task is to act in such a way as to change the perception of Christians and Christianity throughout an entire society, such that we can show Christ for who He really is.

AREAS OF FOCUS: RACISM

Racially, our society seems to be moving further apart rather than closer together. The bitterness and rage in our politics, the recent eruptions of white supremacists, myriad fights over everything from school funding to immigration rights to voting laws, and a general lack of uprightness within our society have led to the bitterness that continues to divide many blacks and whites. Sadly, our churches are, for the most part, not stepping up and into this fray to take the opportunity to shine light on a better path and instead, often serve to support the divisions. Our racial siloes, whether benign or malignant, keep us from collaboration.

Thus, where racial unity within our society can be found, it is often not being driven by churches. And where churches are making headway, the word isn't getting out through traditional and modern forms of news and media. Churches may be doing great work towards racial solidarity, but like a tree falling in the woods, it only matters if someone notices.

This book has therefore largely been focused on the racial divisions within God's church and its impact on our ability to unite in action to bring glory to God and solutions to America's most intractable problems. There is little doubt that racism played a huge role in the divisions we now see in the American body of Christ and within our communities. Nor is there doubt that, in many communities, these divisions are as strong as they have ever been, with a plethora of racially focused denominations peppering the Christian landscape.

Furthermore, the divisions that were started by segregation of the races are now bolstered by the more benign personal preferences, familial history, socio-economic variation, and geography as well as the more toxic and malignant racial animosity, mistrust, age-old resentment, and politics. Of course, this cannot go on if Christ's church is to effectively and summarily impact the racial tensions within our society in the way we could or should.

Therefore, we must rise above society and think, speak, and act uprightly, as our Lord called us to do. Doing so will allow us to have any painful conversations necessary to release our historical grievances.

Our uprightness will then allow us to put aside age-old animosities, stereotypes, biases, and historically derived preconceived notions in favor of objectivity, honesty and the purest of integrity as we discuss and develop holistic solutions for these focus areas and others. Without full uprightness, as ordained by God and shown in Jesus, we will not fully unite, either in thought, speech, or action. And without this, we will show ourselves to be no better than the world. Indeed, we will show ourselves to be worse, as hypocrites who preach one way and act just as society acts.

God's church is the only entity now capable of bringing solutions to the racial divisions that continue to plague our nation. *Only* Christians have mandates on how to treat other Christians who have sinned. *Only* Christians have examples of Christ's teachings to guide our thoughts and deeds and compel us to reach out in both repentance and forgiveness. And *only* Christians have the power of our faith in God to overcome personal and historical obstacles and heal the age-old scars of centuries of oppression and hate. And *only* we can come together and show forth our Christian love for one another and set an example for all of society to see.

And if we don't, Satan will surely be glad to continue to step in and fill that role.

So, as Christian blacks and Christian whites come together for unity in action, race relations and issues should be a key focal point. Herein, I have recommended that Christian whites take on specific roles (e.g. "Race Police") while asking Christian blacks to take on some seemingly impossible tasks. But through the showing of Christian unity and Godly uprightness we will be set apart from the ways of society and the satanic worldliness that seeks to keep blacks and whites in separate war camps. With our renewed relationships we can delve deeply into the issues facing our communities and objectively create holistic solutions that strike at the heart of these and other major social issues. Rather than point fingers of blame or create feel good solutions that leave problems unsolved, Christians will be able to create better and more sustainable solutions to the problems that prevent our people from living in harmony, equality, fairness, and love.

Now is the time for such action. Christians are now in a unique historical position to influence our society in ways we have not seen in centuries. Our numbers are strong. The need is great. Breaching the racial chasm that splits Christianity will be an example to society that no one will be able to ignore. We will boldly proclaim the uprightness it will take, admit our faults and errors as they inevitably arise along our way, and show our determination by continuing to march towards our goals of unifying American Christianity and bringing glory to God. We cannot pass up this unique opportunity to have such a profound influence on our society, our children, and our faith.

We must begin immediately. Doing so will set the stage for what might be the Next Great Awakening of our faith in our nation.

THE NEXT GREAT AWAKENING: A CALL TO BOLD ACTION

*[42] They devoted themselves to the apostles' teaching and
to fellowship, to the breaking of bread and to
prayer. [43] Everyone was filled with awe at the many
wonders and signs performed by the apostles. [44] All the
believers were together and had everything in common.
(Acts 2: 42-44)*

PERSPECTIVES AND BACKGROUND

Since our nation's beginnings, there have been at least two, and as many as four, "Great Awakenings" within the Christian faith. Each short but impactful, these movements served to expand Christianity and diversify church membership. In doing so, they forever changed the American religious landscape by bringing Christ to more and more of America as new denominations were given life and new preaching and teaching styles were brought forth. These movements brought with them changes to doctrinal emphasis as well as important political and social impacts.

For instance, the first two Awakenings helped spread Christianity to those who might have been otherwise untouched, including Native Americans, slaves, and freed blacks. They also spurred the Abolitionist movement and help bring about the end of slavery and birthed charities and service organizations that remain with us today. Indeed, the rapid evolution of the American Christian church that took place during these movements can still be seen in our churches, church culture, and society today.

There is no single start date to the Great Awakenings as there might be to the beginning of a war or a single incident that starts a movement, such as the death of Michael Brown. Nor were there centralized bodies for management, oversight, and guidance. In today's terms, these were more like the spread of Twitter movements than well-constructed, organized campaigns. Many preachers were lone and itinerate, and only joined with others as the movement spread. And while several denominations sponsored missionaries during the Second Great Awakening, there were no formal doctrinal structures, nor did the preachers all come from the same schools of thought on scripture and theology.

Thus, the messaging throughout these movements was inconsistent, even if within broader, similar themes of the times. It is therefore only through retrospection that we identify these movements and see the connections, trends, and causalities that led to their inception and impact.

But it is now rather easy to retrospectively see the hand of God moving amongst His peoples. Through individuals called by their faith and a spirit that moved them to challenge the existing norms, these many men and women, both known and unknown, made an indelible mark on our history and our society. Put in the context of their times, without the ease of the instantaneous spread of information we have today, these movements were even more impressive in the power and breadth of their impact.

In reading these brief accounts and perhaps studying deeper on your own, consider where our nation, our churches, and our children are today. Consider the parallels between those historical periods and the America of today. Consider how these movements spread the message of Christ through new means, new messages, new approaches, and new venues. Consider how, through the inspiration of these movements, Christianity went on to do even greater things within our society. Consider how the equalizing message of the Gospel was spread to the least among us, offering salvation and hope in the face of tribulation.

Then consider how a Great Awakening, enabled through the unity in action of churches in communities throughout the land, might impact everything we seek to change in our society and the very spirit of our nation.

Just as it did as far back as the 1700's, our nation now yearns for the same kind of direction and uplifting compassion that only God's word can bring. And just as it did during our nation's early history, our nation is drifting away from its spiritual roots as life and worldly influences push our people into complacency and a reliance on themselves, mankind, government, and science rather than God.

Perhaps our nation is once again due for a nation-wide movement of God such as these.

AWAKENINGS OF OUR FAITH

The First Great Awakening

The First Great Awakening came in the early 1700's. Its roots were on the other side of the Atlantic, in England, Scotland, and Germany, where preachers began to break with the stylistic and doctrinal traditions of the existing denominations. In Germany, the rise of Pietism promoted a more emotional and personal commitment of faith, while Methodism grew in England to juxtapose the style and doctrine of the State-ordained Church of England. In Europe, the general growth of the movement is thought to have been a counterweight to the rise of the Age of Enlightenment and its emphasis on reason rather than faith, mankind rather than God. Furthermore, some Christian leaders began to see that the enthusiasm of the faithful and the emotional attachment to God and the church had waned, in part due to rigid doctrine and the stoic reverence of the worship experience. Rejuvenation would therefore come from reforming the preaching styles and messages of the Awakening preachers.

The movement came to America in New England in the early 1700's. Here, just as in Europe, traditional worship styles had become associated with a decrease in enthusiasm for church attendance and membership amongst colonists. Moreover, economic and trade stresses of the period put pressure on the lives and livelihoods of the colonists, further negatively impacting church engagement. Thus, the new theological emphasis and preaching styles served as a similar alternative to the formalized services and styles that had been adopted from Europe in the popular Congregationalist, Anglican, and Puritan churches.

The First Awakening was spread by iterant preachers who held meetings in barns, fields, and on riverbanks as well as in churches. Despite the lack of organized infrastructure that we would typically see today, the First Great Awakening evolved quickly from the works of just a few great preachers, each with new styles and messages. One key figure involved in the initiation of the movement is said to be Theodore Frelinghuysen, a minister of the Dutch Reformed Church, who began his pastoral work in New Jersey during the 1720's. Having come from Europe to preach and teach, he was shocked by the deadness of the churches in America, and preached the need for conversion and a profound, life-changing commitment to Christ, not simply perfunctory participation in religious duties.[lxxviii]

Presbyterians Gilbert Tennent and his four sons, preachers all, were heavily influenced by Frelinghuysen and brought a revival to the Presbyterian denomination. Tennent had emigrated from Ireland to Pennsylvania when he was fifteen, after which he went into study to become a minister like his father. He became a pastor in 1723 and led a church in New Jersey, where he discovered and began to follow Frelinghuysen's ideas.

Led by the Tennent family, the Presbyterians not only initiated religious revivals in those colonies during the 1730's, they also established a seminary to train clergymen whose fervid, heartfelt preaching styles would bring sinners to experience evangelical conversion. Originally known as "the Log College," it is better known today as Princeton University.

Tennent's new style and message were not always welcomed, of course. He preached against "Old Sides" (a.k.a. "Old Lights"), preachers who he claimed were not imbued with the Holy Spirit and were therefore not worthy of leading congregations. Eventually, this led to a split in the Presbyterian denomination during which the Tennent's were expelled from the Presbyterian Synod of Philadelphia by Old Side ministers who opposed the Awakening. In 1745, Tennent and others led the formation of a new Synod in New York, from which Tennent and his sons carried on their work.[lxxix]

In 1739, Tennent connected with another European pastor who had come to American to spread the word of God, George Whitefield. Whitefield (pronounced "whit-field") had been a member of the "Holy Club" at Oxford University under the spiritual guidance of Charles and John Wesley. The Club was a group of students dedicated to fasting, prayer, and spiritual exercises and from which would later come the beginnings of the Methodist movement.[lxxx]

Whitefield's more flamboyant preaching took him throughout the colonies where he was connected with other important Awakening preachers, including Sam Davies and Jonathan Edwards. As an itinerate preacher, Whitefield is said to have delivered some 18,000 sermons during his lifetime and was known to be one of the most traveled men in the colonies of the day. Perhaps the most popular preacher of the time, it is said that he preached to an audience of 30,000 in Boston, a gathering greater than the population of the entire city.[lxxxi]

Generally, the messages from these New Light preachers stressed the need for a personal, emotional commitment to Christ rather than salvation at birth via parental consent. They stressed personal sin and guilt and the need for Christ's redemptive grace as they broke away from what they considered to be too much emphasis on the strict observance of rituals and doctrine. They heightened the awareness of inherent human depravity, encouraged personal introspection of lifestyles and words, and demanded a new level of personal piety, scriptural study, and a purity in living. And through their preaching styles, they opened their followers to more emotion and enthusiasm in worship.

This had several impacts on the broader society as the adoption of this thinking spread. It served to "level the salvation playing field" by showing a personal choice in salvation while teaching that all were inherently depraved, including both the poor and the wealthy. Those in upper classes were just as sinful as those in lower classes, and both could become equally embodied with Christ's love.

Furthermore, there was an emphasis on learning and scriptural studies, which led to the establishment of schools including the Princeton as well as other universities such as Brown and Rutgers. Thousands upon thousands were brought to Christ.

As some churches were split between the New Lights and the Old Lights, Methodist and Baptists grew as denominations of choice for the newly converted. Importantly, a new emphasis on missionaries, the spread of the Gospel, and the general equality of all in the eyes of God led to attempts to convert Native Americans, slaves, and freed men and women. Indeed, some New Lights preached about the spirituality of American slaves and encouraged slave owners to acknowledge their slaves' spiritual freedom. John Wesley, like others of the movement, wrote and preached passionately against the use of slaves[lxxxii]. However, some, like Whitefield, continued to own and advocate for the use and legalization of slaves while simultaneously advocating for their fair treatment.[lxxxiii]

The First Great Awakening went on until the mid-1740's when its impact slowly began to fade. Yet, it is said to have started American Christianity down the path towards diversification of theology and liturgical practices. Through the rejuvenation of enthusiasm for Christ, Biblical teachings, salvation through grace, and personal accountability, the movement forever changed the American church landscape and expanded the reach of Christ to a greater number of Americans, especially slaves.

The Second Great Awakening

As with the First Great Awakening, the Second Great Awakening was a response to a decline in religious enthusiasm. By the late 1700's, many people had ceased church attendance due to a variety of factors. Some believed that God did not play an important role in everyday life. Other people had become too consumed with earning a living to have time to worship God. (Any of this sound familiar in modern-day America?) As a result of declining religious convictions, churches began to sponsor religious revivals throughout the country. Thus, erupting less than one hundred years after the First, the Second Great Awakening began around 1790.

Like the doctrinal messages of the First, these emphasized human beings' dependence upon God[lxxxiv] and His power to provide, yet opened the door to salvation for all humans, no matter their class, education, or status. This led to tens of thousands to convert and served to further lessen the influence of the more restrictive Calvinist teachings.

Importantly, the movement's emphasis on the individual's salvation and attention to the plight of slaves laid the groundwork for the Abolitionist movement, which many evangelical Christians joined and supported. The roots of the Abolitionist ideas born in this Awakening became increasingly prominent in Northern churches and politics, growing throughout the period and into the 1830's, which contributed to the regional animosity between North and South leading up to the Civil War.[lxxxv]

Religiously inspired authors and leaders such as Theodore D. Weld, William Lloyd Garrison, Arthur and Lewis Tappan, and Elizur Wright, Jr., all spiritually nourished by revivalism, took up the cause of "immediate emancipation." In early 1831, Garrison began publishing his famous newspaper, the Liberator, in Boston, supported largely by free African Americans.

In December 1833, the Tappan's, Garrison, and sixty other delegates of both races and genders met in Philadelphia to found the American Anti-Slavery Society, which denounced slavery as a sin that must be abolished immediately, endorsed nonviolence, and condemned racial prejudice.

The movement even bled over into higher education, as Christian abolitionists founded Oberlin College, the nation's first experiment in racially integrated coeducation, the Oneida Institute, which graduated an impressive group of African American leaders, and Illinois' Knox College, a western center of abolitionism.[lxxxvi]

The Second Great Awakening also led to even larger-scale and more widespread evangelical efforts amongst slaves and freed slaves. Grown from the seeds of the First Great Awakening, preachers from Northern and some Southern Baptist and Methodist churches preached a message of individual freedom while their denominational leadership supported a freedom to establish individual churches, particularly for slaves and freed blacks.

Thus, through the expanded availability of the teachings of the Bible and the Gospel of Jesus Christ both slaves and freed blacks came to see meaning, hope, and power in Christ while the demise of slavery received increasingly vocal support. The evangelism of the both First and Second Great Awakenings led to the rise of tens of thousands of Christian blacks throughout the South, and forever changed the role of Christ in the black communities.

And of course, the Christians of the Abolitionist movement forever changed the course of the history of God's church in America and the history of the nation, creating the foundational framework upon which it rests today.

The Third Great Awakening

There is debate as to whether there were ever subsequent Awakenings. Some scholars argue that the Third was merely a reaction to the economics of the times (mid- to late-1800's), while the Fourth has been explained away as simply a continuation of the evolution of church doctrine and style throughout the modern age.

The Third is said to have occurred between the years 1856 and 1859, though some historians have its impact stretching into the early 1900's. It has been called the Businessman's Awakening due to the New York City gathering of thousands of businessmen in the aftermath of the stock market collapse of 1857. It has also been called the Prayer Awakening due to an emphasis on communal prayer, interdenominational cooperation, and service to the poor.

The messaging of the movement changed from that of the first two Awakenings. The "hellfire and brimstone" messages that accompanied some of the great preachers of the first two were supplemented by an emphasis on the afterlife and wonders of heaven.[lxxxvii] There was also a shift towards a focus on the earthly impact of Christianity and the need to aid the poor, accompanied by a belief that poverty was not the result of personal failings but rather failed societal structures.

Noteworthy results of this period, whether you refer to it as an "Awakening" or not, were the growth of charity missions in large cities, the expansion of prayer meetings and the use of collective prayer as a means to impact society and its people, and a cross-denomination collaboration that aided in bringing Christians and non-Christians together.

The recently formed Young Men's Christian Association (YMCA, or Y), still a Christian organization at the time, was an important element in bringing the Third Awakening to Philadelphia and Chicago. Formed in London in 1844, the YMCA came to the United States in 1851 and quickly spread as an aid for the urban poor. Likewise, the Young Women's Christian Organization, the Salvation Army, and the China Inland Mission were all made more popular during this period.

This period also saw the rise of the Holiness movement, which countered the Calvinist notion of original sin with the belief in the potential for complete sanctification and a life without willful sin. This grew out of the Methodist church and John Wesley's teachings on a "second work of grace" leading to perfection in Christian living. Phoebe Walter, an iterant Canadian preacher, is known as the "Mother of the Holiness Revival" for her extensive writings and preaching. In the black church, this doctrinal focus was picked up in the Church of God in Christ Holiness, one of the denominational splits of the period.

The Fourth Great Awakening

There is even greater debate as to the legitimacy of the Fourth Great Awakening. The concept of a Fourth movement is based on the work of social historians, notably Robert Fogel.[lxxxviii] His theme borrowed from the framework set forth by the previous works of another historian, William McLoughlin, who is credited with much of the work defining the Third. McLoughlin's seminal work on the topic, "Revivals, Awakenings and Reforms,"[lxxxix] was published in 1978, well before the speculated completion of the Fourth cycle he predicted.

Both authors speculate that the Fourth Awakening began somewhere in the early 1960's. The theory behind the Fourth is based in part on the patterns of the previous Awakenings, each lasting for about thirty or more years, each bringing a change to the landscape of the American church, and each reacting to and being driven by changing technology, social structures and norms, and the economics of the period in which they occurred.

However, McLoughlin and Fogel differ on both the length of each movement and the political underpinnings of the latter two. For McLoughlin, the Third and Fourth were more "leftist" in nature, while for the Fogel they are more "rightist." Fogel therefore claims the Fourth to be a reaction to social movements and changes in economics and technology of the 1960's and beyond, which resulted in the rise of the fundamentalist movement, the growth of Pentecostalism and Protestant "Charismatics" along with the associated emphasis on personal responsibility for sin and salvation, a "traditional" work ethic, and dedication to the family structure.

As we have already seen, some sociologists have attributed these latter traits to an underlying racism within the Christian white culture and moral structures, paralleled as they were by the rise and success of the Civil Rights Movement.

THE NEED FOR THE NEXT GREAT AWAKENING

Regardless of whether these latter two movements are to be known as "Awakenings," it is clear that there is and has been an ongoing evolution in the American Christian church. This, of course, should not be unexpected, given the continuous changes that our society is undergoing and our understanding of the role of Christ in the church and world history. The church at large must necessarily react to the times while maintaining the Bible and Christ as steadfast constants, like mighty islands in the rolling seas.

And clearly, the American church and Americans have benefited from the impacts of the Great Awakenings throughout our nation's history. These long cycles of revitalization, evangelism, and scriptural focus brought forth a Christian culture that is still present today, helped free the slaves, stood up for freedom and morality within the U.S. and around the world, brought forth Christian charity as a social norm, and changed the dynamics of the American culture. Our political, social, and religious landscape has been shaped by these movements as the church reacted to changes in secular society and the challenges faced by Christians and non-Christians alike. Because of these movements, the ethics, morals, and constructs of our Judeo-Christian heritage remains alive and well today, though it is constantly challenged by a worldly society seemingly bent on its destruction.

Historically, the start of these movements has been associated with a general need for nation-wide religious revival. But it was the dramatic change that the Awakenings brought forth that make them so notable. These were not minor changes or slow evolutions in spiritual interest. Rather than the incremental movements of churches within their communities over time, these movements reached millions of new converts in short bursts of religious activity, forever shaping our nation's social and moral fabric.

Current status

While there are more Christians in the Unites States than there have even been, there are also more Americans than there have ever been. Thus, while we have roughly between 54 million and 280 million Americans in our ranks (depending on how you count), it doesn't mean that the church is necessarily riding high and thriving. Some feel that the Spirit is alive and well in our nation, while others feel that God's church is on its heels.

Moreover, the image that society has painted of Christians is not positive and is increasingly negative. Christians and Christianity have been portrayed more commonly as something akin to Dana Carvey's comical Saturday Night Live character, "The Church Lady." The long-running animated TV show, "The Simpson's," portrays the devout Christian Ned Flanders and his family as freakishly comical and the local Reverend Lovejoy as part religious cynic, part hypocrite who refers to the Bible as a "2,000 page sleeping pill" in which "everything is sin."

Meanwhile, Christians from Catholic Nuns to everyday Protestants are portrayed as anti-everything, intolerant haters of all activity not considered absolutely Puritanical, from homosexuality to inter-race marriage to dancing, drinking, and generally enjoying life. Society wants to portray us as denying women the right to their health and wellness, denying gays their freedom to choose partners, and refusing to allow even the discussion of evolution in public schools.

Moreover, society consistently ignores the good we already do in the world, perhaps due to our tendency to work as isolated church silos. Rather than show the billions upon billions of charitable dollars we spend and the billions of hours of time we give, society hides our work from view and glosses over the Christian heritage of the largest charitable organizations in our nation. The good works we do are thus discounted due to the bad things we are said to do and the Puritanical restrictions we are said to want to place on the lives of others.

Furthermore, Christians and the Christian church are often not seen as being upright, but rather as hypocrites with same sort of political one-sidedness and non-Christian behaviors and attitudes displayed by the world we call sinful. Thus, Christians are largely seen as being worse than society as we simultaneously claim a higher level of righteousness and closeness to God yet often display a very different, "earthly" way of thinking, speaking, and acting. This all makes it quite easy to pigeonhole Christians and specific denominations into neat, but largely unfair and illegitimate, categories. In doing so, society not only pits some against others, but judges us all to be short of our own rhetoric. And thus, it is no wonder that raised with these portrayals and misinformation, the new generations of Americans are unchurched.

Parallels

This is the hand with which we now play. As we look forward to the future of Christianity in our society and among our young people, we must ask tough questions about how we will respond and what we must do to simultaneously change our image and continue to bring Christ to our society. Thus, parallels to the need for the rise of such a movement exist throughout our society today. In current-day America, the need for a Great Awakening is expressed in the following examples, just to name a few.

- Declining fervor for church attendance.
- Changes to demographics that are causing older congregations in traditional denominations to dwindle and traditional churches to close.

- Stereotyping of Christians, particularly Christian white men, as a sort of social evil, unworthy of consideration, trust or political power.
- Christians and Christianity are commonly mocked, ridiculed, and falsely accused of the most wicked thoughts and deeds. Christianity is seen as a source of repression, harsh rules, and terrible punishments for otherwise nice people; of being hateful, mean-spirited, and repressive; against everything that is good and fun, and intellectually unattractive.
- The use of "freedom" to repress Christian ideals, morals, and teachings in the name of diversity and an open, free society.
- God becoming a "little g" god, prayed to in times of trouble, but no longer deserving of respect, being followed, or even precise characteristics and attributes.
- Increasingly violent, anti-Christian groups whose volume and bullying have allowed them to steal the role of judge over what is right and wrong, good and evil, and permissible speech and belief.
- General cynicism about Christianity and religion among our youth and young adults (much of which is self-inflicted by Christians themselves).
- Distrust of organized religion and the "Church."
- Political splits amongst Christian blacks and whites that keep us separated in racial silos despite commonalities in our faith, showing us to be hypocrites to the secular society around us.
- The rise of non-Christian faiths, especially Islam, as a secular society resentful of Christianity's long-standing dominance, tries to subdue it and instead supports the rise of non-Christian faiths.
- Government pressure to tax churches and reduce any local and national political power.
- The rise of the "Christian consumer" who wants to be entertained and made to feel positive while avoiding service and deep scriptural understanding.
- Worship as a "feel good" experience rather than a deep contact with an almighty and all-powerful God.
- A stunning and disturbing lack of honesty, integrity, objectivity, and general uprightness throughout society, in the news, politics and leadership, government, business, and science. This pervades our dialogue and interactions as truth becomes less important than winning an argument, opposing the other side, and supporting the

current group-think. Sadly, this is not limited to our society, but has infected many pulpits and congregations.

- Right and wrong are increasingly subjective, to be determined by the individual rather than a guiding set of moral principles. "Don't judge" as the mantra of our youth (unless you are a Christian, in which case a negative judgment has already been made). Common-sense norms as are put forth in the Ten Commandments are considered overly restrictive and even racist.
- A self-focused mentality that only seeks to do good when the self is elevated. Charity is only important if the giver gets credit.
- Focus on the "here and now" rather than the future and an afterlife.
- Increasingly secular generations which have far less faith in God and far more in human action, technology, and "self as savior."
- An ongoing and increasing focus on money rather than joy, having things rather than having purpose
- The numbing of our children to violence, suffering, and death.
- Increases in mental health disorders, particularly among our young, which is leading to high rates of depression and exponential growth in the use of drugs, both illegal and legal, for relief.
- A rising general sense of malaise and fear.
- A rising sense of being lost rather than content with a "peace that surpasses understanding," combined with a rapidly growing reticence to recognize Christianity as a source of hope, happiness, and strength.

The list could go on for pages, of course. But, clearly, our society is both in many ways tired of Christianity and yet desperately in need of it. Clearly, just as in the 1700's and 1800's, we are a people in need of revitalization, rejuvenation, and the uplifting hand of God.

Think of the Awakenings within the context of their influences and outcomes and as part of the ongoing evolution of our presence within American society.

The first two Great Awakenings spread the gospel across the nation and brought more and more blacks and whites to believe in Christ. Evangelism changed the way in which Christ's message was taught while the number of denominations through which it was delivered expanded. Both paved the way for the destruction of slavery and the deep spread of Christianity into the black community. By reaching out to the lost through new approaches and preaching styles, generations of Christians were brought to Christ.

The Third helped further spread the word and works of Christ and set the stage for the vast social and charitable influence churches and Christian organizations now have. Contributing literally tens of billions of dollars in funds, time, goods, and resources, Christians now give far more than any other single group.

Importantly, these movements shaped the course of American religion in a relatively short period and without the assistance of the real-time communications, streaming video, and nation-wide access to the internet and telecommunications.

Now, just imagine how the First and Second Awakenings might have been different were the internet and the cloud available!

OPPORTUNITY

Thus, from the viewpoint of American history and our current landscape, we now have the following elements in place:

- **Spread.** The Word has spread over two hundred and more years through a wide array of congregations, both racially split and integrated church bodies. Now, the name of Christ is known by nearly everyone, whether believers or not.
- **Commitment to serve and give.** There is a general Christian commitment to the betterment of society through giving, service, and Christian love for our fellow man, as exhibited by our many ministries and outreach efforts. Godly love is poured out every day, in the most selfless ways, by Christians from every walk of life. And we, as a group, give, do, and contribute more than any other group in our nation. Our generosity, service, and selfless commitment to our fellow man is a story rarely told!
- **Numbers.** If you total up the entire American population who claim Christianity as a religion, we are well over 250 million believers. Even if that is a lower percentage than it once was, we are still a majority of the nation's population. Furthermore, and ironically, we are by far the most diverse group of people with a singular belief system.
- **Latent capacity to act and influence.** Imagine what we might accomplish if we could deploy all 250 million plus Christians towards some sort of active service? How much might we be able to change? What might we be able to do for our society, for our fellow

Americans and the many injustices that still plague our land? How much glory could we bring to God through our unity in action?

- **A pressing need.** There is obviously a dramatic need for revival of our faith to help our nation through the troubling times it faces. Whether from external hostilities or internal political and social forces, there is much evil arrayed at our nation. Christians must step forward and show the light to a path through the darkness.

As a result of our history, and even our historical faults and errors, we have spread the word through our many denominations to every corner of the nation. We are immensely generous with hearts of service. We are tens of millions strong. And there is a huge, God-sized hole to be filled in our society. What more of an opportunity do we really need?

Therefore, there can be little doubt that it is time for a new Awakening. But the next Awakening will not be realized by historians in the future, years after some unpredicted, unforeseen events and circumstances come together to create a movement. Rather, the next Awakening must and will be a conscious act of the Christian community, at large. Through currently unknown leaders, the efforts of currently unsung heroes and humble servants of our great God, a movement will begin.

ATTRIBUTES AND EXPECTED OUTCOMES OF THE NEXT GREAT AWAKENING

Unlike the first Awakenings, reaching new generations will very likely not happen through preaching, revivals, or mass conversions. At least, not initially. Though these can and do still happen, the world is a very different place than it was in the 1700's and 1800's, requiring a very different sort of evangelism.

We must therefore simultaneously alter the impression society holds of Christians while reaching out to those lost souls who need Christ. Contrary to the approaches of the previous Awakenings, where alterations to preaching styles and messages brought new believers to new denominations, I believe that new generations of believers will be reached through:

- The examples we will set by our uprightness in thought, speech, and action, and our racial and doctrinal unity in action.
- Engagement with Christians in cross-racial, cross-doctrinal, collaborative work on society's largest problems.

- Coming to know individual Christians and the message of Christ through mutual interests in aiding our fellow man, our society, and our world.

The Next Great Awakening will therefore be led not by great orators preaching the gospel in some new way but by "doers" — active Christians working in their communities, united in action with other Christians of all races, doctrines, religious preferences, and political leanings. The word of God won't change, nor will we stop sharing Christ with others. To the contrary, sharing Christ will be made far easier! Our unity will show the world a very different and even godlier church, full of Christians who are very different than society portrays them.

Through our examples of unity, the sheer magnitude of our numbers, the uprightness with which we approach the issues of the day, and the results we will have on the key issues facing our society, we will be recognized as a positive force for goodness and the betterment of our society. "The Church Lady" portrayal will change to a portrayal of everyday Christians, average "Joe Christians," doing good works alongside their brothers and sisters of all races, creeds, and denominations in every community.

United, we will show America how walking uprightly leads to a better way to live, interact, and solve problems. We will show how racism can be eradicated. We will demonstrate that the power of people united by the light of Christ can enable communal responses to poor health, promote justice, and better educate our children. Though we will no doubt be attacked, sometimes viciously, we will demonstrate the power of our faith to overcome obstacles and the evil intentions of wicked men.

Without national infrastructures and vast organizations and bureaucracies to burden us, preachers will unite us across racial barriers and focus their congregants on key issues facing their communities. In neighborhoods, small towns and large cities, churches will align. And through the power of modern-day communications, we will break through the walls of the 350,000 silos that keep us isolated and thereby work together to bring quick, decisive, and lasting change to our society.

As society sees us uprightly working across racial boundaries to do good for our fellow man rather than denying others their lifestyle choices, normal everyday Christians can once again feel confident in living and speaking about God and Christ in a new way, without fear of retribution or being negatively portrayed. Christians will be seen as examples of uprightness, with the purest of integrity and objectivity in our search for and activities in the solutions to key social ills. Being an active, positively engaged Christian will come to be considered a good thing as we point to what we are already doing and what more we will do. All the while, we will display God's love for all humanity.

Our individual churches will change from a source of a weekly obligation to sources of regeneration, revitalization, gleeful tithing, communal bonding, mentoring, creativity, and deep love for those who are in the world doing great works throughout each week. They will seek out other churches with whom to bond, linking members with like passions to make change happen.

The bodies of Christ, churches and congregants united across racial, socio-economic, and historical boundaries throughout tens of thousands of communities, will be fully functional and actively engaged. Enabled by the cross-racial collaboration of many gifted Christians from all walks of life, each working within their talents and passions on key issues facing their communities, the bodies of Christ will serve their communities as never before, bringing glory to God through our uprightness, our work, and our success.

SUMMARY: ACTION BECOMES EVANGELISM

As our new examples of how Christians now think, live, and work together shine forth, we will come to know non-Christians who share our passions for the betterment of our society and our world. We will show that we are simply good-hearted, upright, charitable, and well-meaning people who have a Savior who guides us in everything we think, say, and do. Through these interactions, even without preaching or traditional evangelism, the Spirit will move in the hearts and minds of many of these non-believers.

*Our actions will have their own
inherent evangelical impacts!*

The curious will come not because they were threatened with hell, but because they want to feel the same joy we do from the service and activities in which we participate. Sometimes even without sharing our own testimonies, people will come to learn more about why we do what we do, and what drives us to work with such enthusiasm, passion, and selflessness. Only then can we serve as conduits to a new life in Christ.

Perhaps it will start in a major city where the desperation of a nation is most vividly portrayed; perhaps in the rural South where hate once thrived and congregational segregation still lives on; or in a few churches surrounded by a secular society that mocks their very existence.

Regardless of its source, it will happen. It must happen. Our nation cannot heal itself. Into the vacuum left by the loss of uprightness will come something else, whatever else is strong enough to fill that void. If not us, then something far worse.

It will start when Christian blacks and whites begin to come together and begin a serious, honest, and objective dialogue about the pains in our society. Men and women will come together in places across America, exhibiting the kind of uprightness that Christ calls us to. They will gather in homes, in churches, in restaurants, coffee shops, and community centers.

And then strangely, without thinking, but just as easily as one would remove an overcoat, they will leave behind their biases, historical animosities, their political affiliations and secular loyalties, and the teachings and leanings of the secular world. They will meet. Discuss. Debate. Listen. Love. Decide. And act.

They will choose issues that are important to their communities, staying away from the political and doctrinal issues that have divided us, focusing on issues around which all Christians can unite. They will develop synergies, align strategies, allocate their many resources, and begin a process of unification through action throughout their communities. They will act as equals, united, as God intended them to be.

But make no mistake. We must act. Soon. To turn back the secular winds and redirect the course of the nation. Not through legislative action, for this is the avenue of men. Not through fear or intimidation, for our God should shine as a bastion of love and peace as well as a loving father willing to discipline. We must make ourselves known for being different and making a difference.

Our strength, our passion for people, and our willingness to forgive one another for even the most egregious history comes not from ourselves but from our faith in a God who has given us a new spirit, a new way to live, and new light by which to go forward. Our actions, not our preaching, will make us known.

As action becomes evangelism, we will bring another Great Awakening to our nation.

FINAL THOUGHTS

I am still unclear as to why I felt pulled to become a white man in a black church. For if it has been solely for my edification, then it will have been a wasted effort. Like a tree that falls in the woods, little will have come from these many years of curiosity and learning unless this book somehow, someway, reaches and impacts American Christianity. It is therefore my prayer that this book will, in some way, influence the unity of America's churches so that they might better influence American society.

LEPERS ON AN ELEVATOR

Culturally, the recent years of American history have been eye-opening, as politics and political expression have become increasingly bitter, unyielding, and even violent. Our society is simultaneously more polarized and less open to differing opinions and competing ideas. Many of our young people are increasingly myopic, self-centered, and self-righteous even as the ever-widening breadth of knowledge opens up new avenues for objective exploration of solutions to intractable problems. Blame and revenge have become art forms while concepts such as personal responsibility and hard work are said to be racist subterfuge. Single-parent homes, casual drug use, hypersexuality among our youth, and the near genocidal rates of abortion in the black and Hispanic communities are touted as desirable, enlightened social norms. Pornography is freely available to any teenager with a cell phone. Truth has become whatever someone wants it to be. And hate has become fully justified when the hated target is portrayed to be sufficiently evil.

Meanwhile, society continues to attack Christianity and Christians as irredeemable and racist, portraying the essentials of biblical social mores and values as oppressive, discriminating, old school, racist, misogynist, homophobic, hateful, and wicked, just to name a few. The definitions of racism have been successfully altered so as to keep the negative Bull Conner/George Wallace images of the term alive while widening its application to include nearly all whites, especially Christian whites.

Therefore, Christian white men and women are often as welcomed as lepers in an elevator in many college campuses, social organizations, and workplaces.

The message of Christ now rings hollow to many Americans, as those who have come to know Him through society's viewpoint and the negative impressions of Christians don't like Him or His followers. For the sake of the future of our faith, we must be aware that the next generations of Americans are largely familiar with Jesus via the way in which His followers are portrayed in secular media, the street corner screamers promising hellfire and damnation, the occasional pastor or openly Christian person who falls prey to sin, and the stereotypes of a sort of Puritanism that is anti-everything. What they know of Jesus, they don't like. Small wonder, then, that they are not flocking to our sanctuaries and enjoying what we consider to be outstanding sermons, music, and dance.

THE CHALLENGE IS OURS TO GIVE AWAY

And so, the major social problems that united Christians could help address continue to go unresolved, leaving children, families, and large swaths of our population struggling with intractable issues in education, justice, healthcare, and race. Our churches, however, seem ill-prepared to do much about it.

Whether due to doctrinal, denominational, historical, familial, personal preference, geographic, racial, and/or other causes, our churches seem content to keep mostly to themselves and away from fellow Christians down the street or across town. And as siloed congregations, we have little option but to act as individual soldiers seemingly determined to be singular heroes against a vast opposing army. Indeed, most churches don't know the aggregate strength they have within their congregations, let alone that of their local community of churches. This further reduces our potential impact on society as it limits how we see the strength and power that we might bring to bear.

Yes, there are those churches that are distinctly multi-cultural and multi-racial. These can sometimes serve as examples of what unity should look like. But even these multi-racial churches may be still be acting as silos, rarely going outside to join with the other churches in their community's body of Christ.

Worse still, we often attack one another, whether knowingly or not, by criticizing, attacking, and mocking the social, political, and ethnic groups to which other Christians belong. We turn against ourselves even as society continues to wage war against us all.

Yet the attacks on even one small group of us, whether supported by other Christians or not, damages all of us. Just as a bullet to the arm impacts the rest of the body, so too the body of Christ is impacted when one part is attacked and injured or hampered.

Our silos thereby leave us more open to attack. Like the Jews of Nehemiah's time, spread out along the vast expanse of the walls of Jerusalem, we are inherently more vulnerable in our isolation. And because we too often reflect the ways of the world rather than the uprightness God demands, we are further limited in our abilities to defend against society's onslaught or show the world a better way. Society goes unchallenged as it readily portrays Christians as hypocrites, fools, racists, misogynists, and hellfire-breathing weirdos, rather than the giving, loving, and caring people we can be.

So, how will we reach these new generations of Americans?

HOPE

History shows us that the church has faced similar challenges before. The years preceding the first two Great Awakenings were periods of decline in religious fervor, church attendance, and Christian influence. But the Great Awakenings enabled more than just a few fired-up Christians. Through iterant preachers and new preaching styles, the Awakenings released a flood of Christian passion that helped send missionaries, teachers, and schools to slaves and freed blacks, spread churches across the American landscape from new denominations, helped start the Abolitionist movement, enabled charitable organizations that are still with us today, and brought the love of Christ to millions. Tent revivals, old-style evangelism, and a focus on the pure message of simple salvation changed American culture for many decades.

So, while things might seem bleak, we should always remember that we serve an amazing and all-powerful God. God has provided the numbers we need to be successful. We must provide the will and the drive to achieve His goals.

DOING DIFFERENT, NOT JUST BETTER

The future of American Christianity will not be like its past, nor should it. Our future does not belong solely to the traditional evangelists who spread the gospel so effectively throughout our nation's history. Yes, our preachers are invaluable voices and vital parts of the body of Christ. As leaders of our tens of thousands of churches, their value to their flocks is immeasurable.

Nonetheless, I contend that we will have to prove ourselves to be something other than what the secular media and stereotypes, whether false in part or in whole, claim us to be.

And to do this, we absolutely must tear down our own racial siloes that were built over two hundred years ago via the racial segregation of our churches. We must think, speak, and act with absolute uprightness, and learn to come together as the true body of Christ. This will mean tearing the scabs off decades old wounds, and laying bare our many faults, misconceptions, and premises to deal with the many root issues that keep our people apart and our society from its potential greatness.

Then, we must unite in action while preserving the personality, uniqueness and passion of each individual church and denomination. We should choose issues that are relevant to all our citizens while avoiding those issues that are, by their nature, politically divisive.

Generally, I have recommended that we choose justice, healthcare, and education in addition to race. There are issues pervasive in our communities, but ones which united Christians can help solve. As we keep our uprightness up front, we can bring forth new solutions to society's most intractable problems. And through the influence we will have on these issues, we will simultaneously, but indirectly, address a host of other related issues such as poverty, job creation, family structure and unity, and the general lack of uprightness in our society.

And as we have impact, we will attract the attention of those who seek the same goals and objectives but who do not know Christ as we do. As they see us in our communities, showing a better way to interact and live, some will be curious. Some will see Christianity in a whole new light, different from that which they have been taught and have seen in the past. Some will respond by becoming the dearest of friends and collaborators. They will not fear our involvement, but rather embrace it as genuine and pure. Through this, some will feel the pull of the Holy Spirit and join us our efforts through our churches.

And this could become the Next Great Awakening of our faith in America.

SUMMARY: A TOUGH ROW TO HOE

This will not be easy work. We will have to reach into communities we never thought about contacting. We will have to reach across an aisle when we were expecting the other side to reach out. We will have to put down our egos, our stereotypes, our politics, and our earthly loyalties in favor of a pure loyalty to the purposes of God.

Nor will it always be pleasant work. It will require us all to make sacrifices like we've never made before. We will spend time, treasure, and resources. And make no mistake, society will not like it and will attack us for even meager efforts to unite. We must struggle diligently in the face of strong opposition, entrenched interests, and societal blow-back, for God's success will be a loss for others. Even as we have positive impacts, there will be those whose vested, moneyed, and political interests will be harmed. And they will not sit idly by and watch their influence wane.

But it will be rewarding work. Any time Christians do the work of Christ in our society, God is pleased. And as we unite to do more and show our society how to better interact, collaborate, think, speak, and act, we will bring glory to God and a new light on His word.

And so, I challenge you, the reader, to start today. Unite with churches in your community on this grand journey of faith, action and the spread of Christianity to parts of our society that do not know the real Jesus.

Through our unity in action we will create a movement that will not only impact the most intractable issues of our society, but bring glory to God, a new appreciation for the message of the Gospel, and an entirely new way to reach those who need God's grace, power and love.

STUDY GUIDE

This Study Guide is designed to provide you with thought-provoking questions and discussion topics to allow a deeper understanding of many difficult racial issues. These can be considered through both personal reflections and introspection and dynamic group dialogues. If your group discussions can include both Christian blacks and Christian whites, the Study Guide will be even more beneficial. However, this is not a requirement for learning.

Study Guide content for some chapters provides separate questions and topics for Christian whites and Christian blacks, so as to allow for racially-specific perspectives and responses from each group. But, whether as an individual or a single-race group, it would be worthwhile to try to answer the questions for another racial group, so that you see the questions and topics from a different perspective. Note that some chapters do not have study questions and topics, as some did not lend themselves to this sort of reflection.

It should be noted that Christian uprightness is a requirement for these discussions. The Study Guide questions and topics are neither easy nor simple because racism remains a complex, difficult subject for our society and our churches. But, though Christian uprightness, you, your group, and your congregation will see a clearer path to a better place for our faith, your community, and our society.

REFLECTIONS OF A WHITE MAN IN A BLACK CHURCH
This chapter tells the story of the author's exploratory journey and shares some of the insights that were gained. The experiences and lessons spanned many years and attendance in many churches, both black and white. Through this story, the author hopes to offer the reader foundational perspectives to consider when reading the rest of the book. By asking tough questions and describing the challenges and emotional struggles he faced, the author hopes to open minds and hearts to the book's major messages and purpose.

Christian blacks
1) Have you ever attended a predominately white church?
    a) If not, why not?

b) If so ...
 i) What were your perceptions of the experience?
 ii) How were you greeted and welcomed? Did the greeting make you think about how any newcomer might feel in *your* church?
 iii) Did you feel out of place or did you fit right in?
 iv) How does what the author called "meet, greet, and hug" time differ from the practices at your church? Should your church consider a different way to greet one another?
 v) Can you envision how a white person might be received at your church? For instance, would they be greeted as warmly as friends of members?
2) What does the author's experience at a large, black church say about how we greet anyone not of our congregation? What does the experience tell us we should or could do differently?

Christian whites
3) Have you ever attended a predominately black church?
 a) If not, why not?
 b) If so ...
 i) What were your perceptions of the experience?
 ii) How were you greeted and welcomed? Did the greeting make you think about how any newcomer might feel in *your* church?
 iii) Did you feel out of place or did you fit right in?
 iv) How does what the author called "meet, greet, and hug" time differ from the practices at your church? Should your church consider a different way to greet one another?
 v) Can you envision how a black person might be received at your church? For instance, would they be greeted as warmly as friends of members?
4) What does the author's experience at a large, black church say about how we greet anyone not of our congregation? What does the experience tell us we should or could do differently?

Politics and the pulpit
Politics from the pulpit were an obvious concern of the author, due in part to what the author described as infrequent toxic messages put forth to the congregation. (It is worth noting that the AME pastors' political stances differed at least in part from the author's). This led the author to the realization of the

severity of the political divisions within the American church, potential constraints to unity, and the potential damage that might be done to our youth.

5) What do you think about politics in the pulpit? Should politics be left out of the pulpit, or are "men/women of the cloth" obliged to deal with the politics and issues of our day as part of their teaching, preaching, and leadership?
6) Is politics "preached" at your church? If so ...
   a) How often? Is it a regular, accepted practice? Or a rarity based on some external factors such as legislative activities or an incident that ignites deep and passionate feelings in your congregation and community?
   b) What does the "politics in the pulpit" say to visitors or even members about Christianity, your church, your members, and Christ's message?
   c) Do any political messages seem one-sided, biased, or even toxic? Do they say, "Our way or no way!" or is there an invitation to open and upright political and social dialogue within the congregation?

WHAT CHRISTIAN WHITES NEED TO KNOW ABOUT BLACK CHURCHES

Through a brief historical overview, the author describes the history of Christianity in the American black community from the arrival of slaves to the earliest black churches of the 1700s to its deep role in the Civil Rights Movement. The major goals of this chapter are 1) to educate Christian whites who might not know the complete history, both positive and negative, of Christianity in America, and 2) to offer some insights into the opportunities that historical racial divisions offer American Christianity today.

The author bases much of this chapter on a few, key suppositions. Specifically, the author states that the racial split of the churches allowed Christianity to have a deeper and wider reach into the black community than it might otherwise, enabling a far larger number of souls to be saved and more Christian work to be done. Furthermore, by allowing Christian blacks to come together during the long, arduous journey through slavery, segregation, oppression, and ongoing racism, the black community was made more resilient through the support and comfort of both our omnipresent Lord and the fellowship of saints. Lastly, the black church produced the great Christian leaders who were the face of the Civil Rights movement and showed the world a better way to be, act, and think.

Thus, the author contends, the split of the black and white church may ultimately be a good thing. Through the increase in Christianity's reach and numbers, there is a unique opportunity if Christians can now unite and use the current circumstances for God's glory.

For Christian blacks
1) What, if anything, would you like for Christian whites to take away from this chapter? Is there something that stands out as important to you?
2) What, if anything, would you like Christian whites to know or understand that was not covered in this chapter?
3) Did you learn anything about the history of the American black church from this chapter?
4) Do you agree with these premises?
   a) If not, explain how the author got this wrong and why you disagree with all or part of the above statements. Share your thoughts on the results of the divisions between black and white churches, and what, if anything, these divisions mean for the future of Christianity in America.
   b) If so, explain how you see that the racial divisions of black and white churches may be an opportunity to bring glory to God through racial harmony and unified action. Share your thoughts on the results of the split and where American Christianity might go from here. Do our past moral failures present opportunities to impact society?

For Christian whites
5) What did you learn from the exploration into the history of the American black church?
   a) Were you aware of the denominational splits that took place in the 1800's and the resulting expansion of church denominations?
   b) Did this chapter change your viewpoints on the racial divisions in the American body of Christ? If so, please elaborate.
6) Do you see these divisions as benign and unworthy of concern, or do you feel they could be harmful to the faith or our efforts to impact American society?
7) Do you agree that the historical divisions of the American Protestant church now present a greater opportunity for Christianity if Christians can unite?
   a) If so, what is the most exciting opportunity that you foresee?
   b) If not, explain how the author got this wrong and why you disagree with all or part of the premise.
8) How do you see the current and future racial divisions in the American body of Christ? Are these divisions benign, or do they need to be addressed? Please elaborate on your answer.

RACE AND RACISM FROM A CHRISTIAN WHITE MALE PERSPECTIVE

In this chapter, the author attempts to describe the evolution of racial terminology since the 1960's and the impact the changes are having today on our public discourse, our nation's ability to seek racial accord, and Christianity's potential to come together as a body of Christ. From a Christian white male perspective, the author sets forth stark differences in the interpretation of racial nomenclature, suggesting that modern terminology may be doing more harm than good in overcoming racial divisions and uniting our nation. Importantly for the faithful, the author demonstrates how Christian mores, values, and teachings have been blended into the modern racist terminology, making unity between Christian backs and Christian whites more difficult.

By outlining some of the many impacts of terminology on modern discourse, the faith, and our children, the author recommends a different approach to the use of what may have become overly toxic and misused words.

An important premise of this chapter is the linkage that was constructed between racism and Christianity within the modern definitions. This occurred as sociologists and others wrestled with identifying the sources and manifestations of racism after overt racism began to die away. This led to both the direct and indirect linkage of Christian values, behavioral norms, virtues, and lifestyles with the negative thoughts and feelings that whites are said to harbor against blacks. This theme carries throughout many of the modern racial nomenclature, whether explicitly stated or only implied.

1) How do these definitions and their linkages to Christianity impact the past, current, and future relationships between Christian blacks and Christian whites?
2) Does this impact their capacity and ability to unite as a body of Christ across racial boundaries?
3) How might racism's links to Christianity impact the capacity and ability to reach non-believers, particularly young people, with the message of Christ?
4) What other inhibitions and challenges, if any, does the new terminology present to the body of Christ?

For Christian blacks

5) What do you mean when you use the terms "racist" and "racism?" Is racism an all-encompassing, generalized term with a fluid definition that depends on the context of its use? Or does it have a specific, more fixed definition?

6) How do you use the terms "racism" and "racist" and what do you think of when you use these terms? Are there life and personal experiences, specific people or groups of people that come to mind?
7) Many modern definitions hold that whites are inherently racist, even though they may not actively and consciously think it. Do you consider *all* white people to be racist, whether intentionally, consciously, or unconsciously? Many whites? Some whites?
8) Do you personally know, or know of, white people whom you consider to be racists?
   a) If so, what attributes, actions, words, or attitudes make them racists?
   b) Is their racism conscious or unconscious, intentional or unintentional, learned or engrained?
9) How sensitive do you think white people are to any internalized, even unknown, racism?
10) How sensitive are white people to the racism (or, bias, prejudice, and/or stereotypes) around them, such as within the nation's healthcare, justice, education, and other social systems?
11) How can you educate whites without offending them?
12) Some authors, sociologists, and academics state that racism is the sole reason for the plight of blacks in America. Do you agree?
   a) If not, is racism the cause of any of it?
   b) If so, how much of the plight of today's blacks has its root cause in racism, both past and present?
13) How does this impact the nation's future and the future of relationships with whites, both Christian and non-Christian?
14) Are there any negative impacts on our children from the use of modern racial terms such as institutional racism and systemic racism? How might children, particularly black children, see their future impacted by the use of these terms and the constraints they are meant to describe?
15) Do you think the modern definitions of racism make it easier or more difficult for white people to address the problem of racism?

Some psychologists and sociologists argue that we all, whether black, white, or of any other race, carry stereotypes, biases, and prejudices. Often, these are either positive or benign, depending on their purpose in our psyche and daily lives. Others say all are essentially various forms and degrees of the same core issue, racism.

16) Which side of this argument would you support? Why?

17) Do you carry stereotypes, biases, and prejudices toward any other groups or peoples, whether from your past, your recent experiences, or the experiences of others?
18) If so, what are they? Please share an example.
    a) Do you consider these to be negative, positive, or benign?
    b) If negative, what can you do to change your "reflexive perceptions" and historical biases towards others?
    c) How are they part of your daily life and your interactions with others?
    d) What might these do to your ability to communicate with others?
    e) How might these impact your ability to minister or evangelize to certain segments of the population?

For Christian whites
19) Are you a racist?
    a) If so, what makes you a racist?
    b) If not, why do you believe you are not a racist?
20) What is your definition of racism?
21) What do you think when you hear the word racism? What images, people, situations, and social constructs does the term bring to mind?
22) What would you think if you were called a racist (particularly by someone you do not know)?
    a) What is your initial, "gut" reaction to being called racist?
    b) Are you intrigued, angry, etc.?
23) Do you know anyone, either personally or otherwise, who you would consider a racist?
    a) If so, why do you think that?
    b) Have you ever openly confronted anyone about their racism?
24) Many modern definitions hold that whites are inherently racist, even though they may not actively and consciously think it. Do you believe that all white people are racists, or prone to be racists?
    a) If not, why not?
    b) If so, why?
25) When you consider the definitions of the following terms from the book, what do you think? Do you find them to be appropriate or excessive?
    a) Anti-racism
    b) Systemic racism
    c) Critical Race Theory
    d) Systemic and institutional racism
26) What does "white privilege" mean to you?

27) Do you have it?
   a) If yes, should you get rid of it?
      i) How do you go about releasing it, and to whom would you give it?
      ii) How would you make amends for it?
   b) If not, why not?
28) Many authors, sociologists, and academics state that the sole reason for the plight of blacks in America is racism. What do you think?
29) Are there any negative impacts on our children from the use of terms such as institutional racism and systemic racism?
   a) How might children, particularly black children, see their future impacted by the use of these terms and the constraints they are meant to describe?
   b) How might white children feel about being known as racists by society?

For everyone

Some will differentiate racism, stereotypes, biases, and prejudice as having different attributes, connotations, and psychological purposes. Others say all are essentially the various forms and degrees of the same core issue, racism.

30) What do you think?
31) Do you carry stereotypes, biases, and prejudices toward any other groups or peoples, whether from your past, your recent experiences, or the experiences of others? If so, what are they? Please share an example.
   a) Do you consider these to be negative, positive, or benign? If negative, what can you do to change your "reflexive perceptions" and historical biases towards others?
   b) How are they part of your daily life and your interactions with others?
   c) What might these do to your ability to communicate with others?
   d) How might these impact your ability to minister or evangelize to certain segments of the population?
32) Christians once used Biblical passages to justify slavery and oppression (among other social ills). What would Jesus say about:
   a) Racism
   b) Stereotypes and prejudices
33) Do you think the modern definitions of racism make it easier or more difficult for white people to address the problem of racism?

THE CALL TO UPRIGHTNESS

The Bible calls us to be upright in our thoughts, words, and deeds, just as Jesus was and is. In this chapter, the author delves deeply into the concept and makeup of uprightness, why it is a difficult trait to obtain and maintain, and its importance for Christians and Christianity.

Uprightness is defined as being made up of several key attributes. Specifically: honesty, integrity, and objectivity. Uprightness requires us to go beyond what we have learned and thought in the past and what we hear from political leaders, pundits, the news, the internet, etc., to what the most objective and honest analysis tells us. Without pure uprightness, we cannot adequately evaluate the issues our nation faces and what we, as united Christians, and our society and government should do to resolve them.

1) Do you consider yourself to be upright in your thoughts, words, and actions?
   a) If so, why?
   b) If not, why not? What's missing?
2) Of the three main attributes of uprightness, which do you see as the most challenging?
   a) Why is this one more challenging that the others?
   b) Are any of them easy?

In defining the major attributes of uprightness, the author describes intellectual honesty.

3) How is intellectual honesty different from honesty?
4) Why does the author make a point to call this out?

The author describes a theory on how the brain processes information which suggests that we don't actually consciously consider much of what we think. Rather, the subconscious brain processes some information quickly and efficiently, eliminating the need to consciously evaluate each similar situation anew, thus speeding up reaction time and decision making. Whether these theories are true in part or in whole, they beg the question of how hard and deeply we consider each new, but similar, circumstance, scenario, person, and situation.

5) What role does the "auto pilot" portion of your mind play in how you evaluate current events, people, and situations?
6) What stereotypes do you hold on to? Give two examples from recent experiences.
   a) Where did they come from?

b) How do they impact how you might judge the next situation in which the stereotype might play a role?

The author describes the four attributes of Holy Conversations. They make us vulnerable, they are time-consuming, they require big questions, and they bring big surprises.

7) Why might they be difficult for us to manage?
8) Which of the four seems hardest to you? Why?

SILOS

In this chapter, the author delves into the many reasons that our congregations have become siloed, doing good work in their communities and respective congregations but rarely, if ever, strategically collaborating with churches across town or around the corner. There are many reasons why this happens, many are based on either human nature or group survival "instincts." However, if Christians are to protect the faith from the ongoing onslaught of the world around us and have any significant impact on society, we must necessarily break down our silo walls and create "unity in action."

1) What are two of the main reasons for churches operating in silos?
2) Why are silos seen as a benign part of the faith by most Christians?
3) What are the primary dangers of our ongoing silos to the faith and our churches?
4) Is your church a silo of worship and community activity?
    a) If so, why do you think this is the case?
    b) If not, describe some of your collaborative efforts with other churches? Is it enough, or are your efforts just a start?

SYNERGIES

In this chapter, the author details a church structure and organizational strategy that would allow for more and better collaboration with the larger body of Christ. Such a structure is focused on building service and collaborative opportunities through harnessing the passions, capabilities, and strengths of congregation members and aligning them with similar members of other churches. This will allow for each component of the body of Christ to flourish and have more impact on their chosen ministry efforts.

1) Does your church have an external focus on the broader community and city where you live?

2) What percentage of your church congregants are activity engaged in some form of service, ministry, or program that touches the community outside your church and congregation?
3) How well does your church engage with other local churches with like-minded ministries and programs?
4) Would an organizational emphasis and structure, like the one outlined in this chapter, offer advantages to your church and its efforts to impact the community around you?
   a) If not, why not? What is missing from the structure or the organizational emphasis?
   b) If so, how far is your church from this or similar models?
5) What would it take to move your church from the great works it does in isolation to collaboration across local denominations, geographies, and social, racial, and economic boundaries?

WHAT CHRISTIAN WHITES NEED TO DO

This chapter begins to answer the "So what?" question by offering specific yet challenging recommendations for how Christian whites should approach the racial divisions in God's church. Because some of the recommendations are rather radical, readers may have a hard time envisioning how they might be implemented within their own local communities. However, the author contends that only bold action will allow proper and effective unity and move God's church to its rightful place in our society. Only through upright dialogue among believers can we tear down the siloes that keep us divided and show society a better way to interact, love, and live.

For Christian whites
1) Based on your reading of the first sections of this chapter, how educated are you and your fellow congregants on the social, economic, and political perspectives of your black brothers and sisters?
2) What would it take for you to see the world from the viewpoint of someone whose background is very different from yours?

For many white people, discussions of the historical and current socio-economic causalities of the issues now facing black and other minority communities leads to defensiveness and a sense of being accused of wrongdoing.

3) How did you react to the story of the baritone singer, or the story of the middle-aged black father?

4) Detail your thoughts about whether and how to acknowledge the past versus "moving on" from this point.
   a) Do you sense a risk in acknowledgement of the sins of past generations? How should acknowledgement occur?
   b) Do you feel that society should "just move on," start from where we are, and look forward and not backward?

The concept of a Nehemiah Moment is controversial, at best, due to many factors from logistics to the fear of failure and possible rejection by the Christian black community.

5) What would it take for your church and the community of white churches in your area or city to organize such a prayerful event?
6) How would this be received by the Christian white community in your area or city? The Christian black community? Would the latter respond positively or negatively?
7) Would it be worthwhile, even if it failed to draw great attention or the praise of the Christian black community?

In the second section of the chapter (Collaboration) the author highlights some of the do's and don'ts of collaborating with other churches, particularly black churches. These are based on some of the failed efforts of the past, as well as commonsense respect and dignity for the capabilities and passions of fellow believers.

8) Has your church tried to collaborate with churches of different races in the past? If so, how well did it go? Is it an ongoing effort, or was it for a special occasion, unique event, disaster scenario, etc.?
9) Communication and support without overtaking are two common steps in any intra-group collaborative efforts. How can your church best avoid these traps?
10) How would the white churches collaborate with the black churches in your community or city to become the "Race Police"?
    a) Are there divisions, issues, and histories within the community that might make such an effort uniquely difficult?
    b) How would this be received by the Christian black community?
11) What could you and your church do to start or significantly broaden intra-racial church collaboration in your city?

a) What are the pitfalls, snares, and obstacles that might impede your progress?
b) Are there any white people or churches in your community who might oppose such efforts?

For Christian blacks

This chapter is primarily for Christian whites. Yet, there is a message for Christian blacks, as well. The author suggests ways for Christian whites to better engage with their black brothers and sisters, offering some rather radical ideas to promote unity of the faith and collaboration.

12) How would your church respond to a call for cooperation with a Nehemiah moment as described in this chapter?
   a) Would other black churches in your community support it?
   b) Would it have any significant and lasting impact on the Christian relationships in your area, city, and/or state?
   c) What might be the outcome(s) from such an effort were the local Christian white community make it?
13) The author floated several ideas for how Christian whites might better collaborate, and some do's and don'ts of those efforts. What do you think of the suggestions provided?
   a) Will they help?
   b) What might have the most impact?
   c) Beyond those mentioned in the book, what else might you recommend to your local Christian community?
14) What do you think of the concept of Christian whites becoming the "Race Police" for your area or city? Would you stand with them or oppose them?
   a) Why?
   b) If you would not support them currently, is there something they might do to elicit your future support? Or, is this just a bad idea?
15) What else would you suggest for your Christian white brothers and sisters who want to engage and collaborate with the Christian black community in your area or city?

WHAT CHRISTIAN BLACKS NEED TO DO

In this chapter, the author humbly attempts to make actionable recommendations for Christian blacks who are desirous of collaboration with Christian whites in promoting a more powerful and effective body of Christ. There are some seemingly challenging recommendations on the list as well as some that are rather easy. The goal, of course, is to create unity in action from which God's church can do more to bring glory to Him and change to our society.

For Christian blacks

1) Modern racial terminology was the focus of a previous chapter and is important for Christian collaboration. What will be the reaction of your local Christian black community to working with the Christian white community to come to agreement on the proper definitions and uses of important racial terms?
   a) How might agreement here help all to work together better?
   b) What pushback might be offered to Christian white interpretations?
   c) How could the local Christian black community lead the way in these discussions, and what impacts might their leadership have for your community, city, and denomination leadership?

2) Would the local Christian black community work with their white brothers and sisters to make them the "Race Police" of your area or city? What are the obstacles to such an effort, whether in the black church community or elsewhere in the black community?

3) The second section of this chapter deals with other, specific things the author suggests Christian blacks need to do to help foster collaboration. These include outreach, accepting partnerships, and forgiving centuries of transgressions.
   a) What responsibility, if any, do Christian blacks have for initiating and sustaining any collaborative efforts in your community?
   b) Are any of the mentioned changes already being made in your church, area, or city? If so, please elaborate.
   c) What of these, if any, will be most difficult for you and your congregation?
   d) What actions or efforts did the author miss in this chapter? Are there other things that you and/or your church have done that helped bring the body of Christ closer?

CONSIDERATIONS FOR UNITY

Once Christian communities begin collaborating, the author warns that they will likely become targets of worldly forces opposed to their efforts. Furthermore, there may be constraints and obstacles that come from within our congregations and Christian communities that inhibit our efforts toward unity in action.

1) Why is dignity such an important concept when working in your communities?
2) Do your current charitable efforts offer dignity as part of the aid and support they give?
3) What do you see as the largest impediments to unity in action that might come from your church or church community?
4) Are they due to historical divisions, current politics, socio-economic strata, past and current racial tensions, or other reasons?
5) What external groups, political parties, politicians, organizations, individuals, or other entities pose the biggest threat(s) to your efforts to unite?
   a) How will each be threatened?
   b) How and why might they attack your efforts?
   c) How might you respond to the inevitable pushback?
6) How might the non-Christian whites and blacks react to your efforts toward unification? Will they be threatened or excited?
7) How would you and your newly unified community of Christians respond to any attacks?
   a) What resources could you bring to bear to counter the attacks?
   b) How proactive should the Christian community be in warding off potential attacks and threats?

INTRODUCTION TO THE FOCUS AREAS

In these four short chapters, the author outlines some specific areas that are ripe for Christian unity in action. The author starts with some preliminary thoughts on "Systems Thinking" and how this approach will help you in your efforts to analyze, test ideas, and create solutions for difficult social problems.

1) Setting goals and priorities is obviously important in any effort. How good is your church or church ministry in setting SMART goals and prioritizing activities?

Part of the difficulty in creating and implementing large-scale change is the complex interdependencies of the problems. Tendrils tend to run in places we don't anticipate and foresee, while the dynamics of the situation may cause the issue to evolve and shift even as we are trying to fix it.

2) Name one significant social problem your church or ministry might be trying to address (e.g. local homelessness).

a) What are the interdependencies that are involved with the problem? How do they impact the problem?

b) How do those interdependencies make the solutions more difficult to develop and implement?

Uprightness requires Christians to be wholly objective about our thoughts, words, and actions. And this very often requires us to challenge our own thinking, deeply consider alternative opinions, perspectives, and solutions, and find data that will help us understand the problem better. Of course, data analysis can be as biased as the opinions that sometimes guide it. So, the data we use, and the way in which we analyze, manipulate, and present it must necessarily be completely upright.

3) What data sources have you used, or could you use, to evaluate the problem from the question above?

4) Are there multiple sources? Can you find data from a second source that might confirm or dispel your current data source(s)?

5) Are you comfortable that the data and sources you are using are pure and upright? Or is there some doubt as to the data, its source(s), integrity, or analysis?

6) Offer an example of how you used data to create information and then strategies for attacking your problem.

7) How can you be assured that all the data and analysis you are using would pass the "God test?"

AREAS OF FOCUS: HEALTHCARE

The author begins the discussion of focus areas with an emphasis on health and healthcare. God requires us to treat our bodies well. Through proper diet, exercise, and habits we can all live healthy lives. Yet, too many Christians and non-Christians have poor diets, smoke, drink excessively, and fail to achieve even modest exercise. Some of this is due to our work culture, life stresses, and the demands of family and raising children. Some is due to our "have it your way" culture that both glorifies unrealistic physical beauty and promotes bad diets and health habits. Given the growing cost of the healthcare system and the tolls bad habits, obesity, smoking, drug and alcohol abuse, etc. take on our citizenry, healthcare could and should be a focal area for Christian activity.

1) Does your church currently have a healthcare ministry or other health-related efforts?

a) What is the focus or focuses?

b) Does your healthcare ministry collaborate with other churches to expand your impact into the surrounding community or city?

c) Does your healthcare ministry collaborate with local health officials and agencies, schools, and non-profits?

   i) If so, how are they working together?

   ii) If not, how could they start working together?

2) Does your healthcare ministry do enough to help create "Health Ownership" in your communities and city?

3) What should be the top health priority for your congregation's overall health?

4) What should be the top priority for your community's overall health?

Chronic disease takes a tremendous toll on a small percentage of the population, which in turn drives a high percentage of the total national healthcare expenditure.

5) How might your church engage in a healthcare ministry related to one or more chronic diseases?

6) How might a group of churches united in action develop a community- or city-wide chronic disease management and prevention effort?

AREAS OF FOCUS: EDUCATION

Many churches already have efforts that are focused on childhood education. Many have their own schools, kindergartens, or K-12 schools. Christian volunteers routinely work with kids of all ages to bring additional support to teachers and Christian teachings to after-school programs. Yet, as our education systems continue to fail to achieve adequate results, particularly in low-income and rural areas, much more is needed.

1) What is your church currently doing to support the education of children in your congregation? In your community or city?

a) Do your efforts include kids who are most in need?

b) What percentage of your church congregation is involved in education efforts? Is that enough, or should more be involved?

c) What keeps your members from further and deeper Involvement in this and other external ministries?

2) How might technology help your church help kids in distant areas be more successful?

3) How might you collaborate with churches nearby and across town to be more effective and efficient in aiding the local education system?

AREAS OF FOCUS: JUSTICE

The author points out that the need for justice is called out in the Bible. From Micah to the Apostles, justice is a common theme in God's word. And because justice requires uprightness to be properly administered, Christians are called to promote it.

Furthermore, justice is meant to be proactive and an integral part of the fabric of our society. Indeed, justice is needed throughout our society, not just in our courts of law. It is a core component of the other areas of focus, such as education.

Thus, the administration of upright justice should not be ignored by our churches.

1) Why is uprightness such a key part of justice?
2) Does your church or community have ministries related to justice? If so, what are they?
3) What could a justice-related ministry look like in your church of community?
4) What resources could your church or church community bring to bear, and in what areas?
5) How might a justice ministry help churches bridge current racial divisions in your local body of Christ?
6) How might a justice ministry help create the environment through which Christian whites become the Race Police for the community or city?

THE NEXT GREAT AWAKENING: A BOLD CALL TO ACTION

In the final chapter of the book, the author offers a glimpse into the possibilities of a rejuvenation of Christianity in America, the Next Great Awakening. For comparison and perspective, the author details the history of the previous religious Awakenings in American history. This is to show the reader that our faith has faltered several times before, requiring a broad revival that not only reenergized the saved but brought forth many newly saved saints. Through descriptions of the parallels to the circumstances that Christianity faces today, the author shows both the need and unique opportunity Christians have to create a new Great Awakening. Unlike previous Awakenings, the next will likely not be achieved through tent revivals and famous preachers, but rather through the actions of newly aligned Christian blacks and Christian whites. This, in turn, will bring new excitement and opportunities for sharing Jesus' message with those from whom it has been hidden.

1) Do you feel that America needs a Great Awakening? Why or why not?

2) How did the first two Great Awakenings help set up the opportunities that we now have in America, in terms of our numbers and the breadth of reach of the faith?
3) Can you see God's hand in the long-term positioning of His church in America?
4) Jesus' message and God's love have never changed. How might the tools, techniques, delivery, and messaging of the early Great Awakenings work in today's society with today's youth, many of whom were raised with a disdain for Christians?
5) Will the message work even if the method of delivery changes?
6) Name a few of the parallels between the needs of the nation that spurred the previous Awakenings and the circumstances we face today.
7) Why are these relevant to the need for a Great Awakening?
8) List two of the five major opportunities described in the chapter and how you feel they help Christians put forth Christ' message?
9) Name a few of the key attributes of the author's vision of the Next Great Awakening.
10) Do you agree with this assessment?
11) If you think America is in need, what do you think the best route to success would be?

NOTES

[i] Gonzalez, Justo. For the Healing of the Nations: The Book of Revelation in an Age of Cultural Conflict (New York: Orbis Books, 2005).

[ii] John 15:19, etc.

[iii] Ray, B. African Religions: Symbol, Ritual and Community (New Jersey: Prentice-Hall, 1976).

[iv] BBC World News Service, "The Story of Africa: Christianity." Last accessed March, 1, 2019.
http://www.bbc.co.uk/worldservice/africa/features/storyofafrica/8chapter4.shtml

[v] The so-called "Curse of Ham" is an interpretation of Genesis 9:18-29. In these verses, Noah cursed Ham's son Canaan, damning him to be a slave to his brothers Shem and Japheth. By some "Curse of Ham" interpretations, since Canaan was said to have fathered nations in Africa (e.g. Ethiopia), Noah's curse applied to all Canaan's descendants, thus damning African people to slavery. Further, the name "Ham" is translated from Hebrew as "hot," which some interpreted as "burnt" and as indicative of dark or black skin color. Thus, Ham's son Canaan and his descendants were likely black. Thus, by Noah's curse, blacks were doomed to be slaves. Because it is such a manipulation of the book, this theory did not take hold among mainstream Christianity but was nonetheless used as justification for everything from slavery to segregation.

[vi] Pierson, P., "Why Did the 1800s Explode with Missions?" Christianity Today, Issue 36, 1992. Last accessed on March 1, 2019.
http://www.christianitytoday.com/history/issues/issue-36/why-did-1800s-explode-with-missions.html

[vii] "The History of Slavery in America." Last accessed on March 1, 2019.
https://www.ocf.berkeley.edu/~arihuang/academic/abg/slavery/history.html

[viii] Guasco, M., "The Misguided Focus on 1619 as the Beginning of Slavery in the U.S. Damages Our Understanding of American History", Smithsonian.com. September, 2017. Last accessed on March 1, 2019.
https://www.smithsonianmag.com/history/misguided-focus-1619-beginning-slavery-us-damages-our-understanding-american-history-180964873/

[ix] Austin, Allen, African Muslims in Antebellum America: Transatlantic Stories and Spiritual Struggles (New York: Routledge, 1997).

[x] Yvonne P. Chireau, Black Magic: Religion and the African American Conjuring Tradition (Berkeley: University of California Press, 2003).

[xi] Walker, David. Walker's Appeal, in Four Articles: Together with a Preamble, to the Coloured Citizens of the World, but in Particular, and Very Expressly, to Those of the United States of America, Taken from "Documenting the American South." Last accessed on January 18th, 2018. http://docsouth.unc.edu/nc/walker/walker.html

[xii] Maffley-Kipp, L., "African American Christianity, Pt. I: To the Civil War." National Humanities Center, June 2005. Last accessed on March 1, 2019. http://nationalhumanitiescenter.org/tserve/nineteen/nkeyinfo/aareligion.htm

[xiii] Ibid.

[xiv] Raboteau, Albert. "The Secret Religion of the Slaves." *Christianity Today*, Issue 33, 1992.

[xv] Multiple histories of this movement have been penned. This book was paraphrased from www.ohiohistorycentral.org/w/second_great_awakening, the National Humanities Center (www.nationalhumanitiescenter.org) and elsewhere.

[xvi] The History Channel. "Abolitionist Movement." Last accessed March 1, 2019. http://www.history.com/topics/black-history/abolitionist-movement.

[xvii] "First African Baptist Church Founded", African American Registry, last accessed March 1, 2019, https://aaregistry.org/story/first-african-baptist-church-founded/.

[xviii] Emanuel A.M.E. Church, "History." Last accessed March 1, 2019. https://www.emanuelamechurch.org/staff/

[xix] Davidson Presbyterian Church USA. "Blacks in the Presbyterian Church in the USA 1807 – 1982." Last accessed March 1, 2019. http://www.dpcus.org/Blacks%20in%20the%20United%20Presbyterian%20Church%20in%20the%20USA%201807-1982.pdf

[xx] Georgia Encyclopedia. "Christian Methodist Episcopal Church." Last accessed March 1, 2019. http://www.georgiaencyclopedia.org/articles/arts-culture/christian-methodist-episcopal-church-cme-church

[xxi] African American Registry, "The Black Church." Last accessed March 1, 2019. http://www.aaregistry.org/historic_events/view/black-church-brief-history

[xxii] Hopkins, D.N., *Introducing Black Theology of Liberation* (New York, Orbis Publishing, 1999).

[xxiii] Paraphrased from Luke 4:16 - 20

[xxiv] Matthew 25:40

[xxv] Examples include:
- Swift, David Everett. *Black Prophets of Justice: Activist Clergy before the Civil War* (Louisiana: Louisiana State University Press, 1989).
-Taylor, Clarence. Black Religious Intellectuals: The Fight for Equality from Jim Crow to the Twenty-First Century (New York: Routledge, 2002).
- Calhoun-Brown, A. "Upon This Rock: The Black Church, Nonviolence, and the Civil Rights Movement," *Political Science and Politics*, Vol. 33, No. 2 (Jun., 2000), pp. 168-174.

xxvi Taylor, Clarence. The Gilder Lehrman Institute of American History, "African American Religious Leadership and the Civil Rights Movement." Last accessed March 1, 2019. https://www.gilderlehrman.org/history-by-era/civil-rights-movement/essays/african-american-religious-leadership-and-civil-rights-m

xxvii The Highlander Research and Education Center (a.k.a. The Highlander Folk School), was founded by three Christian white men in 1932 and is a social justice leadership training center. It was instrumental in the Civil Rights Movement, training key figures in non-violent approaches to social change. Students of the Highlander Center included Dr. Martin Luther King, Rosa Parks, Rev. Ralph Abernathy, and Rev. John Lewis. https://www.highlandercenter.org/

xxviii Evans, C.J., White evangelical protestant responses to the civil rights movement. *The Harvard Theological Review*, Vol. 102, (Harvard Press, 2009), 245–273.

xxix Ibid.

xxx Blackwelder, J.K., Southern white fundamentalists and the civil rights movement, *Phylon*, Vol. 40, No. 4, (Clark Atlanta University Press, 1979), 334–341.

xxxi Ibid, p. 336.

xxxii "Letter from a Birmingham Jail." African Studies Center at the University of Pennsylvania. Last accessed March 1, 2019. http://www.africa.upenn.edu/Articles_Gen/Letter_Birmingham.html

xxxiii As you will see later in this book, terms such as "articulate" and "well-spoken" are now seen as "code words" used by white racists.

xxxiv Matthew 12:25, Mark 3:25, and Luke 11:17

xxxv Ironically, the phrase "black friends" is thought by some to be "racist" when stated by a white person, as it is said to imply that blacks can be collected like trophies and shown off for their social value.

xxxvi "Racism," Merriam-Webster Dictionary. Last accessed on March 1, 2019. https://www.merriam-webster.com/dictionary/racism

xxxvii "Racism," New Oxford Dictionary. Last accessed on March 1, 2019. https://en.oxforddictionaries.com/definition/racism

xxxviii "Racism," Dictionary.com. Last accessed on March 1, 2019. www.dictionary.com/browse/racism

xxxix Katz, P. and Taylor, D.A., "Eliminating Racism: Profiles in Controversy." (MA, Springer Press, 1988). P. 53-54. Last accessed on March 1,2019. https://doi.org/10.1007/978-1-4899-0818-6

xl Sears, D. and Henry, P.J., "Symbolic Racism," in *Encyclopedia of Social Psychology*, edited by Baumeister, R. and Vohs, K. (Thousand Oaks: SAGE Publications, 2007).

xli Depaul University of Chicago. Sears, D. and Henry, P.J., "The Origins of Symbolic Racism," *Journal of Personality and Social Psychology*, Vol. 85, No. 2. (2003): 259 - 271. Last accessed March 1, 2019. http://condor.depaul.edu/phenry1/2003%20Sears%20&%20Henry,%20JPSP.pdf

[xlii] McConahay, John B. "Modern Racism, Ambivalence, and the Modern Racism Scale." in *Prejudice, Discrimination, and Racism,* edited by Dovidio, J and Gaetner, S. (Orlando: Academic Press, 1986). pp. 91 - 126.

[xliii] McConahay, John B. and Hough, J.C., "Symbolic Racism," *Journal of Social Issues,* vol. 32 (1976). 23 – 45.

[xliv] McConahay, John. B., 1986, p. 100.

[xlv] Glaude, E., *Democracy in Black*, (New York: Broadway Books, 2016).

[xlvi] Dovidio, J.F. and Gaertner, S. L. "The aversive form of racism" in *Prejudice, Discrimination and Racism*, edited by J. F. Dovidio & S. L. Gaertner (San Diego: Academic Press, 1986), pp. 61-89.

[xlvii] Sue, D.W., *Microaggressions and Marginality: Manifestation, Dynamics, and Impact* (New York: John Wiley and Sons Publishing, 2010), p.1.

[xlviii] This "don't judge" approach is now used to justify accusations of hate and intolerance against Christianity and Christians by other groups, including the LGBT community, immigrants, and those promoting what might be considered immoral behavior.

[xlix] DeAlgelis, T., "Unmasking racial 'microaggressions'," *Monitor on Psychology, American Psychology Association* (February, 2009), p 42.

[l] UCLA School of Public Affairs. "What is Critical Race Theory." Last accessed March 1, 2019. https://spacrs.wordpress.com/what-is-critical-race-theory

[li] Delgado, R., Stefancic, J. "Critical Race Theory: An Annotated Bibliography." *Virginia Law Review*, Number 79, No. 2 (1993), pp. 461–516.

[lii] "Institutional Racism," English Oxford Living Dictionaries. Last accessed March 1, 2019. https://en.oxforddictionaries.com/definition/institutional_racism

[liii] "Institutional Racism," Urban Dictionary. Last accessed March 1, 2019. http://www.urbandictionary.com/define.php?term=institutionalized%20racism

[liv] Feagan, J., Racist America: Roots, current realities, and future reparations (New York: Routledge Press, 2000), p.6.

[lv] I use the term "nearly" here, since there remains an element in our society that remains devoutly racist, in the harshest and most traditional sense of the term. Dylann Roof, the young man who murdered nine AME congregants in the historic Emanuel AME Church in Charleston, SC, is an example of this tiny but still present group. Wherever they exist, we must continue to pray, teach and love, as Dr. Martin Luther King suggested, in hopes that they will see the error of their ways We must also reject their thinking as deeply un-Christian. As Christian whites, we should seek to extinguish this thinking anywhere it is found, as it remains a curse in our society.

[lvi] DiAngelo, R., *White Fragility: Why It's So Hard for White People to Talk About Racism* (Boston: Beacon Press, 2018). The original article: *White Fragility,* International Journal of Critical Pedagogy, Vol 3 (3) (2011) pp 54-70

[lvii] *White Fragility,* International Journal of Critical Pedagogy, Vol 3 (3) (2011) p. 57.

[lviii] Ibid, p, 57.

[lix] Kendi, I., *Stamped from the Beginning: The Definitive History of Racist Ideas in America* (New York: Nation Books, 2016), p.10.

[lx] "Zero sum" refers to economic or game theory in which each participant's mathematical gain or loss is precisely balanced by the loss or gain of the other participant(s). It is common in Economic and political theory, used to represent total "utility" or opportunity for utility. Total gains by participants are equal to the total losses of participants, yielding a net change of zero.

[lxi] Firing Line (or, Firing Line with Bill Buckley) was a television show that debuted in 1966 and ran for the next thirty three years and over 1,500 episodes. It remains the longest running public affairs show hosted by a single person. Firing Line's host, the late Bill Buckley, was famed for offering a debate environment that allowed the polite exchange of perspectives and ideas, giving guests time to fully answer and vet ideas without interruption. This environment seems almost alien in today's world where debate is replaced with shouting and talking over those with opposing viewpoints.

[lxii] Wilson, T., *Strangers to Ourselves: Discovering the Adaptive Unconscious* (Cambridge: The Belknap Press of Harvard University Press, 2002).

[lxiii] "Upright" is also used in reference to posture when standing (Genesis 37:7), physical uprightness or a vertical position of someone or something (Exodus 26:15), and a support column or beam (1 Kings 7:29).

[lxiv] Gallop, Inc. U.S. Approval of Congress: Gallop polling data, Gallop.com. Last accessed on March 1, 2019. http://www.gallup.com/poll/205565/congress-approval-levels-off-higher-2016.aspx?g_source=CONGRESS&g_medium=topic&g_campaign=tiles

[lxv] D. Besharov, A. West, "African American Marriage Patterns," Hoover Press (2000) in *Beyond the Color Line: New Perspectives on Race and Ethnicity in America*, edited by A. Thernstrom & S. Thernstrom. (Stanford: Hoover Institution Press, 2000).

[lxvi] I have heard this terminology used repeatedly as I've discussed this concept with fellow Christians. Adoption is for parentless kids who cannot take care of themselves. It is not meant four Christian brothers and sisters who are as empowered with the Holy Spirit as any of us. Adoption, by the nature of the term, brings with it a sense of dominance, superiority and control, none of which are appropriate as we unite as Christians. God may have adopted us as sinners, but we should not expect to adopt other Christians and their churches.

[lxvii] There remains a small minority of whites who would take pride in such an accusation and freely admit their pure, traditionally defined racism. Let the reader assume that I am not trying to change their minds, at least for the moment.

[lxviii] "Racism," Merriam-Webster Dictionary. Last accessed on March 1, 2019. https://www.merriam-webster.com/dictionary/racism

[lxix] *White Fragility,* International Journal of Critical Pedagogy, Vol 3 (3) (2011) p. 56.

[lxx] Lupton, J., Toxic Charity: How churches and charities hurt those they help (and how to reverse it) (New York: Harper Collins Press, 2011).

[lxxi] Similar writings include John Lupton's follow on books, and Corbett and Fikkert's *When Helping Hurts* (Chicago: Moody Publishing, 2009).

[lxxii] Lupton, J., *Toxic Charity*.

[lxxiii] Tufte, E., *The Visual Display of Quantitative Information* (Cheshire, CT: Graphics Press, 2001). Other books by the same author are also valuable. You can find more at edwardtufte.com.

[lxxiv] Senge, P., The Fifth Discipline: The Art and Practice of the Learning Organization (New York: Doubleday/Currency, 1990).

[lxxv] Story, P., Developing a Poly-Chronic Care Network: An Engineered, Community-Wide Approach to Disease Management (New York: CRC Press, 2012).

[lxxvi] M. Aldridge, et. al., The Myth Regarding the High Cost of End-of-Life Care, *American Journal of Public Health*, December 2015, 105(12): 2411–2415.

[lxxvii] Nehemiah 5:1-13

[lxxviii] Retrieved from Christianity.com. http://www.christianity.com/church/church-history/timeline/1701-1800/the-great-awakening-11630212.html . Last accessed March 1, 2019.

[lxxix] Retrieved from "The Great Awakening Documentary." Last accessed March 1, 2019. http://greatawakeningdocumentary.com/exhibits/show/biographies/gilbert-tennent

[lxxx] Retrieved from https://edsitement.neh.gov/lesson-plan/first-great-awakening#sect-background.

[lxxxi] Ibid.

[lxxxii] Wesley, J., "Thoughts Upon Slavery" in "A Collection of Religious Tracts," Electronic edition. Retrieved from "Documenting the American South" of the UNC-CH Digitization Project. Last accessed March 1, 2019. https://docsouth.unc.edu/church/wesley/wesley.html

[lxxxiii] Galli, Mark., "Slaveholding Evangelist: Whitefield's Troubling Mix of Views," *Christianity Today*. Last accessed March 1, 2019. Retrieved from https://www.christianitytoday.com/history/issues/issue-38/slaveholding-evangelist.html.

[lxxxiv] Multiple histories of this movement have been penned. This text was paraphrased from www.ohiohistorycentral.org/w/second_great_awakening, the National Humanities Center (www.nationalhumanitiescenter.org) and elsewhere.

[lxxxv] "Abolitionist Movement," A&E Television Networks, October, 2009. Last accessed March 1, 2019. Retrieved from https://www.history.com/topics/black-history/abolitionist-movement.

[lxxxvi] Ibid.

[lxxxvii] Choinski, M., The Rhetoric of Revival: The Language of Great Awakening Preachers, Vandenhoeck and Ruprecht, Bristol, CT, 2016, p. 45.

[lxxxviii] Fogel, R., The Fourth Great Awakening and the Future of Egalitarianism, University of Chicago Press, Chicago, IL, 1999.

[lxxxix] McLoughlin, W., <u>Revivals, Awakenings and Reforms</u>, University of Chicago Press, Chicago, IL, 1978.

Made in the USA
Columbia, SC
14 December 2020